THE
BAR MITZVAH
AND THE
BEAST

THE
BAR MITZVAH
AND THE
BEAST

One Family's Cross-Country
Ride of Passage by Bike

MATT BIERS-ARIEL

THE MOUNTAINEERS BOOKS

THE MOUNTAINEERS BOOKS
is the nonprofit publishing arm of The Mountaineers,
an organization founded in 1906 and dedicated to the exploration,
preservation, and enjoyment of outdoor and wilderness areas.

1001 SW Klickitat Way, Suite 201, Seattle, WA 98134

First edition, 2012

10 9 8 7 6 5 4 3 2 1

Distributed in the United Kingdom by Cordee, www.cordee.co.uk
Manufactured in the United States of America

Copy Editor: Joan Gregory
Cover, Interior, and Map Design: John Barnett / 4 Eyes Design
Family Photograph on Cover: Erron Evans
Author Photograph: Laurie Friedman

Library of Congress Cataloging-in-Publication Data
Biers-Ariel, Matt.
  The bar mitzvah and the beast : one family's cross-country ride of
passage by bike / Matt Biers-Ariel.
     p. cm.
  ISBN 978-1-59485-672-3 (pbk.)—ISBN 978-1-59485-673-0 (ebook)
  1. Bicycle touring—United States. 2. Tourism—Religious
aspects—Judaism. I. Title.
  GV1045.B54 2012
  796.6'4—dc23
                                2011045878

The poem, "Much Madness Is Divinest Sense," by Emily Dickinson is reprinted by
permission of the publishers and the Trustees of Amherst College from *The Poems of
Emily Dickinson: Variorum Edition*, Ralph W. Franklin, ed., Cambridge, Mass.: The
Belknap Press of Harvard University Press, © 1998 by the President and Fellows
of Harvard College. © 1951, 1955, 1979, 1983 by the President and Fellows of
Harvard College.

From *The Diary Of A Young Girl: The Definitive Edition* by Anne Frank, edited
by Otto H. Frank and Mirjam Pressler, translated by Susan Massotty, translation
copyright 1995 by Doubleday, a division of Random House, Inc. Used by permission
of Doubleday, a division of Random House, Inc.

SUSTAINABLE FORESTRY INITIATIVE
Certified Fiber Sourcing
Label applies to the text stock   www.sfiprogram.org

To Seabiscuit, Sprite, and Wooch

CONTENTS

ACKNOWLEDGMENTS

FIRST AND FOREMOST my heartfelt thanks to Ken Giles, partly for providing beer in a dry county but mostly for his companionship and good humor. Mark Schwartz and Sharon Strauss schlepped our gear up the Sierras and brought Solly a lifesaving ice cream cone. Kevin Murphy, Jennifer Oman, Daniel Wallach, Catherine Hart, Rabbi Tom Gutherz, and Carmi Weiner opened their homes and hearts to us. The bicycle ministries of the First Baptist Church of Sebree, Kentucky; the Presbyterian Church of Booneville, Kentucky; the Methodist Church of Rosedale, Virginia; and The Place run by the Methodist Church of Damascus, Virginia, all provided succor when we were hot, tired, and crabby.

Lori Lipman Brown helped set up our congressional meetings. *Sacramento Bee* writer Janet Fullwood wrote fabulous articles and was a great help. Rabbi Sydney Mintz sent us off with a beautiful benediction. I would be amiss to forget David Moss, who planted the idea of this alternative rite of passage when he told me how his oldest son had celebrated his bar mitzvah with a cross-country bike ride.

This book would not have been possible without input from Amie Diller, Cyndi Toy, Raoul Adamchak, and Pam Ronald. Thanks to Frank Babbitt, who convinced me to start the blog that greatly tightened the writing. Also to Aunt Yvette whose collation of the trip blog proved an invaluable aid.

Thank you to Amy Smith Bell and Joan Gregory, whose editorial comments were spot on. To Ingrid Emerick for being an awesome Girl Friday. Finally, a great big thank you to Kate Rogers, editor in chief of Mountaineers Books, for taking a chance on a book that is perhaps not their normal fare.

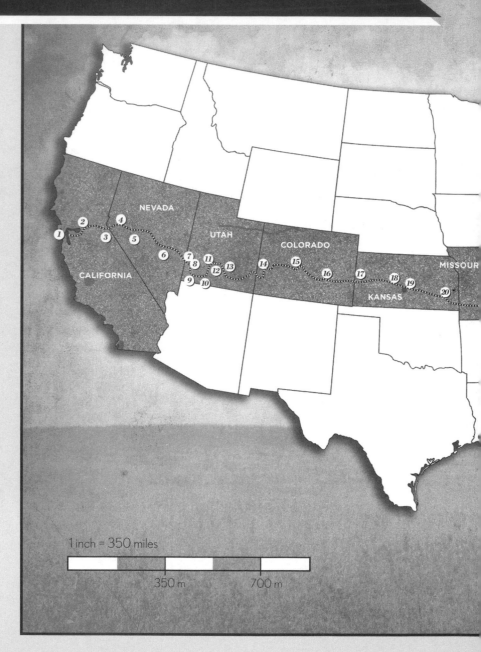

RIDE OF PASSAGE ROUTE

NEVADA

UTAH

COLORADO

CALIFORNIA

MISSOUR

KANSAS

1 inch = 350 miles

350 m   700 m

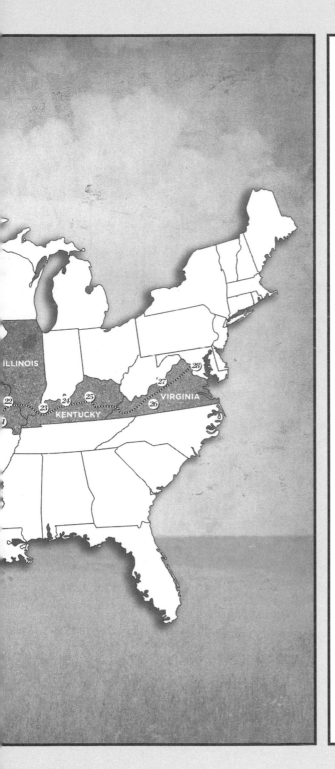

MAP KEY

CALIFORNIA
1. Baker Beach—Yonah and Matt dip rear wheels
2. Davis—pick up Djina and Solomon
3. Carson Pass (8,594 feet)

NEVADA
4. Great Basin—Triple-digit weather commences
5. Middlegate and Shoe Tree
6. Electrolux Café

UTAH
7. Middle of Nowhere—The Beast breaks down
8. Headwinds join heat
9. Cedar City—Ken rescues us
10. Bryce Canyon
11. Pangwitch—Matt and Solly hit 45 mph
12. Escalante—14% grades
13. Hite—Colorado River

COLORADO
14. Ridgeway—pulled over by police twice in one day
15. Monarch Pass (11,312 feet)
16. Pueblo—link to TransAmerica Bike Trail

KANSAS
17. Corn and humidity join heat and wind
18. Yonah and Solomon sick of ride
19. Hutchinson—The Great Debate
20. Chanute—first one-hundred-mile day

MISSOURI
21. Ozark Mountains—self-propelled roller coasters
22. Ash Grove—second 100-mile day

ILLINOIS

KENTUCKY
23. Sebree bicycle ministry
24. Ken rescues us again
25. Appalachian Mountains

VIRGINIA
26. Troutville—Djina's bike breaks down
27. Charlottesville—Leave TransAmerica Bike Trail

WASHINGTON D.C.
28. Dip front wheels in Lincoln Memorial Reflecting Pool

GENESIS OF AN ATHEIST

IT DIDN'T BEGIN as sudden inspiration. I didn't leap out of bed, wake Yonah, and holler, "Son, we're biking across America! Fill your water bottle! Pump up the tires! Grab an extra pair of underwear! Let's go!"

No. It began with a conversation the two of us had seven years prior, when he was in kindergarten. While finishing dinner, little Yonah asked, "Daddy, what happens after you die?"

I remember scant little from Yonah's early childhood except for the times when I caused him bodily harm. Once I walked through a low doorway with him sitting astride my shoulders, giving the toddler a man-sized bump on the head. While changing his diapers, I almost sent him to the emergency room, twice. The first time, I shish-kebabed his delicate baby's butt with a safety pin while pinning his nappy. I pushed and pushed, trying to get the pin through the thick, unyielding cotton. And then it was through, and I closed it. Initially, he didn't make a sound, but his face had a strange look of surprise, and I knew I had done a bad thing. A few months later, I gave him a penny to play with, so he'd stop squirming while I cleaned his tush. Then the penny disappeared. It wasn't in his hands, it wasn't on the changing table, the carpet was bare. I stared at my smiling infant.

"You didn't . . . no . . . don't tell me you . . . your mother is going to *kill* me." For the next two days, my wife, Djina, and I went through his poop. If the penny didn't pass, it would be a possible surgery and a probable divorce. Fortunately it passed.

With a father like me, no wonder the five-year-old was curious about death.

Yonah's first words, his first steps, and the first time he slept through the night are stored somewhere in my brain, but I cannot access those memories. But that question, the question that launched a thousand religions, is burned into my brain as though Yonah asked it ten minutes ago. I remember thinking that this was the essence of fatherhood: conversing with your child on issues of truth and passing wisdom from one generation to the next. "That's a great question, and the truth is that no one really knows what happens when a person dies because no dead person has ever come back to tell us. But there are at least three ideas that people have. The first is that the part of you that makes you you, your soul, goes to a place like heaven or to somewhere else and lives on. The second one says that people are reborn into something different. It's called reincarnation. Maybe you'll be born as another person or maybe as an animal. What kind of animal would you like to be reincarnated as?"

"I like cheetah-birds," he replied.

"That's nice. The third possibility is that when you die, nothing happens. You're dead, and that's the end."

The third possibility sounded harsh, and I didn't want to burden a young soul with existential nightmares, so I softened it with, "It's like being asleep."

Yonah digested it all. I could sense his frontal lobes cogitating. When he finished, he announced, "I'm the kind who thinks that when you're dead, you're dead." He climbed off his chair and skipped to his room to play with Thomas the Tank Engine.

I sat dumbfounded because my five-year-old was more definite about the nature of life and death than I was at thirty-nine. I was a liberal Jew who had some amorphous faith in God or a higher power imbuing the universe with meaning. I also believed, or at least wanted to believe, in the immortal nature of the soul. But here, as I sat at the dining room table cluttered with junk mail, mismatched dirty socks, and plates smeared with spaghetti remains, I had witnessed the genesis of an atheist.

Not only am I Jewish, but I attended graduate school at Hebrew Union College, a liberal seminary, to study the Bible and its commentaries. I did not come from a religious household. My family attended synagogue twice a year for the High Holidays, where

I sullenly sat, watching the prayer book page numbers slowly trudge to the end of the service. Whenever the rabbi mercifully skipped thirty pages, my heart leapt, only to sink when, in a fit of sadism, he sent us back twenty. Passover was a week of choking down stale matzo sandwiches and scrubbing bright-red lipstick off my cheeks after being kissed by relatives as old as the children of Israel themselves. For three years, I suffered in Hebrew school, and at age thirteen had my bar mitzvah. Following that day, when I became a man in the eyes of Judaism, I vowed never again to step into a synagogue.

So how did I wind up at a Jewish seminary?

After graduating from college, I traveled to Israel to work on a kibbutz, a collective farm, partly because of my socialist leanings but mostly to meet blond Scandinavian volunteers. One day in Jerusalem, I happened upon a poster featuring a bagel smothered with cream cheese and lox. Underneath the bagel was the message: "Is this the culmination of thirty-five hundred years of culture?" No doubt about it. That poster perfectly captured my relationship to Judaism, but it gave me pause. Thirty-five hundred years. That's a chunk of time. Could there be something more to my heritage than smoked salmon? After all, while Jews number fewer than one-hundredth of 1 percent of the world's population, they have taken home 20 percent of all Nobel Prizes. Perhaps it was worth giving Judaism one more chance. I enrolled in a yeshiva, a religious college, and spent two months studying the Talmud, Judaism's sacred post-biblical text. Though I was a UC Berkeley graduate, I had never found more serious students than the ones arguing over these ancient books. And there was wisdom. I had fancied myself an environmentalist, and here was Yahweh, two thousand years before the first Earth Day, proclaiming in Ecclesiastes Rabbah: "Take care of My Creation, for if you destroy it, there is no one to clean up after you."

I became religious, returned to America, and enrolled in Hebrew Union College. Following grad school, I taught in a variety of Jewish educational settings for fifteen years. I co-wrote a Jewish naturalist guide. Turning my hand to fiction, I penned three books of Jewish short stories. Christ, you couldn't be much more Jewish than me. But as Yonah approached age thirteen, his bar mitzvah year, the joke about the shoemaker's shoeless son became personal. Yonah didn't want to go through the Jewish rite-of-passage ceremony. If, at age five, he was only theologically opposed to immortality, by twelve, he had developed a severe loathing toward religion.

Djina, and I spoke of Judaism as more than a religious belief. We explained that Judaism could be thought of as a culture. Plenty of Jews have little patience for the religious doctrines but are proud of being Jewish. Yonah would have none of this. He saw religion as a way to dumb people down and as the root of the world's conflicts. I felt he was rejecting a child's version of religion, the one represented by the long-bearded, muscular God of Genesis painted on the Sistine Chapel's ceiling. I, too, had rejected that God and religious view. For me, religion meant community, beautiful stories, and a taste of the spiritual world. It was not a dogma of rules and rites; rather, religion was a conduit to finding meaning in life. Yonah's rejection seemed like a Christian rejecting the fellowship and charity that come with Christianity after reading about atrocities committed by Crusaders in the name of Christ. But nuances and paradoxes are difficult for young teens. The bottom line: My son had no desire to be a Jew.

Should Djina and I have pushed the bar mitzvah on him as many parents do? Wasn't there a Jewish teaching: If first one acts, understanding will follow? But even if the coming-of-age ritual were meaningful, insisting that Yonah participate could more likely breed resentment and fury. Perhaps if religion weren't forced down his throat, our son would find his Jewish soul in his own time, as Djina and I had.

Ironically, the atheist himself decided to attend Hebrew school at age twelve. He didn't do it at the behest of his parents or because of some change of heart about spiritual matters. It was a cold Machiavellian calculation. He had decided to become president of the United States. But he came to learn that Americans would more likely elect a Jew than an atheist because the most disliked people in America are those who do not believe in God. (A 1999 Gallup poll found that while 6 percent of Americans would not vote for a Jewish presidential candidate, and 8 percent would refuse a woman, a full 48 percent would not cast their ballots for an atheist.) So Yonah dutifully went to Hebrew school.

"What have you learned so far?" I asked after a month.

"There's like a hundred prayers, and they all say, 'God, you're great!' You'd think if God were so great, he wouldn't need us to keep telling him."

In addition to learning prayers, Yonah studied Jewish thought. He enjoyed debating the great philosophical questions, such as the nature of good and evil. Unfortunately, much of the curriculum dealt with the "boring" Jewish laws such as *kashrut*, and why one must never eat chicken and cheese together. Yonah had been a strict vegetarian since age eight and, without realizing it, had been living a de facto kosher life.

"See—you're more Jewish than you thought!" I told him.

"Right, Dad."

After six months he announced, "No more." The chance to pontificate on a Torah passage in front of an audience held no appeal. The chocolate fountains of the bar mitzvah party did not entice him. Even a vision of the presidency didn't exert a strong enough pull to get him to wear a *yamulke* for a single Saturday morning. His thirteenth birthday would come and go like all his others. And I'd be sad.

The truth was I didn't want Yonah to become zealously religious. But thirteen is an auspicious age. While a boy is not a man at thirteen, he is clearly no longer a child. Almost every ancient culture recognized puberty's importance, but in America it is mostly ignored. We wanted Yonah to mark his thirteenth birthday with a ritual, a rite of passage. But if not a bar mitzvah, what?

I had always admired the Native American vision quest (or at least the popular impression of it): a solo physical journey into the wilderness with the express desire to experience a spiritual awakening. The fasting boy hikes deep into the wilderness, pushing beyond his physical endurance until he reaches a sacred space. Through prayer, the boy enters the dream world and learns his true name, the essence of his spiritual being. Upon returning, he is no longer a boy, but a young man.

A spiritual journey wouldn't appeal to Yonah, but a physical one might. Physical challenges allow us to measure our fortitude and spirit, to find our limits, push against them, and learn who we are when the veneer of personality disintegrates in the face of challenge and danger. Maybe if the challenge was profound enough physically, the spiritual might ride on its coattails.

I love to bike and had some friends who had cycled across the United States. Maybe Yonah could do that, and I'd join him. It would be a real father-son bonding experience. Besides being a physical challenge, it would be an eye-opener for a blue-state, West Coast kid to experience the heartland of America and go beyond the stereotype of gun-toting pro-lifers who think Darwin should have been burned at the stake. It would be like exploring a foreign culture without having to learn a new language. I ran the idea past him.

"Are you kidding?" he said.

"I'm serious."

"It's like three thousand miles."

"Actually, because you take backroads instead of freeways, it's more like four thousand."

"There is *no* way."

"C'mon, you love American history. Here's a chance to see where history was made. It'll be fun and a challenge. You'll probably be like the youngest kid ever to do it."

"Bike riding's boring."

"Did Mom tell you *her* idea? Going to Israel and visiting the holy sites like the Western Wall . . . "

"Definitely no!"

"Got any other ideas?" Silence. "Okay, then it's back to Hebrew school."

"No, no, no! That bike thing sounds okay."

So in order to avoid a single day of chanting a small section of Torah, leading a congregation in a half-dozen prayers, and dancing with his grandmother at his bar mitzvah party, twelve-year-old Yonah Biers-Ariel, an ambivalent cyclist, decided to pedal a bicycle from San Francisco to Washington, D.C., with his dad.

THE BAR MITZVAH AND THE BEAST

Now that we had decided to bike across America, I asked myself, "Is it possible?" Ten weeks of summer vacation to cover four thousand miles. The farthest that Yonah had ever biked was twenty-five miles, an all-day extravaganza with innumerable rest stops. Even if Yonah could manage the mileage, he'd have to do it with camping equipment and food strapped onto his bike, not only riding a twenty-five-pound bike up the Rocky Mountains, but lugging an additional twenty-five pounds of gear. And so much could go wrong. Bust a wheel in the Nevada desert and it's days waiting for new one. Midwest thunderstorms could force us to hunker down for a week. And if either of us got even a cold, the delay would sink us. Though no bookies would give us even odds, it was at least worth a try. As that poem in the Reform Judaism prayer book says, it's the journey, not the destination, that counts.

"And if you don't try, you'll never know what you're capable of. If we need to, we can leapfrog Kansas and Missouri by bus. I mean, how much corn do you need to see?"

"I'd rather leapfrog the Rockies."

The plan of the two of us biking across America by ourselves lasted until son number two walked through the front door. Solomon, at eight years old, was clearly too young to ride across the country, but upon hearing the adventure, there was no way he was staying home due to Little Brother Rule #1: Anything big brother does must be done by little brother. Impossibility of task adds to the allure.

"Solly, we're going to be on our bikes at least four hours a day."

"So?"

"That's going to be boring for you."

"No, it won't."

"It's going to be really hard. I don't know if Yonah can do it, and he's four years older. I don't even know if *I* can do it."

"I can do it."

"You can't bring your Gameboy."

Long pause. Deep swallow. "If Yonah can do it, I can do it."

So Solomon, who recently had been passed by a seventy-five-year-old jogger while riding his bike to school, was coming. While he would add fun, Solomon would make the trip significantly more challenging because it meant he and I would ride together on a tandem bicycle. Tandems are notoriously difficult in hill climbing, and we were not just negotiating hills, but mountains: the Sierras, the Rockies, the Appalachians. If a tandem with two strong adults is hard going, how about one with a middle-aged man sporting chronically sore knees seated in front of a third-grade graduate? For those unfamiliar with young boy energy as played out on a bicycle, it goes like this: Thirty seconds hell-bent sprinting to the finish line of the Tour de France followed by ten minutes of recuperation while naming favorite baseball players and reciting their statistics before another thirty seconds of sprinting. Repeat until sixth grade.

When Djina came home from work, I proudly announced, "Yonah wants to ride cross-country. Solomon's coming too."

"Are you crazy? There is no way!"

"We looked at the maps. It'll be tough, but it's possible. As Theodore Herzl said, 'If you will it, it is no dream.'"

The corners of her mouth slowly lifted and her blue-green eyes sparkled. "I mean there's no way I'm letting you take them on your own. I'm coming too." Despite my perfect record with Solomon on the changing table, Yonah's diaper debacles still weighed on her mind. But to be fair, this was about more than her progeny's safety. Djina loves cycling and adventure. There was, however, a timing obstacle. As a high school English teacher in a public school, I shared summer vacation with the boys. She's a midwife and can't say to an eight-month pregnant woman, "Can you put off pushing until, say, Labor Day?" But like Solomon, Djina would not be deterred. She went to her colleagues, they made a coverage agreement, and the whole family was signed on.

Biking across America would be an extreme physical challenge. But would it be a sufficient rite of passage for Yonah? Most synagogues do not consider leading a religious service adequate to complete the bar mitzvah. There is usually a social action element, such as collecting money for food banks, working at a homeless shelter, taking part in a river cleanup. Yonah needed something too. And it was Yonah who suggested tackling global climate change. Every other issue paled compared to rising water levels, mass extinctions, and the whole panoply of requisite disasters that comes with atmospheric carbon dioxide buildup. And wasn't cycling a carbon-free way to travel? Even if we made it only as far as the Sierras, we'd be an example for others to view biking as a legitimate means of transportation.

The idea was simple: Write a petition, gather a million signatures, present it to the White House and Congress, and watch the country suddenly become carbon neutral and lead the world toward a green future. As a humble family, we did not expect a ticker-tape parade, but if the president insisted. . . .

The petition focused on practical ideas. While arguably the best action an individual can take to arrest global warming is dig a hole, drive his car into it, and then fill the hole, this idea would not win the day. Our ideas focused on improving gas mileage, decreasing car trips, and creating a green energy industry. The petition would be a kick in the pants for our country to stop dragging its humongous carbon footprint and show leadership. I imagined a media field day as we would, Pied Piper–like, lead thousands of cyclists into Washington, D.C., converge on the White House to deliver half-a-million signatures, and then climb back on our bikes and ride up Constitution Avenue to deliver the other half-million to Congress. The glacier of American lethargy on global warming would melt. Angelina Jolie would hand us frosty smoothies made with organic fruit, and George Clooney would present us with keys to a brand-new Prius.

Riding coast to coast would be Yonah's rite of passage, moving him from child to adolescent. On a larger scale, we hoped that our petition might catalyze America to undergo a transformation from our petrochemical present to a noncarbon future. Like riding across the country, changing our energy usage would be a difficult transformation, and like a rite of passage, not without pain. At least collecting signatures would be easy. Besides a few troglodytes, who wouldn't sign? No one wants to combat malaria mosquitoes in Alaska or to tour New York City in a submarine. But how to gather so many signatures? The internet. Just turn the petition into an electronic format and glom it onto an already existing organization's website. How about the Sierra Club?

"Yes!" their media guy exclaimed enthusiastically when we called. Unfortunately, it was early 2007 and then-President George

W. Bush was keeping the club's fingers engaged in plugging up the dikes protecting the Arctic National Wildlife Refuge and the Endangered Species Act. They didn't have time.

How about MoveOn.org? Aren't they the voice of liberal, grassroots electronic organizing? While they never have a problem getting in touch with me with weekly action updates, try and contact them if you're not Al Gore. I combed through their website. No contact info. I called 411. "I'm sorry but we have no listing."

A few days later the phone rang. "This is David Henderson from MoveOn.org."

"Did you say MoveOn.org?"

"Yes, we are starting a campaign to close Guantanamo Bay . . . "

"I've been trying to reach you guys for months! Listen to this amazing idea [five minutes of blather about the trip and petition]. Whom do I contact about getting the petition on your website?"

"Well, uh, I don't know. I was sent campaign information on my computer. I've never spoken to anyone either."

"Oh."

"Would you like to get involved with the—"

"Maybe next time. Bye."

Finally, after trolling the internet a few more weeks, we found Cool Capital, a consortium of environmental, business, and other Washington, D.C., groups dedicated to greening the nation's capital. We emailed them. The next day the executive director called and said she was so moved by our trip that tears splashed onto her keyboard. Not only would they set up an electronic petition, but they would host a blog and help organize the thousands of riders who would converge on D.C. the day of our arrival. Our dream was actually going to become reality. I suggested Yonah start writing the speech he'd deliver from the Capitol steps. I went to the Prius website to look at car colors.

Alas, Robert Burns put it best when he wrote, "The best-laid plans o' mice an' men / Gang aft a-gley, / An' lea'e us nought but grief an' pain / For promised joy." Here's a translation for those whose eighteenth-century Scottish-tinged English is rusty: "We plan, and then through no fault of our own, we fail. And then we cry." An old Jewish adage puts a different spin on it: "Man plans, God laughs." An atheist might venture: "Man plans, and maybe another man plans against him, or maybe a hurricane comes, or who knows what, but it won't work."

The point is that the director at Cool Capital assigned an intern to coordinate everything. The intern had other plans and did nothing. By the time we realized this, the director, who had earlier been moved to tears, had moved to a new job, and we were left adrift, alone on a piece of melting arctic ice. But the petition would not be abandoned. If the glacier would not come to Muhammad, we would go to the glacier and collect the signatures ourselves on the old standby, paper.

O═O:O═O:O═O:O═O:O═O:O═O:O═O:O═O:O═O:O═O:O═O

A trip of this magnitude needs preparation. The right equipment is critical. Topping the list: bicycles. The bicycle is a technological marvel that can move a human being four times a walking pace using one-third the energy. A human on a bicycle is more efficient in terms of calories per mile than any other mode of transportation. It is the most ubiquitous form of transportation in the entire world (excluding the United States, of course).

Yonah had a cheap, hand-me-down bike. The Sierras would laugh it off the mountain, so we bought him a touring bicycle, thereby going from the biking equivalent of a 1993 Ford Fiesta to a new Toyota Camry Hybrid. Djina already had a bicycle, but it was a racing bike, not a touring one, with a carbon-based graphite frame that could be lifted by an index finger. If Yonah's new bike was a Toyota Camry, Djina's was a Porsche Boxster. Loading this bike with sleeping bags and tents would be as inelegant as hitching a U-Haul trailer to a Porsche. It wasn't right, but it would work.

Solly and I needed a tandem, and they were not cheap. A decent one was in the three- to four-thousand dollar range. I was never much for tandems, and since this ride would be a onetime thing, I refused to pay retail.

Djina advised me to buy a new one and then sell it later.

"Why buy a new bike when I can get a used one on eBay?" I protested. "It's better to reuse than buy new, and it's common knowledge that tandems are bought by guys who want their significant others to get into biking. The guy buys a four-thousand dollar bike, and they go for the first ride. She hates that most of what she sees is his back, and she's hoarse from screaming at him to slow down. But she's a good sport and goes out with him on Saturdays for a month. On the fifth Saturday she refuses to mount 'that thing,' and she tells him the only way he is going to ride the tandem is with another woman. So after two hundred miles, the tandem is retired to the garage. One year later, it's moved up to the rafters. Five years later, she makes him sell it, so they can buy a bike trailer for the baby. And then I get it cheap."

"I'd buy a new one."

My thought bubble chuckled, "I'll show her."

As it turned out, the tandem was not a single mouse click away. There were lots of guys looking to get their significant others into biking, and those bastards were too cheap to buy new, so I learned eBay strategic bidding, which is to hold off until the auction's last minute. Unfortunately, others employ the same strategy, and as a teacher, it's hard to do personal business from school.

" . . . and the reason the theme of my short story is loss of innocence is that when I was six, my dad left us and . . . "

"Paul, can you hold that thought for a second? I just have to do something real fast."

I lost three sweet bikes to final buzzer bidders. After the third one, Djina reiterated her "I'd buy a new one" mantra. My thought bubble could barely contain itself screeching, "I'll *really* show her!"

I discovered Esnipe, a service that automatically slips your bid in thirty seconds before the auction closes. Pay a nominal fee, tell them how high you're willing to bid, and—voilà—you've got a new (well, used) bike. A Burley tandem came up. It looked good. The seller, however, didn't know anything about it. He couldn't tell me the year or model. But that hardly mattered. In fact, it was better because it proved he didn't ride it. It had been mothballed in the rafters since the fall of the Berlin Wall. Lots of people wanted it and the bidding war was on. I contacted Esnipe, observed from the sidelines, and four days later received the "You're a winner!" congratulatory email.

The bike arrived and looked fine. Perhaps it had a few more than two hundred miles on it, but that baby was solid. If Yonah had a Toyota Camry and Djina was cycling a Porsche, Solomon and I were going to cross America in a good-condition 1985ish Ford F350 one-ton pickup.

"See," I crowed to my wife. She smiled, but her thought bubble was easy to cipher: "I would have bought a new one."

○▬○▪○▬○▪○▬○▪○▬○▪○▬○▪○▬○▪○▬○▪○▬○

To carry gear and food, some transcontinental cyclists have a friend or family member follow in a sag vehicle to haul everything. Since this defeated the low carbon footprint message, we had two options: panniers (saddlebags) or bike trailers. For panniers, a bicycle needs brazons, threaded nuts in the frame that a bicycle rack can be screwed into. The panniers then attach to the rack. Racing bikes don't have brazons, so Djina got a trailer. We put panniers on the other two bikes because a trailer might be too difficult for Yonah to handle, and a trailer on the back of an already stretched tandem might make it longer than an actual Ford pickup.

Now the gear itself. The plan was to camp most days, so it was to Recreational Equipment Incorporated (REI) for lightweight equipment. There was a three-pound, eleven-ounce tent for $168. For $329, we could purchase a three-pound, three-ounce tent.

Me: "Let's get the $168 tent." (I had already put it in the cart.)

Djina: "Half a pound is a lot of weight." (She put the other one in.)

Me: "That's like five Clif Bars. And it's $160 more."

Djina: "Trust me, every ounce counts. It's not that much money to save your knees."

Twenty more minutes of arguing/discussion, and like Solomon's namesake, we cut the baby in half. One $168 tent, one $329 tent. (One month later, still two months before the trip, the $329 tent went on sale for $159.)

The other items weren't any easier. Titanium or aluminum pots? This time the difference was three ounces and thirty dollars. We went titanium. Then the stove. There were twenty stoves from which to choose. Djina liked a particular MSR model. It was lightweight and dependable, but it required special fuel canisters. I was skeptical about finding them in Kentucky, but the salesman assured us: "You can buy MSR canisters everywhere." So it went into the cart. The camping equipment was rounded out with stuff from home: sleeping bags, ensolite pads, matches, sporks (combination spoon/fork/knife utensils), bowls, and our friend Ken Giles's special pencil gift: a number-two pencil wrapped with duct tape. "Duct tape can fix anything," he told me. "It'll come in handy."

Other equipment included my Leatherman, a Swiss Army Knife on steroids. With its pliers, knife, and thirteen other gadgets, which I hadn't the foggiest idea how to use, we were covered for exigencies such as opening beer bottles that weren't twist-offs. I bought a bike tool. It had tire irons (for removing the tire from the wheel to repair flats), assorted wrenches, and a chain link remover.

"A chain link remover?" I asked incredulously. "Why would I ever need that? I've been biking for over forty years, and I've never broken a chain."

"Well," the salesman said, "if you do happen to break your chain in the middle of the desert, it'd be good to have."

"Whatever," I said, and he rang it up along with spare tires and tubes.

Djina compiled a first-aid bag anchored with sunscreen and ibuprofen. The final piece of equipment was a set of Adventure Cycling Association (ACA) maps. This organization produces ten or so map sets that crisscross the United States. These maps are genius. Each one covers between three hundred to 450 miles of roads that avoid heavy traffic and big cities. In addition to giving the safest, most scenic route, the maps provide elevation profiles and locate campgrounds, grocery stores, hotels, libraries, and bicycle shops. Yonah and I pored over the maps and made an itinerary based on mileage, elevation changes, and campground locations. At about sixty miles a day, the trip would take sixty-three days riding plus six rest days.

The sleeping bags and tents went in the trailer hooked to Djina's bike. The two other bikes carried four panniers each, two small ones in front, two large ones in back. Each person had a large one for clothing. The small ones were for equipment and food. Unlike a multiday backpacking trek, we didn't need to pack all of our food. We brought some essentials that would be hard to find in the Ozarks, such as eighty packets of a vitamin supplement that promised to save my knees. We kept the panniers stuffed with at least ten energy bars. (Note: We decided in the Nevada desert that chocolate-covered bars would henceforth be forbidden.)

SINGING YOUR SONG

TIME TO TRAIN. We live in Davis, California, a college town ten miles west of Sacramento. Since 2002, I've taught in Winters, thirteen miles away, and have commuted by bicycle, so I was more or less trained. Djina took a spin class a few times a week, where twenty stationary bicycles are crammed into a space the size of a living room, ventilated by industrial fans. Green Day, The Rolling Stones, and other such truck blare over loudspeakers while an instructor, who makes Arnold Schwarzenegger (circa 1975) look like a wuss, screams, "Push it!" Djina, too, was more or less trained.

The boys played sports and rode their bikes to school, but their in-shapeness to ride across the country was the equivalent of being ready to pilot a jetfighter after mastering the art of folding a paper airplane. Our initial ride was to Winters. After six miles at a poky 12 miles per hour pace on a flat road and carrying no gear, the boys were kaput.

"Are you kidding?" I didn't try to mask my irritation.

"I'm really thirsty," Yonah said.

"I'm hungry," Solomon piped in.

"Yeah," Yonah agreed.

While they took ten minutes to rest, eat, drink, and complain, I calculated. We needed to cover sixty miles a day. At this pace, plus gear, plus mountains, Greenland would be exporting pineapples by the time we rolled into Washington, D.C. It was obvious: We had bitten off too much. Way too much. We needed to amend the trip. San Francisco to Los Angeles was a legitimate long-distance route, and at four hundred miles, it might be doable.

Yet to change the trip would be to admit failure. All the nay-sayers who had pronounced "No way!" when we announced our plan could now crow, "I told you you were crazy. "It wasn't opti-mism that said, "Don't give up, we can do it." No. We had told everyone that we were going to ride cross-country, and—damn it—no matter what, we would stick to the plan because pride was at stake. While pride is often given a bad rap, it is the great motivator. Without it, our species might still be swinging in the trees. So I kept quiet, and after a few more grumbles, the boys mounted their bikes.

It took two more trips before we could reach Winters without stopping. We weren't breaking any speed records, averaging 12 miles per hour, but I figured that by the end of our training regi-men, we'd be at 15 miles per hour. That would mean four hours on the bikes to do the daily sixty miles. This would allow time to indulge in Djina's pre-trip fantasies: eating at Rotary Club pan-cake breakfasts, swimming in lakes, and taking in matinees to avoid the midday sun.

After mastering Winters, we increased our mileage to a forty-mile loop around Lake Solano. Two months into training and it was hill time. Going coast to coast means over 150,000 feet of vertical climbing. That's thirty miles straight up, high enough to wave to the Space Shuttle. Davis is located in California's Central Valley, an ancient seabed where the "hills" are the freeway over-passes. Cantelow Road is the only local topography. It is relatively steep, at about an 8 percent pitch, but it's short. Nevertheless, it was our training mountain. It takes an average rider six min-utes to reach the top. It took Solomon and me twenty minutes to struggle up it. Average speed: 4.3 miles per hour.

"Well," I said, "if we need to, we'll get off and push the bike up the steep roads. No shame in that."

The next step was to add the panniers and trailer, and ride with weight. At this point, the tandem's metaphor, a Ford F350 truck, was jettisoned and replaced by the bike's true name, The Beast. If it was on the heavy side without panniers, there are no adjectives to describe it fully loaded. The tired allusion of Sisyphus did not do justice to pedaling the fully loaded Beast up Cantelow. It was more akin to pedaling through seven-inch-thick, newly poured cement. We crawled up Cantelow at 3.2 miles per hour, the same pace of my eighty-year-old mother's daily constitutional. The silver lining: We didn't get off and push.

The goal of a fifteen-miles-per-hour average was discarded like a banana peel on the side of the road. Twelve miles per hour was the new goal, but doubtful. Ten miles per hour seemed more likely. Six hours of actual riding time. With breaks and everything, probably on the road eight hours a day. In other words, good-bye to those matinees. I didn't care. Most summer movies suck.

While both Djina and Yonah's bikes worked like the well-tuned machines they were, The Beast, well, I was not as right as I could have been about buying a used tandem. This bike had been some couple's workhorse for twenty years and was tired and ready to go to pasture. Components failed on a regular basis.

"You can still get a new bike," Djina offered. And admit I was wrong? Never! Sure the bike wasn't perfect, but it still was cheaper than a new bike and rode pretty well—most of the time. It just needed some TLC. So I replaced chains, shifters, and cables. I reconfigured the brakes and adjusted the gears. But it still got grumpy. And struggling with it always led to getting busted by the family's language cop. Solomon's mission was to stamp out curse words. If someone said, "Damn!" "Shit!" or any other non-synagogue word, he would shout, "Checkmark!" hoping that through his intervention we would clean our diction and substitute approved exclamations such as "Gosh darn!" But when you strain up a hill at 3 miles per hour, and need one entire breath for every single pedal rotation, and you can't take your hands off the handlebars long enough to wipe the sweat stinging your eyes, and the hill becomes even steeper, and you steel yourself for more pain as you shift into the lowest gear you have, and the chain decides at that moment, that very moment, to leap off the chain ring and wedge itself between the chain ring and the frame as if it had been super-glued into place, and your pedals come to a dead stop, and so do you, and you fall, and your knee, hand, and shoulder get bloodied, and all those part replacements and adjustments you made over the last month prove themselves worthless, then "Gosh darn!" or "Jeez!" just won't cut it. The only words to act as balm are "Goddamn motherfucking piece of shit!"

And then, standing above his sprawled-out father is Solomon, hands on hips. "Checkmark, checkmark, checkmark."

The Beast's most significant problem was its cluster of three chain rings. The largest diameter one was for going fast. The middle one was where the chain lived 80 percent of the time. Then came the small—actually tiny—ring, which was the only way to get The Beast up a climb. Unfortunately, shifting into this low gear was tricky due to the wide gap between it and the middle chain ring. Occasionally the chain shifted too far and wedged itself between the chain ring and the frame. As a devotee of Murphy's Law, the chain would wedge at only the worst of times. To free it meant yanking it with both hands, in conjunction with a good strong oath, and then repeating these steps until the chain, satisfied that my hands were sufficiently blackened with grease, relented.

○━○▪○━○▪○━○▪○━○▪○━○▪○━○▪○━○▪○━○▪○━○▪○━○▪○━○

I thought my last book, *The Triumph of Eve and Other Subversive Bible Tales*, would be so controversial that I considered using a pseudonym in case a crazed fundamentalist wanted to deliver a personal fatwa through our living room window. In the end, I kept my name and hoped a large, conservative organization would ban the book. Outside of an appearance on *Oprah*, nothing guarantees the success of a book like being excommunicated. But no one called for a book burning, Oprah's administrative assistant never left a message on my answering machine, and outside of the 1,987 people who bought the book, nobody knew it existed. The lesson here is that writing a book is the easy part. Getting people to take notice—there's the real work. And so too with the ride. If we wanted publicity for the petition, it was on us to get it done.

Four months before the trip, we contacted the local paper, *The Davis Enterprise*, and pitched the idea. The reporter said, "Call back in two months." Not a promising start. If he decided to write a story, it would be buried below the obituaries. It must have been a slow news week when I called back. He interviewed us, and then splayed across the top of the next Sunday's front page was our picture under the headline: "Gearing Up for Change." A long, flattering article followed.

That day we rode up Cantelow and stopped at the top. Another rider pulled up. "You're the family in the paper. It's a great thing you're trying. Good luck."

At that moment, the ride became real for Solly, and he worriedly asked, "If we don't go on the ride, is there going to be an article saying we didn't go?"

"Of course, so when we get to the bottom of Cantelow, you'll have to start pedaling harder." When we hit the flats, I felt a power surge from the rear for the first time.

The local publicity helped as the next Saturday, the boys and I went to the farmers market to set up a table with our petition. People crowded around to sign. Our line was longer than the one at the Gold Rush Kettle Corn booth. Forget the online petition. We were going to get a million signatures ourselves.

Janet Fullwood, travel editor of the *Sacramento Bee*, said she would like to follow the trip's progress with a series of stories. The day after the initial article, my email box was for once not dominated by penis-enhancement ads, but by people requesting petitions to circulate and offering places to stay when we crossed the Sierras. KGO, a large San Francisco AM radio station, sent out a reporter. Not to be outdone, *Good Morning, Sacramento* put us on live TV.

Suddenly we were minor celebrities. Here was a real family adventure. Though completing the ride across the continent was still less than an even bet, it wasn't something unattainable. A family might be able to do it. Unlike an elite athlete or an extreme mountaineer, we were relatable. People also responded because we were putting ourselves in the public eye to do something about global warming. If we could somehow bottle and then deliver the desire that people had for Washington to take the lead on global warming, it would knock our representatives over, and they would have to act. It would be that clichéd bumper sticker come to life: "If the people lead, the leaders will follow."

We contacted newspapers along the route, but Kansas's *Hutchinson News* was the only one that wrote an article. When I asked the editor of the Carson City, Nevada, paper why he passed, he replied, "Do you know how many bicyclists come through our city each summer trying to raise money or get a petition signed?"

"But this is about global warming," I said.

"Lung cancer, diabetes, animal testing. Everybody thinks his ride is the only one."

"I bet none of them do it with kids," I said.

"Last year a guy crossed the country on a horse."

◦▬◦▬◦▬◦▬◦▬◦▬◦▬◦▬◦▬◦▬◦▬◦▬◦

The newspaper articles all focused on the family challenge and global climate change, but it was a single line that caught a certain people's collective attention. To us, it was almost a throwaway line. But to this subset of readers, it was the only line that counted. The line wasn't "Parents forcing children to cycle through Nevada desert; Child Protective Service notified." It wasn't "Fight to end global warming takes to two wheels." Nor was it "Family vows to try every variety of French fry in the country." It was "Yonah Biers-Ariel did not want a traditional bar mitzvah because he is an atheist." While this was a true statement, and was the seed of the trip, once the trip was decided, we hardly gave it a thought. But to the people who were struck by this statement, the sentence "Yonah Biers-Ariel enjoys dipping kittens in gasoline and lighting them on fire" would not have evoked a stronger response.

We should have seen it coming. Remember the Gallup poll? Forty-eight percent of Americans hate atheists. But why? Why are they reviled? Fear. If an atheist were elected president, people would fear that he'd have no religious moral code to guide him, and he'd rule like a heathen. What would prevent an atheist president from, say, playing footsie in an airport restroom with a person of the same sex? More likely than such a far-fetched scenario would be an atheist prez creating a death panel mandated to pull the plug on Granny.

Yet the strong reaction runs deeper than the fear of amorality. It is at the subconscious level where our true fears rule. It is at this level where the religious-minded fear that the atheists might be on to something. The more science unlocks the secrets of life, the smaller God becomes. At some point, God may become superfluous. Without God, there is no afterlife, and the raison d'être for practically every religion evaporates. Without God, the foundation of billions of people is destroyed as they undergo an extreme existential crisis attempting to make meaning out of a meaningless universe.

America, we have a problem.

The opening salvo was launched at work. I posted the *Davis Enterprise* article alongside the petition in the teachers' room. One colleague, whom I respect as a great teacher, clings to a different theological view of the world. Specifically, she believes that one day in the not-so-distant future, she will be raptured to Heaven with all those who have taken Jesus into their hearts. Though she genuinely likes Jews in general and me in particular, she believes that I will earn a one-way ticket to Hell for not letting Jesus save me. She read the article and instead of "What an amazing trip you and your family are taking!" the first words out of her mouth were "Aren't you concerned about your son's soul?"

As much as any parent. But was I bothered that he didn't believe in God? Not really. Yonah was and is one of the most moral people I know. He gets along with everybody. Excluding tussles with his little brother, he has never been in a fight. The one time he got in trouble at school was when he stood up to his teacher because another student was unfairly punished. He doesn't believe in killing animals for food. How concerned should I have been? Besides, he was young and impressionable. One day he'd likely discover his Jewish soul.

Besides garnering media attention, we contacted elected officials in Washington to set up meetings and present them with the petition. The International Panel on Climate Change (IPCC), the official United Nations research group on global warming, had issued its 2007 report, which stated that global warming was real and that "most of the observed increase in globally averaged temperatures since the mid-twentieth century is very likely due to the observed increase in anthropogenic [human-made] greenhouse gas concentrations." Nevertheless, then-President

George Bush refused to take the scientific consensus seriously. If we were to arrive at 1600 Pennsylvania Avenue with a thousand polar bears, he wouldn't give us a second look; he didn't think the country needed to transform energy policy. His mantra was, "Drill, baby, drill." Therefore, we would bypass the executive branch and go to Congress, since they would write any climate change laws. Unfortunately, in August, when we were planning to arrive, Congress would be on vacation.

At least their staffs would be in town, and the truth of the matter is that the grunts, the congressional staffs, do the heavy lifting on Capitol Hill. Senator Barbara Boxer's chief of staff for the Environment and Public Works Committee agreed to meet us. This committee, charged with dealing with global climate change, made Boxer, as committee chair, the Senate's most powerful player on the issue. With the help of the Secular Coalition for America (read: atheists), we set up a meeting with David Moulton, the staff director for the House Select Committee on Energy Independence and Global Warming, then chaired by Congressman Ed Markey.

So we weren't going to be pictured on the front page of the *Washington Post* leading a thousand bicyclists while presenting a million-signature petition to W. But we were going to the heads of the committees in the House and Senate that could actually do something about global warming.

The truth is, I didn't want a Prius anyway.

<hr />

We held a dress rehearsal: a three-day, fully loaded ride to Calistoga, sixty miles away. On the way is Cardiac, a fifteen-hundred-foot climb. (Think older, not-in-great-shape bike rider, and you've got the name's origin.) If we could manage Cardiac, the sixty miles, and the panniers, we'd be ready for anything. The ride went well except for a ten-mile stretch on State Route 29 that lacked shoulders. Who would have thought our effort of riding on the far-right white line would be so underappreciated? Though there was only one driver who actually raised a middle-finger salute and said something that earned him a checkmark, there were more glares than smiles. The drivers were not turning to their passengers and exclaiming, "Look, Mary, a family of bike riders! What wonderful transportation role models! Such family bonding! Let's sell the car and buy bikes! Thank you, Biers-Ariel clan! Have a great day!"

No. It was, "Goddamn assholes! Fuck you!" How do I know? While driving, I've been slowed by a peloton of bikers. I've been there.

Because the summer wasn't quite long enough, I made lesson plans for the first week of school that I'd miss and swallowed a bitter pill. I had assumed I'd take the missed week as "personal necessity" days. A personal necessity day is using a sick day when you're not sick. The principal agreed, but the superintendent would not. I was livid. Didn't I have a large stockpile of unused sick days? Wasn't I role modeling transportation alternatives for our students? Well? In the end, I had to take a leave of absence and a substantial loss of salary. I cursed the superintendent's name. What was worse was the amount of time I spent seething over the injustice. Why couldn't I just earn a few checkmarks and move on? That was the logical progression since there was nothing to be done; it was out of my control. But the brain is a funny thing. You can't tell it what to think. So for an entire week, every moment of free thought was "Goddamn superintendent! Fuck you!"

Friends and family had insisted for months that we keep a blog to track our progress, insisting it would be an easy thing to do. But I didn't believe them. I didn't even know how to insert one of those winking smiley faces after making an email joke. Besides, who reads a blog besides your mother? When there were two days left, Djina grabbed the bike by the handlebars and announced that she would set up the blog. That was the impetus I needed. I was the man. Fifteen minutes later, I found Blogspot, and Ride2cooltheplanet.blogspot.com was born.

Everything was set. It was the last night. The better part of a year spent in preparation. We stuffed our bicycle shirts with Clif Bars, mixed Cytomax in water bottles, and I drank a beer. As I lay in bed, I thought about how I had always wanted to make something of my life. As a kid and then as a young adult, I had hopes for fame. First it was becoming a professional basketball player. That dream died when Lance Jackson became the high school's starting point guard, and I gave up the game. In my early twenties, I created a comic strip about a summer camp. Unfortunately, each strip took forever because I'm a lousy artist. After a month, I had ten and submitted them to a newspaper. They wanted to see a minimum of thirty before considering them, and I hung up my pen.

As an adult, I thought I might have a chance to make it as an author when I published a few books, but when I received a $12.73 royalty check for my "breakthrough" book, and it was number 88,342 on Amazon's list of most popular books, I knew I would never quit my day job.

At age thirty-eight, I applied for a mid-career fellowship. During the interview, the fellowship president said that a person had until age forty to make his mark on the world. I didn't get the fellowship, and now I was forty-eight. Thoreau wrote that most men lead lives of quiet desperation and go to the grave with the song still in them. I wouldn't say this was exactly me, but it was true that the images of what I thought I would become and what I had become did not match. But here in front of me was not the possibility for fame, but for an accomplishment I could be proud of, a song to sing.

The trip was as much for me as it was for Yonah.

THE BAR MITZVAH AND THE BEAST

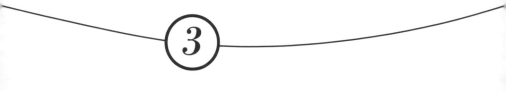

A NOT TOTALLY RELIABLE NARRATOR

THE TRADITION for cross-country cyclists is to dip the rear wheel in the ocean where you begin, and if you make it to the other side, dip the front wheel in the ocean where you arrive. For us to dip, we needed to backtrack eighty miles to the Pacific. Since the Adventure Cycling Association route passes through Davis literally within one hundred yards of our house, Djina said, "Pick me up on Day Two." Solly wanted to spend a last day at school because his class was putting on a play and he was the snake. Cupcakes were involved. So it was Yonah and me.

The plan was to Amtrak to San Francisco, wet the wheels, and cycle back to Davis. There was a 6:50 AM train, but breakfast took longer than anticipated. We raced to the train station and arrived at the ticket booth at 6:48. I was so frantic that in one graceless motion, I yanked my wallet from its pocket and a dozen plastic cards skittered across the tile floor. Not an auspicious start. "Two tickets for the 6:50 Capitol Corridor! It hasn't left yet, right?"

"She's running late. Departing 8:32."

"You are kidding me."

The ticket agent pointed to the electronic arrival/departure board on the wall. "One-way or round-trip?"

We hadn't even begun and already here was that lesson about time, and being in the moment, and not hurrying, and the irony of life, and the humor of God. I should have looked to the heavens and chuckled, "You got me again, but *now* I get it." Instead, I picked up the wayward credit cards, purchased the tickets, and tried quieting my racing heart with a cinnamon bun.

On the train, Yonah played Nintendo. Like every other parent, I bemoan the attraction computer games hold for my kids. Give a kid a Nintendo, PlayStation, or whatever; put them in a window-less room; make sure there is enough pizza; and return in three months. "I'm back!" you announce upon opening the door and ducking the escaping fetid air.

"Huh, what? You were gone?"

In 1989, Bill McKibben argued in *The End of Nature* that the environment had been so abused through technological advances that nature no longer exists. For Yonah and many, many kids, their reply to McKibben is, "So?" This is not to say Yonah does not care about pollution, disappearing polar bears, and global climate change. It is to say that he lives his life indifferent to the magic of the natural world. Yonah can wax eloquent about esoteric US historical events such as William Howard Taft being the only president to also serve as a Supreme Court justice, but a fiery red sunset earns a "Can we go inside now?"

For me, as it did for Emerson, Thoreau, and Muir, religion and spirituality begin with an awe of nature. Sit me outside any-where, and I can see more action than in anything cooked up in Hollywood. "You just need to sit and watch, and the big screen unfolds in front of you."

"Great, Dad."

After Day One, the Nintendo was staying home. I hoped and prayed that the ride would help Yonah feel a connectedness to the natural world in as profound a manner as he was connected to the virtual one. If this would happen, I knew his soul would flower.

From the San Francisco Ferry Building, we rode to Baker Beach, about a mile south of the Golden Gate Bridge. Our good friend, Rabbi Sydney Mintz, was there to send us off with a blessing. Yonah and I removed our cycling shoes, rolled up our tights, and carried the bikes to the surf. We turned the bikes to face east and anointed the rear wheels. With the Golden Gate Bridge in the background, pelicans skimming low over the waves, and a foghorn keeping time, the trip officially began. It was a beautiful, perfect moment. I desperately wanted to say something profound, such as, "Yonah, you have spent almost a year in preparation for this. The anointing of the wheel symbol-izes the commencement of your rite of passage to adulthood, which will culminate when you dip the front wheel into the

Atlantic. Though this will be a true test of courage, I am confident you will succeed. I am proud of you." Instead, I mumbled some inanity about being happy to start the trip. The truth is, it didn't matter what I said because Yonah wasn't listening. He was wiping sand off his wheel, anxious to shove off. My antsyness about time is nothing compared to his. Rabbi Syd beseeched God to protect us from sore butts and flat tires, and then we were off.

We doubled back to the Ferry Building to cross San Francisco Bay to Vallejo. Of course, we would have loved riding across bridges instead of riding ferries, but the bridges we had to cross didn't allow bicycles. And since Yonah and I had to cover more than seventy-five miles to Davis, I didn't feel too bad about the ferry. I was, however, upset about lunch. All I wanted was a baguette and a chunk of cheese. The baguette was easy. The problem was the cheese. The Ferry Building houses a high-end cheese shop, where prices on the unpronounceable cheese wheels started at $28.95 per pound. There was one deal—a quarter-pound of dry cheddar at the we're-giving-it-away price of $14.50 a pound. Bon appétit.

In Vallejo we pulled on fluorescent-green bicycling jerseys. I wanted to be as obvious as the peacock's display feathers, the black widow's hourglass, the highway patrol's flashing lights. My chief concern in riding across the country was getting bashed by a car, and this was no empty worry. In Djina's spin class alone, one woman's fiancé had been maimed and one man's wife had been killed on the road. Twenty-five pounds of bike going against a Mini Cooper is more of a mismatch than Solomon's Little League team going against the Boston Red Sox. Though the statistics show that one is no more likely to die on a bike than in a car, we did everything to increase survivability. Protected by only a one-and-a-half-inch thick helmet, our heads' best defense was avoidance. Hence, jerseys bright enough for the man on the moon to see, and constantly drilling into both boys' brains the bicyclists' First Commandment: "Always assume you are invisible to cars."

A lesser worry was that one or both of my knees would fail. Prior to the trip, I worked with a personal trainer to strengthen them. In addition, I made a pact with God. If God allowed my knees to survive the summer, I would be willing to sacrifice them and never ride again. The trip was that important.

"You really believe that God controls what happens to your knees?" Yonah asked.

"I don't know. Probably not. But I believe there is a nonmaterial reality that through prayer or meditation you can connect with. Maybe that's God. Maybe that can help my knees. And we've got ibuprofen too."

"I bet the ibuprofen's enough."

"Just because you can't measure it doesn't mean the spiritual world isn't real," I offered. "Take love, for instance."

"You can measure that by looking at changes in blood pressure and adrenalin when a person sees someone he loves."

"Where did you learn that?"

"Video games."

From Vallejo we made good time. On one descent, Yonah reached 41 miles per hour, a personal record. "Do *not* tell your mother how fast you went."

We talked and laughed the whole way, eventually rolling into Davis tired but not exhausted. Yonah seemed psyched.

"Think you could do this all the way cross-country?" I asked rhetorically, knowing the only answer would be an enthusiastic, "Yes!"

Yonah, an old soul from his diaper days, sagely replied, "We'll see."

The next morning, Solomon and Djina joined the ride, as did Ken Giles. Already mentioned as creator of the duct tape pencil but not formally introduced, Ken is a professor of agricultural engineering at UC Davis. He invents tractor sprayers. Who knew that one could acquire a tenured position by building a better squirt gun? I exaggerate. He is a real scientist who can explain fractals. He has a side gig consulting with industry giants about soap production. When a detergent is "new and improved," you can partially thank Professor Giles.

For a second day we were sans trailer and panniers. Our friends Mark and Sharon sagged our gear to the campsite. We rode through Sacramento along the American River Parkway, a twenty-three-mile multiuse path that is one of the longest urban bikeways in the country. Zipping along the American River with not a car in sight, watching bright orange tanagers flit from branch to branch of stately oaks and cottonwoods, made it hard to believe that we were in the heart of a metropolis. This urban path and others of its ilk provide habitat for animals and invaluable transportation alternatives to dangerous urban bike riding. If rising gas prices and environmental concerns are to turn more drivers into bike commuters, then safe bike thoroughfares like this one need to be created in every major metropolitan area. I made a mental note to bring this up in Washington.

We assumed the order we would keep for the time with Ken. Solomon and I led. Yonah followed, his front wheel a foot behind our back, allowing him to draft. Ken and Djina lagged a quarter-mile behind, chatting about the important issues of the day, such as which cheese shop is better: the one at the Ferry Building or at Dean & Deluca. Thus we traveled west to east through a city of four hundred thousand. Alas, like the straw sucking up air at the end of a milkshake, all good things must pass. Within thirty yards of finishing the trail and entering traffic, we were lost. The ACA map didn't match the facts on the ground. I claimed, "The map's screwed up."

Djina guffawed. "Right." I asked for directions, and we were on the road again. For the next twenty miles, we cycled past innumerable housing developments of three-thousand-plus square-foot homes.

Tolstoy has a story about how much space a person needs. The protagonist is given the opportunity to cover as much land as he can in a single day. If he can return to the starting point by sunset, thereby creating a huge circle, all the land inside the circle becomes his. The man pushes himself past his limits but successfully attains a huge amount of property. Unfortunately he drops dead from exhaustion. Answer to initial question: The amount of land a man needs is six feet, the length of a grave. Though Count Tolstoy exaggerates, it would be a more sustainable world if contractors wouldn't build and buyers wouldn't demand such large houses; the resources to build and maintain one of these babies is the housing equivalent of driving a Hummer.

On the outskirts of Placerville, we again were lost.

"Damn map!"

"Checkmark!"

"Solomon, 'damn' is not a curse word."

"Checkmark!"

To make matters worse, we were staring at a road that rose at about the same angle as a step ladder. It made Cantelow and Cardiac, the climbs we trained on, look like hills a toddler might make in a sandbox. And wasn't Placerville in the foothills? Wasn't its elevation a thousand feet? Didn't seven thousand vertical feet of the Sierras await us? My thoughts distilled to a single command to the feet: "push/pull." A quarter of the way up "push/pull" was pushed/pulled out by, "This is a real bastard!" Half-way up, the bastard morphed to, "This is a real friggin' bastard!" Then it got so steep that when we looked straight ahead it was clouds and sky. I lost my fire and muttered, "No way."

Had I been on my own, I would have stopped. I've always been a quitter when things get tough. Whenever I find myself racing some guy of equal ability, I usually lose because I just can't summon my inner Lance Armstrong and push beyond. I stop at the high end of the comfort level and don't enter the red zone. Unfortunately, to be truly great at something requires one to go there. But at that very moment, the very second I was about to yank my shoes out of the cleats, I heard deep breathing behind me. Unlike his dad, Solomon wasn't quitting. He was in the infrared zone. He was going to make it. I refocused. Push/pull, inhale, push/pull, exhale. Repeat and repeat and repeat and . . .

"We made it!" Solomon shouted at the top of the hill.

"Did you have any doubt?"

⊙▬⊙ː⊙▬⊙ː⊙▬⊙ː⊙▬⊙ː⊙▬⊙ː⊙▬⊙ː⊙▬⊙ː⊙▬⊙ː⊙▬⊙ː⊙▬⊙ː⊙▬⊙

The Sierras are big. Mount Whitney, the tallest mountain in the continental United States, lives there. The Sierras are bad. Ask the Donner Party. The Sierras kicked our butts. Our *average* speed was 4.5 miles per hour. At one point, when we were doing 3.2 miles per hour, an ant had the audacity to try and pass us. Solomon and I kicked it in and were the victors in a wheel-to-antenna photo finish.

Again we didn't ride with panniers because Mark and Sharon schlepped our gear to Caples Lake. The route followed the Mormon Emigrant Trail. Let it be known that the people who built this were way tougher than us. In 1848, a group of Mormon workers were anxious to return home to the Salt Lake Valley. In an irony that surely an old-school Mormon could appreciate, forty-five men and one woman made their way across the Sierras, building Northern California's first east–west wagon road as they went. Not only did they build this road up wickedly steep grades, but they did it without internal combustion engines or mini-markets in which to purchase ice-cold rehydration beverages.

I explained to Yonah that the social glue that motivated the Mormons was their shared religious belief. "Not only that," I added, "but think about the Jews who built modern Israel. It was their shared religious belief that allowed them to stand up to five invading armies and build a vibrant society out of the desert."

"You told me that most Zionists weren't religious," the religious school dropout countered. "So the Mormons had a shared religious belief, but that doesn't mean they needed one. They wanted to get home. The only way was to work together. Religion didn't keep them together. Necessity did. Same with the Jews."

"But religion *is* a social glue," I said, wanting to have the last word.

"A glue if you're in the religion, but if you're not, it's more like a gun," he countered, and his bike pulled away from The Beast. Not only was the brat besting me in an argument with information gleaned from me, but he was beating me up the mountain. There was something faintly oedipal about the whole thing.

By Day Three, Solomon's initial excitement had worn off. A nine-year-old is not meant to spend eight hours a day, one foot behind the sweaty back of an adult. And dare I speak of the olfactory assault on the young boy? Solomon needed distraction, he needed games. The guessing game Botticello is a riff on the old Twenty Questions standby. One person thinks of a person or character. He gives the others the first letter of the last name, and they have twenty yes/no questions to guess the name. My names were an eclectic mix: George Washington, Homer Simpson, Yonah Biers-Ariel, Michael Jordan. Solomon's names were: Johan Santana, David Ortiz, Ryan Howard, and Alfonso Soriano—baseball players.

"But, Solomon, you have to pick people I've heard of. Dontrelle Willis?"

"Are you kidding? He was the Marlins' ace when they won the World Series!"

We played the Daniel Hill Game, named after its inventor, Solomon's good friend. Someone says the name of a person, say, Albert Einstein. The next person takes the last letter of the last name and says a new name whose first or last name starts with that letter. In the case of Einstein, the next name would start with "N." Here's a typical round.

Solomon: Albert Pujols.

Me: Socrates.

Solomon: Sandy Koufax.

Me: Uh . . . uh . . . Xaviera Hollander.

Solomon: Who's that?

Me: She wrote *The Happy Hooker*.

Solomon: What's a hooker?

Me: Uh . . . someone who has sex for money.

Solomon: Gross.

This game was edifying as we each learned about people we had never heard of. I learned that Nellie Fox, Pete Fox, and Jimmie Foxx all played major league baseball.

Upon arriving at Caples Lake, we were too tired to put up tents or cook dinner or do anything for a good half-hour but watch Solomon racing up and down the rocks pretending he was John Muir.

"He's got to ride harder tomorrow," Yonah observed. I lacked strength to nod.

One of the best things about riding cross-country is that you can practice gluttony and not get fat. Djina, as lead nutritionist, exhorted the boys to eat at every spare moment. She knew that the boys mustn't lose weight. For while it is natural, and even desirable in many cases, that adults on a cross country bike trip lose weight, kids must not. If they do, their bodies shut down and need a week to recover. In other words, if they were to lose five pounds, the trip would be over. Thus the daily milkshake directive. I imagined a day when Yonah would beg, "But, Mom, can't I have some carrot sticks?" and Djina's stern reply, "Only after you finish your cookies 'n cream Dairy Queen Blizzard."

But at Caples Lake, Solomon wasn't hungry. He was too busy climbing rocks and summiting Mount Everest. "Solomon, you better eat, or you'll start metabolizing your muscles," Djina warned.

Ken added, "Sol, you better slow down. You just digested your pancreas." And thus the pancreas joke was invented. When you have no television, Nintendo, or radio, you make your own entertainment. For nearly a week, it was pancreas jokes.

"That chocolate bar sure tasted better than my pancreas."

"Did you sprinkle the shredded pancreas on the pasta?"

We were a riot. But when you go 8:00 AM to 5:00 PM on a bike, even recycled pancreas jokes seem funny. The only thing not funny as we crept our way up the Sierras was the state of my knees. "Feed us ibuprofen!" they screeched. I acceded but knew they better get better, or I'd have to trade The Beast for a rental car and sag Djina and Yonah's gear the rest of the way.

Our sherpas, Mark and Sharon, wished us luck and headed home. The time for us to haul our own gear had arrived. My initial thought at seeing the pile of stuff was: Forget the eight aerodynamic bags and wispy trailer; call U-Haul. We crammed, cajoled, and cursed until the panniers were the density of plutonium. I needed to wheel The Beast to the road from the campsite, but a regular push didn't budge it. I planted both feet and heaved. It groaned in complaint but moved. By the time I reached the road, sweat cascaded down my forehead even though the ambient temperature was 45 degrees. I couldn't imagine how Solomon and I, with or without pancreases, could possibly make it over Carson Pass.

Nevertheless, the two of us mounted The Beast and were off like a tortoise out of molasses. Employing turtle strategy, we plugged along and did not stop. For five miles the tactic worked, but a mile before the pass, the grade increased, and we ran out of gas. The mountain beat us. We would have to walk the rest of the way. I didn't relish pushing The Beast, not to mention the humiliation. (Earlier I had told Solomon there was no shame in pushing. That was a lie.) But at that very moment, the very second before we unclipped from the pedals, a white pick-up truck came alongside and slowly passed us. The driver called out, "Hey! You're that family! Right on!" Suddenly, we no longer needed to stop. With newfound energy, we summited the 8,594-foot Carson Pass. Was the white pick-up guy simply a random man who just happened to have read the paper and coincidently drove by *at the exact moment* we needed him, or was he an angel sent to fuel our final push? It felt too coincidental to be purely random, but on the other hand, I doubt angels sit around waiting to be helpful. Truth lies in the inexplicable middle, somewhere between the faith of the believer and the rationality of the atheist.

I mentioned this to Yonah. He gave me a funny look and said, "That truck didn't come the exact second you were going to give up. You're like those religious people who see the Virgin Mary in a window or a tree trunk because they want to believe."

I was chagrined being caught lying by a thirteen-year-old kid. "How did you know?"

"Because you yelled, 'We're kicking the Sierra's butt!' just before that guy drove up. It got really steep only at the very end."

"Well, I still believe that the truth lies between the extremes."

"I believe I'm God."

"You believe *you're* God?"

"I have just as much proof for my belief as you do for yours."

There was nothing I could utter in retort, but I will say this to you, dear reader, I promise not to exaggerate or lie anymore. I swear to God.

We drained our water bottles, collected petition signatures from the visitors at the Carson Pass Visitor Center; checked wheels, tires, and brakes; and started down the east side of the Sierras. Fact: A mountain descent is far superior to every amusement park ride in the world. As you bullet down a mountain in excess of 40 miles per hour on two rubber tires one-and-a-quarter-inches wide, your adrenalin tap is wide open, the way it is on a rollercoaster ride. But there is no screaming because the danger is exquisitely real, and you are in extreme concentration. First there are animals that don't look both ways before crossing the road. I know a guy who plowed into a deer at 35 miles per hour. Ouch. Then there is going around a curve too fast. Whoops. However, the biggest worry at high speeds is a tire blow out. There is an explosive sound, the metal rim comes in contact with ground, and the bike wobbles like an amphetamine-powered drunk on a tightrope. It is an extremely rare occurrence, but if a tire blows, especially a front one, we are talking a few seconds of uncontrollable bicycle accompanied by pure, undiluted terror, then either slowing down and gaining control, or soft human tissue slamming into rock-hard road. If it is the latter, a helicopter medevac follows.

Despite, and very possibly because of, the possibilities of such scenarios, bicyclists love descents. Perhaps the desire for speed and riding on the edge of safety is an evolutionary response our ancestors needed to escape the clutches of saber-toothed tigers. Flying down a hill provides the adrenalin fix that keeps our fight-or-flight response sharp. Perhaps it is the ecstatic feeling of being fully alive, the enhancement of being, the soaring of the spirit as it hurtles through space. Whatever the reason, evolutionary or spiritual, one downhill is never enough.

I unleashed The Beast and let it run free. It, too, was happy to no longer be creaking its tired body up the mountain. Solomon joyfully screamed. At 43 miles per hour, I remembered my parental obligation to keep my child safe, so I tapped the brakes. At the bottom we waited for the others. I was a bit worried about Yonah. He had never descended a big mountain. Did he have the wherewithal to handle it? Would the speed freak him out? But not for the first time did he prove more competent than I gave him credit. Yonah had been bitten by the speed bug. He arrived less than ten seconds after us and said, "That was good." In Yonahese, this translates to, "Freaking awesome, man!"

At the café/general store in Woodsford, we had our first negative interaction with a local. We stopped for milkshakes to go with PB&J sandwiches. There was a table in the midst of a pandemonium of fishing gear, fast foods, and assorted t shirts with messages such as "I Shot Bambi's Mom" and "Of Course I Hunt Better than You . . . I'm a Girl." No one seemed in a hurry to take our order, so we sat down and made sandwiches. At this point, the guy behind the bar said, "You got nerve bringing food into my restaurant."

"Uh, we were just waiting to order some milkshakes," I said.

He grunted, which I interpreted to mean, "Alright."

For the first time on the trip we didn't mention our petition, and Djina swore he overcharged us on the shakes.

○━○┄○━○┄○━○┄○━○┄○━○┄○━○┄○━○┄○━○┄○━○┄○━○

Into Nevada and the rain shadow. The air off the Pacific Ocean, laden with water, sweeps up the Sierras, rises, cools, and dumps its load. By the time air crosses to the east side, it's nearly empty. If the west and east side of the Sierras were facial hair, the west side with its countless fir and pine trees is a Rasputin-like beard. The east face is a five o'clock shadow. The Sierra precipitation is not just a boon for the ski resorts and timber interests, it is the lifeblood for California's cities and agriculture. Besides being the nation's most populous state, California leads the country in agricultural products from almonds to zucchini, milk to marijuana, all powered by the Sierra snowpack. Global warming computer modeling predicts the snowpack may decrease by up to 90 percent by 2100. Water planners and politicians are grappling with strategies, but the best solution is to decrease carbon dioxide.

Most of us know global climate change must be addressed, but since few of us feel the effects in our daily lives, we live as if climate change does not exist. At least subconsciously, we cling to the hope that it won't be as dire as the climatologists predict. Scientists are often wrong, we tell ourselves, and even if they aren't, American ingenuity will provide technological fixes, right? And besides, why should I spend fifteen minutes hanging my laundry when my neighbors throw their clothes in the dryer?

Unfortunately, by the time we feel the heat, it will be too late. There will be a global transformation, but it won't be to a green future on which we can exert some control. Think the Four Horsemen of the Apocalypse with bad sunburns. They won't be happy. What our country needs is a consciousness raising, an environmental Great Awakening. "What type of plug-in hybrid would Jesus drive?" needs to be preached from the pulpit. We need art to shape a new zeitgeist: country songs bemoaning unrequited carbon diets, art installations made of recycled oil drums, movies where the heroes ride bikes and buses. Chiefly, we need stories telling us how to live anew.

When it comes to confronting the defining issue of the twenty-first century, technology will help, but it may be art and religion that hold the possibility of salvation.

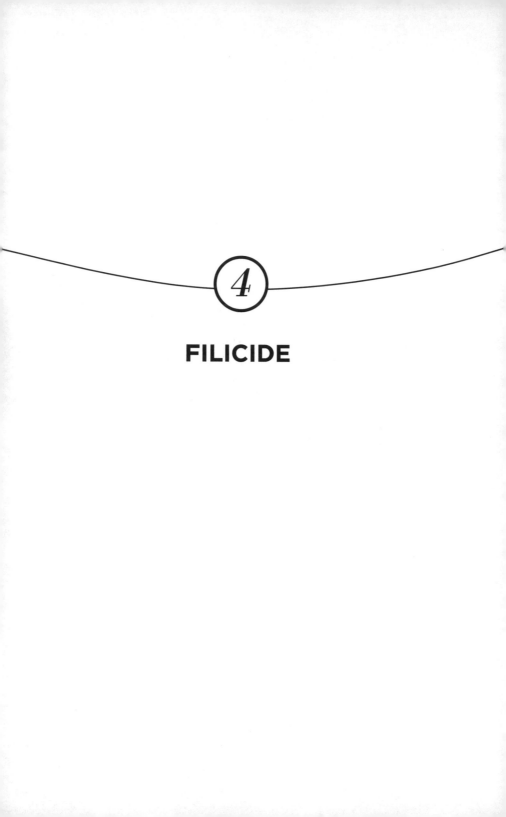

4

FILICIDE

RIDING THROUGH the chaparral of the Eastern Sierra foot-hills, we had an accident. The Beast was leading, Yonah drafting, and Ken and Djina a bit back, mooing at the cows. I stopped to look at an interesting sign painted on a building. Yonah stopped. Djina plowed into Yonah's back tire.

"Why didn't you signal you were stopping!" she yelled at me from a prone position.

"If you weren't mooing, you would have seen us!"

Our first accident and first fight. No one was injured, so we continued on to Carson City, whose roads were not bicycle friendly. Speeding big rigs raced along a main thoroughfare that had neither bike lanes nor shoulders. Then Djina's derailleur went funny. It insisted on staying in the smallest front chain ring, causing her legs to spin like a hamster on a treadmill.

When faced with a bike issue, there is always a choice: (1) Drop bike off at shop. Cross street to Mishka's Coffee Shop. Read paper while sipping a fairly traded coffee and listening to their excellent music. Total cost: $42 repair, $2.50 beverage. Forty-five minute time commitment; maximum blood pressure 110/68. Or: (2) Pick up part at bike shop. Return home. Realize specialized tool is broken or missing. Return to bike shop. Return home. Realize you're short one ball bearing. Return to shop. Return home. Fix bike while listening to neighbor's kid butchering "Twinkle, Twinkle, Little Star" on the violin. Total cost: $7 parts, $15 new tool, $0.35 bandages for bloody knuckles, $2 medicinal beer. Two-hour, forty-five-minute time commitment; maximum blood pressure 137/96.

Money saved: $20.15. A no-brainer: Door #2. Always.

I examined Djina's bike and discovered that part of the front derailleur was cracked. There was nothing to do but find a bike shop and replace the expensive piece of equipment. Bummer. At least a bike shop was nearby. I asked the mechanic about discount derailleurs.

"Let me take a look," he said and wheeled the bike behind the counter. Before I removed my helmet, he wheeled it back.

"The derailleur's fine. The cable just slipped off the track. I slid it back on. Look."

I looked and then examined our other bikes. All of them had the "crack."

"Uh, thanks," I mumbled while fingering the derailleur in order to avoid the embarrassment of eye contact. I might have thought myself a good mechanic, but clearly my view of self did not jibe with the facts. My repair skills would need improvement if we ever got stuck—God forbid—in the middle of the desert forty miles from the nearest town.

It was late in the afternoon and I was beat, so I voted to stay in Carson City. Yonah, whose default setting is sprawled out on a couch, voted to continue. I acceded since this was his rite of passage and any leadership he took should be encouraged. (And I lost the vote four to one.)

From Carson City, a strong west wind blew us thirteen miles in thirty-two minutes into Dayton. This was our first encounter with North America's prevailing westerly wind. We were quite psyched that our future would hold more of the same to sail us across the continent. In Dayton, we camped with Arthur and Raleigh, a father-son team of cross-country cyclists. We also conversed with two young men and a woman in the next campsite, whose skinny bodies were covered with tattoos and who were collectively missing four front teeth. Crystal meth, I thought. Don't ask me why. That is just the way my mind works.

They told us they were locals on their way to Vegas.

"But you live in Nevada," Djina pointed out. "You can gamble in your Laundromat."

"Ain't the same. Last time we won six hundred and seventy-five dollars."

"Everyone knows slots pay better there."

"You really ridin' 'crost country on them bikes?"

If we had come upon these three on my street in Davis, I wouldn't have said a word to them. Instead, I would have double-checked my bike lock, made sure the boys were safe, and then retreated into the comfort of my home to gloat over my moral superiority. The beauty of travel is that you don't get to decide who you will and will not interact with. Instead, you become open to the world and everyone inhabiting it. You see people beyond your stereotypes of them. The three young people told us about a beautiful place to swim on the adjacent Carson River. We told them about our petition. They signed and we swam. And when we gave them the beer we couldn't finish, a friendship was sealed.

⊙━⊙━⊙━⊙━⊙━⊙━⊙━⊙━⊙━⊙━⊙━⊙━⊙━⊙━⊙

Nevada's Great Basin contains a national park, but let's face it, it's a stretch to glorify a quarter-million square miles of desert where the tallest (and only) flora—sagebrush—barely reached Solomon's waist. I, as always, exaggerate. There were trees. Every casino was framed by small clusters of trees, and there were plenty of casinos because the only other leisure activity was sunbathing. Still it was surprising to see so many on US Highway 50 whose well-deserved moniker is "The Loneliest Road in America." Aside from the occasional big rig and the even rarer passenger vehicle, the road was empty. So who was stopping at Captain Jack's Casino?

Located next to the casino stood the area's other economic pillar—the pawn shop. If the gambler was lucky, he went from casino to pawn shop to redeem his wedding ring. If not, the transaction went the other way. It was heartrending passing through this economically depressed hardscape. Could anything be a boon to an area that receives 362 sunny days per year? What could a humongous area with so much sun offer?

You don't need to be a Nobel laureate, a MacArthur Fellow, or even a high school graduate to realize that the Great Basin solar potential could make it the Saudi Arabia of solar electricity. So why aren't we doing it? There are economic, technical, and environmental issues to overcome, but the root of the problem is that America no longer does the Big Project. Didn't we save the world from Hitler? Didn't we build the interstate highway system? Didn't we once take "one small step for [a] man, one giant leap for mankind"? America has lost the fire to go big. But here is the chance for us to lead the world into a sustainable energy future. Instead of spending trillions to secure oil from the Middle East, we could convert Nevada sunshine into kilowatts at a fraction of the cost.

On our blog, I suggested massive arrays of photovoltaic cells. A blog is a two-way street, and NathanWW replied: "The problem is that solar cells are unreliable on that scale. Birds poop on them, cables degrade, they get abraded by blowing dirt, etc. So if a huge solar installation is built, there will be significant portions of it down at any given time. The solution," this electrical engineer continued, "would be to build a low-tech version, such as a series of mirrors feeding into a large parabolic mirror which would concentrate heat on a collector and boil water or other liquid inside. The advantage is you are using very simple installations which have few failure modes. They're cheaper than photovoltaics and a system like this could operate using the same equipment in a coal-fired plant, just using solar energy instead of coal."

It turned out that NathanWW was a fifteen-year-old high school sophomore, the older brother of one of Yonah's friends. His amendment to the photovoltaic arrays makes sense. In fact, there are already a few solar plants that generate electricity. The question is whether the United States should convert large swaths of desert to energy production. On one hand, the desert sun could generate a tremendous amount of clean energy. On the other hand, there are large environmental concerns to be addressed, and a better electronic grid would need to be built to transfer the energy. Perhaps after a spirited debate, Congress might decide the costs outweigh the benefits and scuttle the idea to transform the desert into energy production. But the problem is that no one in Washington, D.C., is seriously debating this or any other Big Project as an alternative to fossil fuels. We would definitely bring this up at our meetings with congressional leaders.

If our country were to give Nathan's idea its just due, he might become the youngest recipient of a MacArthur Genius Award.

Minimally, his contribution to the country's energy independence would look good on a college application.

<hr />

The Great Basin was hot. Since heat became the trip's ongoing motif, I'll not write about it anymore. Please mentally insert "It was hot" every fifth paragraph. In my regular life, I couldn't be in this kind of heat for more than ten minutes before jumping into a pool or entering an air-conditioned building. But we managed to stay in the blast furnace for eight to ten hours a day because the wind generated by riding, mixed with our sweat, prevented us from keeling over with heat stroke. To compensate for the amount of water we constantly lost through our evolutionary air-conditioning system, sweat, we stopped at every mini-mart to top off our radiators with Gatorade. Before the trip, I thought Gatorade came in two flavors, Lemon-Lime and Orange, both more fluorescent than a Jimi Hendrix poster. But there are more, oh so many more.

At the first mini-mart, I, a traditionalist, selected a quart of Lemon-Lime. Solomon and Yonah, risk-taking youths, went for A.M. Orange-Strawberry. The cashier was a bored teen. Our petition had been wildly successful so far, but here was an apathetic eighteen-year-old who was surely stealing condoms from the stock. What did he care about global climate change? But what harm would it be to ask?

"We have a petition about global warming. Want to take a look at it?"

Half-lidded eyes looked up. Zero comprehension. You want a stick of jerky with your Gatorade or not?

It might take a village to raise a child, but it takes a teen to communicate with a teen. Yonah ventured, "We're biking across the country to give it to Congress."

The eyelids lifted. "Really?"

"Yep," Solomon said.

"I'll sign." His eyes emitted a small sparkle, and a compact fluorescent light bulb clicked on above my head. If this kid stuck in the middle of nowhere understood the need to act on global warming, then everyone must.

We wanted to linger in the shade of the gas pumps and main-line Gatorade. It was exactly like not wanting to exit a hot shower in an unheated New England farmhouse in the middle of January. But in reverse. Unfortunately, you don't get to Washington sitting on your butt, unless your butt's on a bike seat.

At Fallon, Nevada, we bid goodbye to the first ACA map. In five days, we had covered 302 miles. It was also goodbye to Ken. Betty, his wife, came up from Davis to take her wayward husband home. What had taken us five days of tough riding took Betty fewer than five hours—and she didn't stink upon arrival. She and Ken left us at Fallon's campground, the county fairground.

Solomon objected. He wanted a hotel, but our plan was to stay in hotels only when there were no camping options available or once every other week to do laundry, sleep in a bed, and shower. Solomon cared not a whit for a bed, and he'd rather eat liver than shower. He wanted television. We are one of the less than 1 percent of Americans who do not own a TV; therefore, Solomon can smell a plasma screen from a half-mile away. He wanted to channel-surf. On and on about Fallon's wonderful hotel he pontificated, as only a nine-year-old who spent dawn to dusk sweating on a bicycle seat in triple-digit temperatures could. But the five-dollar fairground included showers. It was a no-brainer.

Alas, 'twas I who lacked a brain. We paid the five bucks and were told to camp anywhere on the ten-acre lawn. From afar it looked inviting. From up close, dried horse manure mixed with dirty, cottonlike seeds blanketed the patchy grass and stuck to everything. A WPA work crew last cleaned the outhouse in 1936.

After we had pitched our tents away from the fresher manure, a neighbor from one of the two other occupied campsites came to investigate. His site held no tent and no Coleman stove, only a Ford Bronco. The alcohol aroma arrived moments before he did, and then without any prompting, he regaled us with his hitch-hiking trip across the States and the ten-speed bike he'd had since age twelve. He wasn't belligerent, but he seemed irked when I refused the flashlight he tried pressing upon us.

"You don't need no batteries; just wind it up, like this. Try it."

"Thanks, but we already have flashlights, and we need to keep our weight down. The Rockies are going to be tough."

"But it don't take no batteries. You can use it."

Eventually he staggered back to his truck. Djina insisted that she and I sleep in separate tents in case he woke up in the middle of the night to gift us a two-pound can of Chef Boyardee ravioli. The boys were in their sleeping bags when three sheriff SUVs surrounded the large RV parked at the other occupied campsite. One sheriff ambled over and asked, "Did you happen to see a man chase a woman across the campground? He may have had a knife."

"No, but the guy in that truck is really drunk."

"Oh. Okay, I'll check him out."

Solomon was of two minds. On one hand, he wanted to taunt me with, "I told you so," about the cruddy campground. But the excitement of being in the middle of a real-life crime as well as meeting a grown man whose grasp of language was less than his was at least equivalent to watching *SpongeBob SquarePants*.

The sheriff returned, gave us his card, and told us to call him if the Bronco drove off.

"He'll be a hazard on the road," the sheriff said.

"He's not a hazard here?" I asked.

"Pete? Naw, he's harmless. Just needs to sleep it off."

That might have been the case, but as man of the family, I slept with my Leatherman, blade open.

O━O━O━O━O━O━O━O━O━O━O━O━O

Djina is way more enthusiastic than I am. Take five Red Sox fans after Boston broke the eighty-six-year Curse of the Bambino and won the 2004 World Series, add their enthusiasm together on one side, put Djina's on the other, and—well—their enthusiasm would totally cream hers, but she is quite enthusiastic. As self-appointed trip cheerleader, she began each day with a paean to Willie Nelson. Fewer than ten pedal strokes from camp, she'd belt out, "On the road again / Just can't wait to get on the road again," followed by her Declaration of Exuberance: "I can't believe I get to go on a bike ride today!" We'd smile at our crazy mother/ deranged wife and then be off. Fielding a challenge to her routine, she answered, "My work is to stand and be astonished by every day we're on this trip. Isn't it amazing? How can you not start the day like this?"

Solomon, whose genetic makeup is Djina-heavy, developed his own morning ritual. For the better part of a year, whenever Solomon ate chicken, he would salute it and proclaim, *"Gracias, Gallina!"* It was something he picked up from his Spanish immersion school. Thus was initiated the Morning Cacophony for Two in the Key of Loud, with Djina yodeling Willie Nelson and Solomon proclaiming *"Gracias, Gallina!"* to the morning sun. Yet it wasn't until Solomon sang every verse of "One Hundred Bottles of Beer on the Wall" that I realized the operatic quality of his voice. Not in tone or melody, but as he sat twenty-four short inches from my eardrums, I was in awe that a little kid could possess such an enormity of lungs.

Sitting on The Beast's rear end, Solomon could not steer, shift, or brake. He could stare at sagebrush and pedal. But when offered a plane ride to his grandparents' where he could spend the summer hanging out with his cousins and playing Nintendo until his fingers could bench-press a sixty-inch, high-definition plasma screen, Solomon chose to stay.

Still, we needed to deal with boredom. Even if I knew an unlimited number of people whose name began with "X," there was a limit to word games. In the morning, he could hold it together playing games, singing songs, and watching birds, but by midafternoon, when more wood was added to the inferno, it would get ugly. Typically we'd be doing 3 to 4 miles per hour up a hill, and I'd be huffing and puffing like a wolf blowing down a house. The sun in the southern sky would cast our shadow just left of The Beast. Imagine what you would do if you were struggling beyond what you thought was physically possible, and in your shadow, you saw your son with both hands above his head practicing imaginary basketball shots. You laugh, but I can assure you thoughts of filicide would cross your mind too.

Djina anticipated the problem before the trip began. She purchased an iPod and spent tedious weeks filling it with books.

Harry Potter and the Goblet of Fire took a weekend to download. She put on seven more books and fifteen of Solly's favorite songs. Though he loved *Harry Potter* as much as Carlos Delgado, his favorite baseball player, he didn't listen to *Harry* or any other book for more than ten minutes. He plugged into music. But not all the music. His repeated choices were "Smoke on the Water" and "Layla." But even between those two, I conservatively estimate that Solomon listened to "Layla" a dozen times a day. I vowed if we ever made it to D.C., I would track down Eric Clapton and present him with a bottle of 1973 Stag's Leap Cabernet Sauvignon. He had earned it.

To communicate while riding, Solomon and I created a code. "Standing!" meant one of us needed to stand on the pedals either to get more torque on a steep grade or because someone's butt was sore. The reason for announcing was that the sudden shift of weight could throw The Beast off balance. (The Beast always looked for a way to make trouble.) After one rider announced his intent to stand, the other rider needed to respond with, "Go ahead!" because I might be taking a swig of water and not have both hands on the handlebars. Usually Solomon forgot to wait for the countersign and stood as he yelled, "Standing!" Like a cat who sits on the newspaper just when you're about to read it, Solomon was most likely to stand when I was just starting to fiddle intently with something. I wish I could have been more of an actualized person during these near wipeouts, reacting like the Dalai Lama with a bemused smile. I more resembled Edvard Munch's *The Scream*.

I was often short with Solomon. Being together 24/7 and within two feet of each other for a large chunk of it, fueled my lashing out. And it wasn't only on the bike. When we made camp, there were specific chores that needed doing, such as setting up tents and cooking dinner. In the morning, it was a quick breakfast and camp breakdown to cover miles before the heat kicked in. There wasn't much down time to space out and relax. This was not Club Med. But while Djina, Yonah, and I understood the schedule, Solomon was too young to grok it. Ask him to brush his teeth and the first two times he didn't hear. Time three, with a voice at higher decibels and a hint of exasperation, sent him on his way to his toothbrush. Halfway there he'd find a stick, and suddenly it's Solomon Biers-Ariel batting against Roger Clemens in the bottom of the ninth of the seventh game of the World Series. And I'd yell. Yonah, always one to sense blood, was more than happy to join in the parenting. Solomon, feeling Yonah an easier target, shouted, "Yonah, you're such a jerk!" and the fighting commenced. Then I'd *really* yell.

I picture myself as the dad in Bill Watterson's *Calvin and Hobbes*. He's an avid bike rider who is either cajoling Calvin to go outside or delivering some bromide on life that Calvin ignores. But beyond the cartoon image, I often wonder about my parenting. How am I doing? Sometimes good, other times an utter failure. The things that most set me off are when I see one of my foibles or bad habits expressed in the boys. The perverse thing is that I come down harder on them than I do on myself for doing the same thing. Is it because they remind me of what I dislike about myself, or is it because I had hoped my progeny would have advanced beyond their father?

I wonder if my generation analyzes its parenting more than prior generations. Quite a lot has been said about the overprotective baby boomer parent who will do everything for the good of his child yet is paradoxically self-absorbed with his own life. This truism fit the trip: On the one hand, the ride provided an opportunity to test my children as well as have them experience a wider arc of American life. On the other hand, riding cross-country fulfilled a personal desire. So my son's rite of passage was somewhat motivated by selfishness. It's the same with teaching. Teachers who want to make a difference rarely survive more than a year or two. The ones who succeed are selfish: Teaching gives them pleasure. Parenting, teaching, anything: If you don't do it for yourself, you're not going to be that good.

Now if I would only yell less.

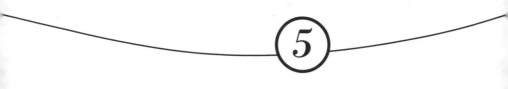

WHY I'M A LUDDITE

TRAVELING CAN STRESS even the most solid marriage. We were no exception. Take our panniers—please! To keep our clothing and personal items separate, I inked our names on each small pannier. Unfortunately, the panniers were too small for jackets and raingear, so everyone got a large pannier instead. Group gear went into the small panniers. They were organized and labeled thusly: Solomon and Yonah = food, Djina = kitchen gear, Matt = tools. Granted the labels were not in the most visible places, and I used a gray marker on black bags. Still, if you tried, you could read them.

Djina was not satisfied with my system, so she took a Sharpie and re-marked the small bags with prominent geometric shapes: a triangle, a circle, a square, and a diamond. We fought over whose markings were better. Sure, "Djina = kitchen" could be misconstrued as sexist, but that was only because Djina, like every woman I have ever known, is way too sensitive. At least, I could remember my mnemonics. To this day, I don't know which of Djina's symbols the kitchen was. In addition, my middle-aged mind could never remember the word for the four-sided thingy with a pointy top and bottom; thus, I sometimes called the diamond a square, sometimes a triangle, but mostly I called panniers by family names. Djina accused me, "How hard is it to remember diamond equals tools? You're so passive aggressive!"

Yonah, whose ear does not register a chore request, is uncannily tuned to his parents' spats. He sang out, "Dad's passive aggressive and Mom's aggressive aggressive!"

Thirst joined the ride. The town of Middlegate, Nevada, is forty miles from Fallon. We figured we'd fill water bottles there, but by mile thirty-five, Djina and I were empty and had severe cotton mouth with none of the benefits. There was a restaurant a quarter-mile off US Highway 50, so we rolled into a dusty parking lot complete with hitchin' posts, two fossilized stagecoaches, and the shell of an Oldsmobile, circa 1950. A bevy of dilapidated hotel rooms formed a horseshoe around its perimeter. "Welcome to Middlegate Station," read the sign on the side of a weather-beaten, wooden building. "The Middle of Nowhere. Population 18 17."

We stepped inside and were welcomed by a blast of refreshing air-conditioning infused with a cumulous cloud of tobacco smoke. Eight people, easily everyone within a twenty-mile radius, sat along the bar chain-smoking and chain-drinking, eyes glued to an eighteen-inch TV where an episode from the original *Star Trek* series played. Had we walked into a joint like this just one week prior, we would have U-turned before a single nicotine molecule could invade the boys' nostrils. Now we dashed to the refrigerator, grabbed four Berry Gatorades, and paid the barkeep, a skeletal, grandfather-type who lit a new cigarette with his dying one.

The walls and ceilings were covered with the wallpaper of choice throughout the bars and restaurants of Nevada: money. One-, five-, along with the occasional ten-, and twenty-dollar bills were pinned to every square inch of space not plastered with posters of Dale Earnhart Jr. posing next to his race car with a Budweiser in hand. "An' this is jus' from a couple year," the barkeep explained. "After 9/11, I packed up the bills an' sent 'em to New York: thirty-five thousand dollars."

The boys and I retreated to the backroom to play billiards. At first they held the cues as if they were wielding swords to stab the cue ball. In the end, they sort of picked it up and enjoyed themselves. Hell, they would have enjoyed themselves if the game was counting dollar bills on the ceiling, because the alternative was cycling in a convection oven.

The bar had a computer for patrons to use. The middle of nowhere was outfitted with DSL. Djina said, "I'm going to write something on the blog you set up."

I asked the barkeep, "How far to Middlegate?"

"Yer here."

"But this is Middlegate Station. There's supposed to be a grocery store, too."

He nodded toward the refrigerator of Gatorade and bottled water.

"But according to the map, it's at least four miles from here."

"Yer map ain't right. You want a room fer the night?"

Thirty minutes in this bar would only give each of us one or two small, benign growths we could easily cough up on the road. A full night in Middlegate would mean third-stage emphysema. I looked at the map for the next town. "How much farther to Cold Spring Station?"

"Ain't nothin' there."

"The map says there's food and camping."

"Next town's Austin. Sixty-five mile. You could go Carroll Summit. Fifty-six mile that way."

From the left came a new voice, "I'm going that way myself." Two guys down from me, slumped over the bar, was a guy wearing a fluorescent green bicycle jersey. How had I missed him amid the flannel, denim, and leather ponied up to the bar?

"There's a topo map over there," the guy continued. "C'mon. I'll show you. My name's Dave." Across the room was a large, 3-D, plastic topographical map of Nevada. US Highway 50 was a thin line. A microscopic dot was Middlegate and an equally tiny dot was Cold Spring Station. There was Austin and the shortcut over Carroll Summit. It was very steep. "I'm taking off as soon as it cools down," Dave said.

"Bike through the night?"

"Nah, I'll pull over somewhere and camp. I got everything. I'll show you."

Dave looked to be my age, a bit shorter, but built. His sleeveless bike shirt accentuated his biceps. I followed him out. Leaning against the building was a bike so loaded down that the frame color was obscured. Think Depression-era Dust Bowl migrants with their beds and pots hanging over the sides of their dilapidated trucks. In addition to standard gear, Dave had a camping chair, a few folded eight-by-ten-foot plastic tarps, electric hair clippers, a portable television, various plastic bags filled with what appeared to be more plastic bags, and a short but stout tree limb.

"My kickstand," he explained and then launched into a monologue about his desire to do something wild, his need to escape his lousy job selling insurance, his sort-of girlfriend who kind-of dumped him, but not really because he would probably see her in Kansas, and his absolute need to get away from everything.

"How much does your rig weigh?"

He grinned. "About a hundred and twenty pounds."

"You are kidding." The Beast was forty pounds unloaded. With gear it was definitely no more than seventy. Add fifty more? No checkmarking way.

Dave was clearly an odd one, but one with legs of steel. People take trips for lots of reasons. Dave's was to escape. Perhaps it wasn't the external things in his life that he needed to escape from; perhaps it was release from his internal demons. After all, what sane guy cycles with a television? I wished him well and went back inside where Djina was ready to leave. She said the smoke was getting to her (read: she finished blogging). I wanted to trust the map about Cold Spring Station, but the fact that it got Middlegate wrong didn't bode well. If the map again failed us, we'd pull over and camp when it got dark. Couldn't be worse than Fallon. After a last toke of air-conditioned smoke, we plunged back into the kiln.

Less than a mile from Middlegate was a uniquely American site. On the edge of a dried-up riverbed stood a huge, lone cottonwood tree. It was the first native tree we'd seen since entering the Great Basin, easily seventy-five feet high with a canopy the same diameter. Hanging from its branches were hundreds, nay, thousands of shoes. Money doesn't grow on trees, but here in the Nevada desert, footwear does. Tourists flock from around the world to see California's giant sequoias as well as New England's deciduous fall color frenzy. Now the Great Basin has a vacation destination: The Nike Tree.

After ten miles of rock, sagebrush, and more rock, there was no sign of Cold Spring Station. The sun was rapidly descending. Maybe that barkeep wasn't just trying to get us to stay. I scanned the roadside for a non-rocky place to camp. But wait, the map did indicate an old Pony Express stop, and there on the left . . .

"What's that?" I pointed.

"Rocks," said Djina.

"But there's a fence around them," I insisted.

"Maybe they don't want people to steal them," offered Solomon.

"Right, Solly," Yonah said. "Look around. What do you see? Rocks."

But Solomon was right. These were special rocks, remnants from a way station of the nineteenth century's version of FedEx, the Pony Express. Minimally 95 percent of US Highway 50 historical markers pointed out Pony Express stations, Pony Express trivia, and Pony Express massacres. No one in the almost one-hundred fifty years since the closure of the Pony Express was happier than I to see those fenced-in rocks, for the map indicated that in less than one mile, just over the next rise, would be Cold Spring Station. And then there it was, exactly where the map promised: civilization! Two glorious buildings. A restaurant and a hotel. "There is a God!" I exclaimed.

Yonah looked at me with the bemused expression of the older monk watching the neophyte burst forth with happiness as he breaks his first two-day fast with a slice of warm bread. "Why credit God?" he asked. "It was on the map."

"It's not that. It's because the map was wrong about Middlegate, and the guy at the bar lied, and—oh, never mind—it's just an expression."

"We're staying at the hotel, right?" Solomon asked. There was camping in the back, but Solomon was having none of that. A room was available, but when Solomon found out that the satellite dish wasn't hooked up, his face went dark and he bravely fought back tears. But the cleaning woman/maître d'/ombudsperson came to the rescue and found a room with a working TV, and all was well. While the boys channel surfed, Djina and I did laundry. The post-wash clothes didn't look much cleaner, but at least they no longer stank. Except for the socks. Only a blow torch could destroy that odor. We hung everything out to dry on the porch. Though the sun had already set, within an hour the clothes felt as if they had been whisked out of an industrial dryer.

After dinner, the exhausted family plopped down on the beds and watched the heroic SpongeBob SquarePants thwart an evil crab's plan to dominate the undersea world.

Did you know that Nevada is filled with plants and creatures amazingly adapted to life in the desert? Did you know that sagebrush uses both deep roots to get water in times of drought as well as shallow roots to capture the rare rain? Did you know that the kangaroo rat rarely if ever has to drink water because it retains its moisture by super-concentrating its urine through an ingenious kidney? Did you know the Biers-Ariels couldn't care less about sagebrush or kangaroo rats, for we were not desert biologists but a sunburned family with 150 miles of desert down and 150 to go? Those mirror arrays churning out electricity were sounding better and better, if only to run bicycle-mounted air-conditioners.

The Nevada desert isn't flat, but mountainous. We slogged to the top of one steep pass and looked across a twenty-mile-wide valley containing not a single manmade item save the solitary, Etch-a-Sketch line of US Highway 50. By the time the line neared the next mountain range, it disappeared. The scene had that "Hey, we're on the moon" kind of look, but with less water.

"C'mon, Dad, let's go!" The only time Solomon hurried me up was on a mountain descent. This was when he pedaled with fervor. The cyclometer ticked off: 10, 15, 25, 35, 40 miles per hour. A scream of joy flavored with a dash of terror emanated from the rear. The tires hummed, The Beast gobbled up yellow road stripes, and the wind whooshed by our helmets. We were one with The Beast and one with each other. Ecstasy. Then suddenly a strange bike sound. On flat ground, cyclists dislike unfamiliar bike noises, but such an event at a speed fast enough to permanently put you in a wheelchair is horrifying. My heart pounded and I slowly braked, praying I would not cause my son paralysis. Solomon screamed in my ear. Even though he was close enough to see my ear's hammer and anvil, I couldn't understand a word. We pulled over.

"What?!"

"The map fell out back there."

The noise was the wind ripping the map from my jersey

pocket. Instead of responding with "Ha-ha-ha! It was only the map! I thought we were going to die!" I said, "It's going to be an ugly ride back to get it." I don't know if we Jews have a monopoly on turning sunny skies into black clouds, but I am an expert at it.

And then Djina raced by holding the map aloft like a scalp. "Ha-ha-ha! Come and get it!"

○━○∶○━○∶○━○∶○━○∶○━○∶○━○∶○━○∶○━○∶○━○∶○━○∶○━○

Prior to the trip, we tacked up a United States map with the route highlighted. Friends spoke about the Austin Hot Springs in north-central Nevada. Djina loves soaking. It was the only spot she circled. We arrived in Austin and asked directions.

"They're easy to get to. Just up the road a bit." He pointed to a gravel road. "'Bout fifteen mile." One mile, fifteen mile. No difference. We weren't going off-route any farther than the bicycles could cycle themselves. Besides, if you added the dripping sweat to the ambient heat, you could argue we'd been in a mobile sauna for six hours. A soak in an actual hot tub would be the equivalent of serving an Eskimo a snow cone.

While we sucked down shakes at a café, Solly's burger arrived, and I salivated. For twenty years, I'd been a practicing, non-dogmatic vegetarian who ate fish, eggs, and dairy. Every year or so, if Djina tempted me with a succulent morsel of lamb on the end of a fork, the aroma would trigger the hardwired, primal hunter receptors, and I'd bite. But a hamburger? Ground cow? Never! So why was my hand inching toward my son's plate? Fortunately, the garden burger arrived, keeping my moral superiority intact.

Onto Austin's antique shop/internet café. In the hour on the Middlegate computer, Djina had become addicted. Blogging is the new postcard, but so much better. By the time you put the stamp and address on a regular postcard, you've got space for, "It's beautiful here. Don't forget to water the plants. Love, Mom." But in a blog, you can post *War and Peace*. Instead of mailing seventeen postcards, just click "Send." No more looking through the postcard carousel to find the cheesiest one. Bring along a digital camera, and *you* become the postcard picture. Who wants to see a picture of Austin's fire station when you can post a picture of Matt and the boys peeing on the side of the road?

"Mom! I can't believe you put that on the blog!"

"He-he-he."

A man was strolling down Main Street with his laptop open, searching for an unsecured wireless connection to borrow. This, we learned, was Eric, a Belgian filmmaker. He, his wife, Axelle, and their four children were touring the New World in a custom-outfitted bus to make a film of the experience for Belgium television. We formed a mutual admiration club.

"You're riding bikes across the country. That's fantastic!"

"Your bus is so cool. What an amazing adventure!"

"No, no, biking is much more cool, and bringing a petition to Washington on global warming. What a concept!"

"Damn it! Exploring the whole hemisphere by bus is way better!"

Luckily, Djina tore open a package of Fig Newtons, and Axelle brought out her stash of Belgian chocolate, and we avoided blows. Eric wanted to interview us, so we camped together at the Bob Scott campground a few miles past Austin on the other side of a 7,500-foot pass. The east side of the summit was as different from the west side as the colorful Oz was different from Dorothy's Kansas. Finally there were trees! Pines and cedars and oaks, oh my! The desert had vanished. The campsite views were gorgeous, the toilets remarkably clean, and the campground free. Thank you, casino taxes!

By the time Eric finished interviewing the intrepid bicycling family, it was 9:00 AM. This might not seem late to a banker, but if you are embarking on a sixty-plus-mile bike ride and fifty-five miles are through desert (one mile past the campground, the Technicolor Oz regressed back to the sepia of Auntie Em's farm), and it's hot enough for Lucifer to chug a fifty-five-gallon barrel of Gatorade, then 9:00 AM is at least two hours too late.

A raven nest sat atop a telephone pole with the nestlings poking their heads over the side. It was a breathtaking vision. At least that was what Djina said. I didn't see it. I was counting how many leg rpms it took Solly and me to travel 12 miles per hour in a higher gear versus a lower gear (seventy-one versus eighty-three). I did, however, catch a glimpse of a golden eagle gliding across the sky as well as four wild horses galloping across the desert. Outside of these three animal moments, the day was sagebrush. For sixty-three miles, the only sun relief was a canvas shade structure in the solitary rest area where we lunched.

There were so few cars on US Highway 50 that we rode side-by-side. Yonah bemoaned how little he learned in school. Most classes moved too slowly, and in eighth grade he was taught what he had already learned in the fifth, sixth, and seventh grades. Alas, for every student like Yonah, there's at least one eighth grader who can't tell a noun from a verb. Cram thirty students in a classroom and watch the top and bottom conversely be bored and stupefied. I encouraged Yonah to learn outside of school.

"Find something you are passionate about and learn everything you can about it."

"I'm passionate about video games," he said.

"That doesn't count," I replied.

"Why not?"

"Because killing aliens doesn't teach you skills or make you a better person."

"You just want me to be passionate about something you think is worthy to be passionate about."

"No!" I exclaimed while thinking, "Exactly!"

Perhaps riding across America would ignite some passion in him, though I wasn't willing to bet the house on it. On the other hand, maybe Yonah and his fellow dispassionate youth are on to something. Passion has a dark side. All those single-minded people, organizations, and religions that are so passionate, they let nothing, be it law or ethics, stand in their way. Still, if Yonah dedicated himself to bicycle racing or poured his heart into a debate team, he might feel better about himself, and I'd definitely feel better about my parenting.

We rolled into Eureka, Nevada, population 600, for a rest day. After eight days and five hundred miles, we were bushed. It felt like an eighty-five-year-old man had sneaked in during the night and traded knees with me. My butt was sore and my shoulders tight. And we were only an eighth of the way across. If only we were French, then our cross-country adventure would be practically over; instead of Gatorade in Eureka, it would be French roast on the Champs-Élysées.

The boys and I headed into a grocery for quarts of Fierce Wild Berry Gatorade while Djina scouted Main Street for a hotel. Raines Market had fifty to sixty mounted heads, skins, and fish lining the walls above the groceries. I don't get the trophy thing. I can see hunting because you're hungry, but the head on the wall? It would be like lining our den with carrot tops from Djina's garden. Oh well, to each his own. Right now, a hunter is regaling his friends with the story of "that family of weirdos biking across the friggin' desert."

To make conversation before bringing out the petition, I feigned interest in the trophies. A thirtyish man, part of the family that owned the store, walked over. "Me and my family took most of them," he said, looking at me with steely, hunter eyes. "I know what you're thinking. You're from the city and think we're ignorant, gun-crazed survivalists who live to kill. I care about this land. I love it. I was born right here, and I've got young kids. I'm a conservationist, and I want to leave a good world for my kids. This land can't carry all the animals and they need to be culled. That's the job of the hunter."

He was earnest and though "culled" is a euphemism for "killed" he did have a legitimate point. After talking to this guy, I could almost condone hunting, though it's a safe bet that neither Yonah, the vegetarian, Solomon, the friend to all critters, nor I will ever get our tags when deer season opens. And Djina? Forget it. Fluorescent orange hunting hats are gauche.

"Uh," I began, "would you be interested in signing a petition on global warming."

"For or against?"

"Read it."

"I don't have to. You're a liberal. Probably vegetarian. Right?"

"Nondogmatic."

"Eh?"

"Uh, yeah."

"So you think the whole planet's heating up, and unless the government gets its rear in gear, we're going to fry. Right?"

"Hey, if you don't want to sign, don't worry about it."

He chuckled. "Give me a pen. Maybe the politicians will listen to you. They sure don't listen to the IPCC. Probably didn't see Gore's movie. He's a hunter you know."

"As is the current vice-president."

"Not a very good one."

Outside, while I was mulling how much more complicated and nuanced people are than their stereotypes lead you to believe, Djina announced she had found a hotel. The two of us have a difference regarding money; the difference is in diction. I claim I am frugal. She claims I am cheap. While I don't quite see her as extravagant, she lists herself as economical with the ability to spend when necessary. So while Djina knew where she wanted to spend the night, she realized she had to sell it as a bargain. And a bargain she had found: eighty-eight dollars for two nights at a hotel that served breakfast.

"Are you sure that isn't for one night?" I asked.

"I'm sure."

As we stuffed groceries in our panniers, a cyclist rode up and told us that he was camping in the city park with his two sons for free.

"Did you say *free*?" I asked.

"Forget it," said Djina.

Bicycle storage proved to be a problem at this and every hotel. While there was always plenty of parking for cars, motorcycles, and jumbo spaces for RVs, we never found a hotel with secure bicycle parking. It was if we were asking the front desk, "Any place to store our four anacondas?" Sometimes we rolled the bikes into our rooms; other times we'd lock them outside and hope for the best, as we did in Eureka.

After settling in and taking a tire iron to pry the remote control from Solomon's fingers, we walked Main Street. A sign on the door of the Department of Motor Vehicles warned, "No firearms allowed in the building." Between "No firearms allowed" and "Join the NRA" signs, Main Street was covered. The only place without signage was the Chinese restaurant, and that's where we ate. What a treat. After a week of greasy fries, Gatorade, and milkshakes, we'd get chow mein noodles with real vegetables and maybe, if the stars were aligned, tofu. Alas, the waitress was an angry Anglo teen who couldn't care less if we stayed or left. It was her last night and she wanted to go home. Eventually she took our order and served a meal that reflected the quality of service.

∞═○═○═○═○═○═○═○═○═○═○═○═○═○═○═○═○═∞

A lepidopterist loves butterflies. Wine is the sommelier's muse. Yonah worshiped the hotel buffet breakfast. That's not to say the rest of us didn't partake, but for Yonah it was a transcendent experience, a passion one might say. And as one always fondly remembers his first love, Yonah will always hold a special place in his heart for his first hotel buffet; a morning when he didn't have to wolf down cereal, yogurt, and a banana; a morning when his parents weren't haranguing him to fold up and stuff the tent.

The buffet had its own room, the hotel's secular chapel. Starting left and sweeping right were boxes of cereals from the mundane (Shredded Wheat) to the sublime (Frosted Flakes). Better-looking-than-tasting pastries and muffins followed; then a score of hard-boiled eggs; a cornucopia overflowing with bananas, oranges, and apples; bagels and bread; a toaster; jam, butter, and cream cheese; orange and cranberry juice; coffee, tea, hot chocolate; yogurts galore; and the waffle maker, the holiest of holies in the Breakfast Buffet Eucharist. Adjacent to the iron knelt a tray of Dixie cup chalices filled with batter. The waffle communion begins with the disciple paying homage to the waffle maker with a spray of oil. Next the pouring of the batter accompanied by the turning of the iron via its swivel. At precisely two minutes and thirty seconds comes the call to worship, the buzzer. The lifting of the lid, and the waffle is gently placed on the waiting double-thick paper plate. Generously anointed with Aunt Jemima and the wafer, er, waffle is taken into the body.

While Solomon had Frosted Flakes and was cajoled into a banana, Yonah stopped only after fifths of everything. Because of the limited menu for vegetarians in Nevada, Yonah took a page from the camel and loaded up. Djina was wrong about the price of the hotel. It was, as I had suspected, eighty-eight dollars *per night*. But with Yonah at the buffet, it was still a bargain.

⬤━◗⫶◖━◗⫶◖━◗⫶◖━◗⫶◖━◗⫶◖━◗⫶◖━◗⫶◖━◗⫶◖━⬤

Perched on stools at the Eureka Laundromat in the middle of a balmy day were laundryless people pitching quarters into slot machines. And they stared at us as though we were the strange ones wheeling in a bicycle trailer brimming with smelly spandex. Could the petition bridge the chasm between us? Could we find a common purpose in protecting our fragile atmosphere? Perhaps. Alas, we had left it in the hotel room, so neither group spoke to the other, thereby leaving all our prejudices intact.

Believe it or not, the Pony Express is not mentioned in the Eureka Sentinel Museum. Instead, it houses a press room from the 1800s, old household appliances, and office machines from a bygone age when form stood on equal footing with function. The beauty of these old machines is matched by the fact that their workings are transparent and understandable. Take the typewriter. Push the "t" button and a little arm rises in conjunction with an inked-ribbon to whack the paper creating a "t." The "shift" key actually *shifts* the entire array of letters, so the "T' whacks the paper. If I was typing this manuscript on a typewriter and the typewriter broke, I might, after the requisite checkmarks, be able to fix it. At the very least, I could apply a temporary duct tape fix.

Now take a computer. If you are anything like me (i.e. a sentient being), you have absolutely no idea how it works. Oh sure, there are bytes, hard drives, and semiconductors. We *all* know that. But as soon as a computer breaks down, we're totally clueless. Let's face it. We don't know how any piece of modern technology works. Unless you are an engineer, I'll wager you can't even explain how a plug-into-the-wall phone works, how your voice spoken into a small box runs through a wire and reappears half-a-world away out of another box. Well? Then there is the wireless internet. I could right now take a writing break and in thirty seconds get commodity prices from the Kazakhstan stock exchange, discover Shakespeare's father was a glove maker, and download man-on-dog porn. But explain it? In an earlier age, it would have been considered magic. Theologians would claim it was evidence of God. What I know is that whenever we are under a satellite or near some kind of transponder, we are bombarded by millions—nay—trillions of quanta of information 24/7, and if we had the proper receiver implanted in our heads, we could get it all. Such an implant sounds Big Brotherish to me, but Yonah, Solomon, and most kids I know would call it a species upgrade. Instead of wearing a dorky-looking bluetooth, in a few years a computer wired to one's brain will be planted in his scalp with eyeglasses doing double duty as screens.

Perhaps I am a Luddite because this future unmoors me, but I believe that technology moves far too fast. I don't have any answers, except that we should be discussing the direction and speed that technology is taking us.

The Eureka Sentinel Museum was like being cuddled in a down comforter on a frosty night with a cup of hot cocoa by the fireplace because it felt good to see a time when we understood our technology. Of course, I'm a hypocrite and would never exchange my computer for even an electric typewriter, but still, to see a wood-fired kitchen stove makes my heart thrill.

OਵOਵOਵOਵOਵOਵOਵOਵOਵOਵOਵO

The boys and I swam in Eureka's ginormous indoor pool while Djina lay on the lawn to do the important work of evening out her tan. It's not that she necessarily needed or even wanted more sun than the ten hours a day we'd been getting, but her tan lines followed the contours of her bicycle shorts and jersey instead of a bikini top and bottom. She strategically placed towels to get her tan right. If you're confused, you're a guy.

THE BAR MITZVAH AND THE BEAST

Therefore it was upon me to defend the older generation's honor in pool basketball. And it was here, in Eureka's public swimming pool, that Yonah truly became a man. It wasn't the bar mitzvah: "Son, now that you've chanted Torah, you are a man." It wasn't the cycling across the Sierras: "Son, you rode that mountain like a man." Here was manhood's true test. Son versus Father. Mano a mano. Oedipus versus Laius. Up to this point, I had been easily able to crush Yonah and Solomon in two-on-one pool basketball, tossing them into the air like juggling cats. But here was Yonah shoving me away from the basket. Not only couldn't I get around this broad-shouldered behemoth, but he was dunking over me at will. After the grand humiliation, I watched the two of them go at it. One of the great joys of parenthood is watching your kids. When they're little, it's enough to watch them coo, smile, or lick ice cream. When they are older, it's enough to watch them shine at sports or school. Here it was enough to watch them play without fighting. Yonah was lucky to have Solomon as a built-in friend, for Yonah, with all of his intellectual gifts, athleticism, and moral goodness, was quite shy. In school, he was well-liked and respected, yet he never had the desire to call a friend. So, when they were not at each other's throats, his best mate was Solomon.

As we were leaving, Yonah pointed out the high school mascot painted above the pool: The Vandals. Suddenly, I remembered the bikes attached to a rail at the back of the hotel with a wimpy-ish lock. I rushed back to find that the bikes were safe, but The Beast's back tire was flat. Normally, a flat tire takes five minutes to fix. But like its owner, The Beast had reached middle-age and was a bit crotchety. Unlike a normal bicycle with one brake on the back wheel, The Beast had two—a regular pull brake and a drum brake. The regular pull brake scrunches two pieces of hard rubber against the wheel's rim to slow its rotations with friction. But because the weight of a tandem creates so much kinetic energy on a descent, the heat buildup on pull brakes can cause the rim to get so hot, the inner tube occasionally explodes. That, in an understatement, would be bad. Therefore, The Beast also had a drum brake. (The drum brake was not quite an anachronism, but by 2007, any decent, self-respecting tandem's rear wheel was equipped with a single, high-tech disc brake. Not so The Beast.)

Drum brakes work fine unless the need arises to change a tire. Then you might as well be repairing a busted airlock on the International Space Station with a dull toothpick. First, the brake needed to be unbolted from the frame. Theoretically no problem, but the brake's bolt had been happy where it was. It took one checkmark to loosen while slightly stripping it. Next, I slipped out the cable that was threaded through a hole and held in place between a nut and a second bolt. This bolt, too, did not surrender without a fight and relented only after I had bloodied three knuckles on the rear sprocket. Steps three through six: remove the nuts holding the wheel onto the bike, yank off the tire, replace the tube, and reverse the process. Reversing the process . . . aye that was the rub. The cable from step two had unraveled at the end and no longer fit through the hole, so I cut an inch off the end. Once the cable was in, the wheel had to be positioned exactly right to reattach the brake to the frame. The whole assembly had to be lightly bashed for everything to fit.

Now that everything was back together, the brake had to be adjusted. Too tight and the wheel wouldn't move; too loose and the brake wouldn't work. Goldilocks would never have been able to do it because the "just right" spot could be found over the course of six microns along the cable, and I am sure her mouth was too pure to utter the expletives needed to find it.

Total time: One hour, five minutes. It wasn't so bad because it was a day off, and I fixed it in the shade of the hotel's veranda rather than in the middle of the desert.

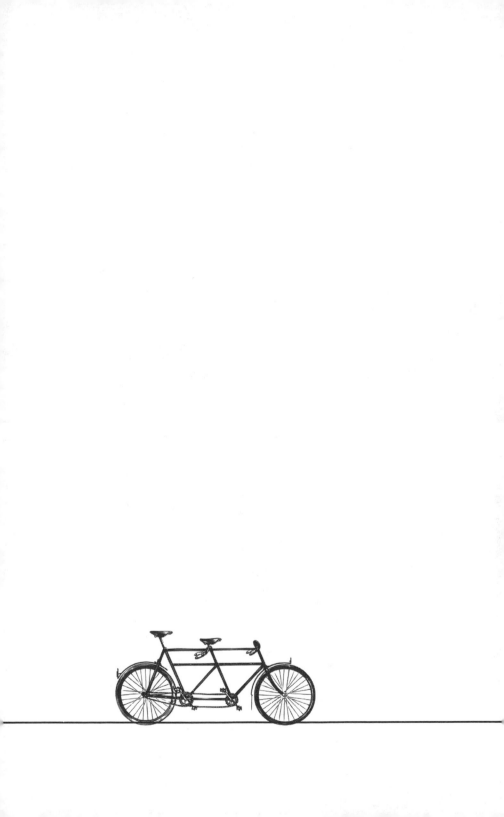

6

WORDS ARE NOT NECESSARY

THE DAY FOLLOWING EUREKA was eighty-four miles sans towns, convenience stores, shade. Forced to schlep all our water, Djina packed an extra four-and-a-half gallons into her trailer. Bonus question: What does a gallon of water weigh?

To avoid as much heat as possible, we arose at 4:00 AM and powered down cereal and bananas filched from the buffet the night before. Yonah bid a wistful good-bye to the waffle maker, which was ensconced behind a glass door that would remain locked until long after we had departed Eureka's darkened Main Street. Though we crossed four named summits—Pinto, Pancake, Little Antelope, and Robinson—nothing was too steep, the heat stayed below triple digits, and there was a slight tailwind.

It was hard to believe Yonah was only thirteen as he blasted up the ascents. However, though physically he was becoming a man, he still asked questions about commonsense things that he could have easily figured out had he trusted himself. A few days earlier, he had asked, "How do I wash my socks?" followed by "How will I know they're clean?" and "How do I hang them up to dry?" Had he trusted his intuition, he would have arrived at successful solutions, if not at first, certainly by the second or third time. But he hated failure and wanted his first attempt to be perfect. Perhaps he felt failure would reflect poorly on his character. The paradox is that the road to success always runs through the towns of Failure, Fiasco, and Defeat. As a youth, I was unlike my son. Once I convinced a commercial rafting company to employ me as a guide after boating with a friend down the American River in his raft and figuring out that all one needed to guide was to paddle around a few pesky rocks. Heck, any moron could do *that*. Here let me insert more evidence to support the notion that there is a God who watches over idiots, or at least a patron saint of imbeciles, for no one died or was permanently maimed in my single season on the river as I habitually flipped rafts in rapids with such names as Satan's Cesspool, Troublemaker, and Meatgrinder.

Djina's the same as me. Expert in areas she knows little about. She has never met an issue that she couldn't pontificate on. Sometimes she'll know the pertinent facts, sometimes she won't. It really doesn't matter. So given our natures, how did Yonah become so tentative?

My hope was that the trip would give him the confidence to make mistakes and figure things out for himself. As the old saw goes, while parents can't solve their children's problems, they can give them the tools and confidence to figure them out on their own. This would work if I answered his sock question by stopping what I was doing, smiling, and calmly replying, "If you were on your own, how would you wash your socks?" I would patiently wait and he'd eventually come up with his own solution. What an excellent parent! Only it wasn't me. The incredulous father who could not believe his son was incapable of washing his own socks stared at the boy and huffed, "Are you kidding? Soap and water!" The boy's tentative nature continued.

It was Father's Day, the Mother's Day afterthought holiday invented by Hallmark and the tie cartel. The only use for a tie on The Beast would be to keep Solomon's hands on the handlebars, and I knew there must be a law against that. Instead, Djina cajoled the boys into saying something they appreciated about me at the top of each pass. Despite the earlier sock remark, Yonah joined Solomon and came up with something sweet, thoughtful, and at least partially true. It was the best Father's Day gift ever.

The day's only difficulty was that after seven hours on the bike, Solomon started nodding off. I knocked him on his helmet to keep him awake. While other nine-year-olds were spending their summers running around playing sports, Solomon was sitting from sunrise to sunset on the back of a bike in the middle of the desert. Again he was offered a plane ride to his grandparents, and again the budding masochist declined.

We rolled into Ely expecting another pleasant town like Eureka. But though it was significantly bigger, at over four thousand souls, half of the town's beautiful buildings were boarded up. Young unemployed men created an angry vibe in the air. Think Main Street at Disneyland. Think crystal meth. Mix together in a cocktail shaker and pour out Ely, Nevada. We stopped at Sportsworld for tire tubes. A large sign on the side of the building advertised, "Cheapest beer in town."

Djina wondered, "Is the beer next to the guns or the chainsaws?"

Though there were cases of beer that nearly reached the ceiling, aisles of guns and hunting equipment, and enough fishing gear to deplete the western states of trout, Ely's single sporting goods store had not a single road bike inner tube.

Three miles out of town was a KOA campground. Its registration desk was located in a large convenience store. Besides us, there were about a dozen people inside, all elderly, all sporting yellow shirts. "Here to camp?" inquired a bright-eyed seventy-year-old wearing a straw cowboy hat, Bermuda shorts, and white knee socks to complete his cheerful outfit. A badge identified him as "Bill, Texas."

"Yes."

"Well," continued Bill, "You've come to the right place. Just fill out this registration form."

The other yellow shirts inched their way toward us. Bicyclists were a novelty in this campground, which catered to the RV crowd. Everyone was so nice that my cynicism antennae interpreted the feel as cultish. Of course it wasn't. It was simply that if you were retired on a fixed income, this was a good place to be. Make a little cash, hang out with your peers, and be helpful. Given the future fears surrounding Social Security and the stock market, I filed KOA onto my cerebral hard drive. Two KOA women engaged in a heated discussion about who would escort us to the "tent area." "Fran, Minnesota" won, and with a toothy smile, she took us to a large lawn, possibly the only grass within a five-hundred-mile radius.

After helping us raise the tents, Solomon found the basketball court. A couple of kids showed up, and Solomon had two new friends. While Yonah tended to keep his own counsel, Solomon made friends with any sentient being: kid, dog, beetle. If there were no life-forms around, he'd bring out one of his imaginary friends. Jamie was a family fixture for years. He ate with us and had sleepovers. Jamie was a nice kid, but it was irritating when he left Solomon's room a mess.

Three Harley-Davidsons set up camp next to us. Though they are loud to the point of hearing loss and conjure up images of those famous bad boys, the Hell's Angels, Harleys are panache materialized. The bad boy image gives mystique to the accountants and marketing vice presidents who buy the bulk of them. It's the sparkling chrome, the leather, the custom touches, and the patented engine rumble that tell everyone, "I'm here. I'm bad. I'm cool. I'm Brando." (Of course, Brando rode a Triumph in *The Wild One*, but that's only fact. We're talking myth here.).

After the riders shut off their machines and their eardrums settled, these bikers became quite friendly. First the usual comments. "You're coming from where?" "I doubt if I could bike this stomach of mine more than a mile." Then we handed the most loquacious a petition, and after reading it, he handed it back *unsigned*. Was there a mistake? Didn't he know that petitions get signed? Or did he see us as part of the liberal scare campaign making something out of nothing. Hadn't Rush Limbaugh warned them about us? And even if there was a smidgen of truth to what those elitists were saying, which there wasn't, who cares about polar bears? You can see them in zoos. Then again, maybe it was part of the Harley mystique not to get involved. They were, after all, rebels. But every way we looked at it, the truth of the matter was, after six hundred miles, this was the petition's first rejection.

Answer to water question: One gallon of water weighs 8.33 pounds, so Djina began the day carrying an extra *37.5 pounds* in water. That's a woman of valor.

Seven miles from the day's destination, Baker, The Beast had the squishy feel of riding on a flat. Because of Murphy and his accursed law, it was the rear tire. Though fixing it was down to

THE BAR MITZVAH AND THE BEAST

fifty-five minutes, there was a larger issue between The Beast and me. The trust we had built over the half-year relationship was teetering. While an occasional chain wedgie was an inconvenience, a bad tire or tube was dangerous. The next bike shop was 140 desert miles away. The perceptive Djina knew better than to point out the advantages of a new tandem.

Baker consisted of a dozen dilapidated wooden houses set in the middle of the Great Basin. Electricity didn't appear to be a town feature. Its residents probably had never beheld an ice cube. Most definitely there would be no Gatorade. From the outside, the Silver Jack Inn/Electrolux Café looked like a reject from Warner Brothers' Wild West B-movie back lot.

Yet not for the first time, the veneer blinded the eyes, for in we walked and were greeted not by tobacco's vaporized carcinogens, currency stapled to the wall, or life-size pictures of Dale Earnhardt, Jr. about to drink and drive. Rather there were poster-sized, museum-quality photographs of wildflowers, New England foliage, and elephant seals. Just as Moses lost his way to the land of Canaan, these photographs lost their way to a SOHO art gallery. An Electrolux vacuum cleaner hung from the ceiling as either a chandelier or a warning against excessive cleanliness. There was a refrigerated glass case that held not only Gatorade and Budweiser, but tarts, chocolate truffles, and—what's this?—Sierra Nevada Pale Ale!

We ordered Thai stir-fry with peanut sauce, whole grain bread, and chocolate brownies, each as large as an elephant seal proboscis. The café's four tables were occupied, so we shared the large one with a clutch of local artists who had left the big city to pursue their art and eccentricities in the rarified air of Nevada's high desert. There was the eighty-five-year-old who told us of the house she had been building since 1968. There was the weaver who used horsetail hair for her yarn and lived in a hole in the ground.

"I'm sorry, I thought you said, 'hole'?"

"It's got everything I need except having to haul water every other day."

There was another person at the table, but after someone claims to live in a hole, there was nothing memorable he could say short of admitting to be the Zodiac Killer.

I wanted to talk to the owner of the café/hotel because besides creating gourmet plates, he was the photographer. He was too busy to chat because he also ran the five-room hotel. Therefore, here is the fictional biography of Terry Marasco. Terry began his career as dishwasher at Berkeley's world-renowned Chez Panisse, working himself up to chief pastry chef before being discovered by Ansel Adams, who bequeathed him his large format camera on his deathbed. Writing recipes for *Saveur* and going out on assignment for *National Geographic* proved tiresome for this eccentric genius. "I vant to be alone!" he screeched at his agent before packing up his knives and camera to find the middle of nowhere. He found it and settled in Baker. The rest is history.

"Here's a guy with passion!" I exclaimed to Yonah. "What do you think?" Yonah did not respond because he too was occupied, working on his second brownie. After the gourmet feed, we checked into the hotel, our stomachs and souls satisfied but blissfully ignorant of one of the universe's primary laws: Life is a zero-sum game; therefore, a magnificent evening, like a tan, needs to be evened out.

○■○:○■○:○■○:○■○:○■○:○■○:○■○:○■○:○■○:○■○:○■○

Eighty-three desert miles from Baker to Milford with no services? Cake. Eureka to Ely was eighty-four, and this time, our tummies were filled with whole grains, not greasy chow mein. Again we lit out before the dawn, bid goodbye to Nevada, and waved hello to Utah. A river otter frolicked in a small lake. Prairie dogs poked their heads from their holes to yell encouragements, and pairs of ravens rode the thermals towards the heavens. A grand day to be alive. But as soon as the sun was three fingers above the horizon, the sun went from simmer to boil and the winds from angelic to satanic. The great day to be alive morphed into survival day; our pace was the bicycling equivalent to backpacking up a sand mountain with seventy-five-pound packs. There was a bad omen: a dead cow that was soon followed by a second bad omen, a second dead cow. Neither were roadkill. These bovines died of thirst.

Though we had started with an extra four gallons, by the second cow it was clear we would not have nearly enough water.

On a bike, you never know how hot the ambient temperature is until you stop because the wind/sweat air-conditioning masks the heat. At mile forty we got off our bikes and discovered true heat. Up until this moment, the trip's heat had been a bother, an inconvenience, a running joke. Today the fires from hell leapt forth from fissures in the earth. The Sahara and the Gobi were comparative Gardens of Eden. The wind turned the heat into a convection oven. An egg tossed into the air would come down hard-boiled. There is an apocryphal story that in the time of the Ottoman Empire, a man committing murder during a summer khamsin wind would not receive full punishment due to a temporary insanity caused by the heated wind. I understood why, for this unrelenting wind brought violent thoughts. I cursed it to stop. It paid no heed and blasted more heat.

We were down to a quart of water. And we still had two significant passes to climb. And Milford was still forty-three miles away. Terry, the Electrolux Café's proprietor was mistaken. He had not reached the middle of nowhere. We had. And for the first time on the trip, we were in real danger. You might be wondering why we got off our bikes in the first place. It wasn't to rest or to lunch or to even out tans. There was a flat. Between the three bikes and one trailer, there were eight tires. Seven of the tires take no more than five minutes to change. What are the odds that the flat would be on the eighth? Twelve point five percent. Yep. The rear of The Beast.

I was despondent. Not from the heat, the wind, or the water situation—any of which had the potential to put us in serious jeopardy. It was that The Beast had decided it had enough of this misadventure. It was calling it quits. Including training rides, The Beast had put on over two thousand miles without a flat. Now it wouldn't go fifty miles without getting one. The air leaking from the tire hissed, "You should have bought a new one."

I multitasked. While fixing the flat, I scanned the road for a car to shake down for water. It wasn't promising, for we were no longer on US Highway 50, the Loneliest Road in America. We were on one of its smaller tributaries. We were utterly alone. Finally, a vehicle appeared. I waved my blackened hands and stood in the road. It stopped and the elderly couple's expression was no different had Baby Face Nelson demanded their money. They quickly handed over two pints of water and did not stick around to schmooze. I meant to save the water for the boys. I didn't mean to drink three-quarters of a bottle. I only took a sip. I swear.

When replacing a tube, you must run your fingers inside the tire to feel for any protruding glass or thorn ready to puncture the replacement. Everything seemed fine, so in went a previously patched tube. The operation was down to forty-five minutes and we slogged on.

The next summit, Wah-Wah, was aptly named. Near the top, a Subaru pulled over. A family of four climbed out, opened the back, pulled out a cooler, and handed each of us a pint of chilled water. A carafe of Rothschild 1965 Cabernet Sauvignon would not be smoother on the palate. Here was the one command every religious tradition is clear about: kindness to strangers. Other drivers passed us with a one-word thought bubble: morons. But this family's small act of kindness, a five-minute delay in their four-day drive, saved us. A Jewish teaching claims that by saving a single person, one saves the world. Why? Because a single act of kindness holds the possibility of transforming the world in the same manner that dislodging a single pebble might lead to a rock slide. The fact that these Good Samaritans stopped when we needed help showed the goodness of religion. I said as much to Yonah.

He replied, "Atheists can be nice too."

"Sure, but if a person is in a religion that preaches kindness to strangers, then isn't it more likely that a person in the religion will be kinder than an atheist who has no such teaching?"

"Every year on the first day of school, my teachers make class contracts. Being nice to each other is always at the top."

"Don't you think they get the idea from the Bible?"

"Where did the Bible get it from? It must have been from people because the Bible was written by man."

"Inspired man."

"Inspired by what?"

"The soul or the thing we call God."

"It could be an evolutionary thing. Societies where people act nice to each other are selected over societies that kill each other."

"I bet that family was churchgoers."

"Or bicyclists," Djina chimed in.

"Or bicyclists," I admitted, glaring at my wife as she unwittingly subterfuged my attempt to get Yonah to see the beauty in religion.

East of the summit was another desolate valley floor. Twenty miles across stood Frisco Summit. Our destination, Milford, lay on the other side. More water was necessary. We flagged down a large pickup with the license plate ILUVBEEF.

"Wish I could help, but all I got is a half-gallon of water we've been swigging from."

"We'll take it!"

"Uh, I got a quarter bottle of warm Gatorade?"

"Yes!"

"How 'bout I sling your bikes in the back, and we just take you to Milford?"

Pause. Begging drink is one thing, but begging a ride? "Thanks. We're going to try and make it on our own."

"Well, okay. Good luck. It's mighty hot today."

As we approached Frisco Summit, the day was no longer a child, or even middle-aged. But it was nearly the summer solstice, so at 6:00 PM, we still felt confident about making Milford.

"Dad," Solomon tentatively called as we started the climb. This nine-year-old was smart enough to know what would set his dad off and broke the bad news gradually. "I think we might have another flat."

"No way!" But sure enough he was right. Wise Solomon did not issue checkmarks for words that would have made Beelzebub's ears burn. These flats didn't make sense. I examined the wheel, tire, and tube. Everything seemed fine. It was like the coroner who examines the body and pronounces, "Nothing wrong except for the fact that he's dead."

I wanted to cry, but the wind and sun would have dried the tears, and I had no water to lose. Plus, I had to pretend everything was all right for the kids. There was nothing to do except put in another patched tube, even though The Beast smirked that it wouldn't last. We shook down another truck and scored a full gallon of water. Close to the top of Frisco Summit, the sun was beginning to descend, and The Beast called it quits with its third flat. The ride was over for Solomon and me. There wasn't enough daylight to fix it. Yonah and Djina continued to Milford while I stuck out a thumb. A large pickup with four migrant workers wedged into the front seat stopped. We loaded everything into the bed and settled between the bikes. I thought Solomon would be excited about riding in the back of a pickup, speeding along with the wind in our faces like a pair of desperadoes watching the setting sun paint orange and red streaks across the sky. But he was sullen and angry. We were breaking the law.

"Solomon, we didn't have a choice."

"You have to wear seatbelts."

"Not if you ride in the back of a truck."

"You have to wear seatbelts. It's the law."

"This is Nevada. It's not like California. They don't have seatbelt laws."

"We're in Utah, *Dad*."

"Utah has a law *against* wearing seatbelts."

"Yeah, right, Dad. You're such a jerk."

And so it went to Milford. While waiting for Djina and Yonah at the city's main intersection, his anger did not abate. Perhaps he has forgiven me, but I suspect that at an auspicious family gathering—say a fiftieth wedding anniversary—he'll raise a glass, "I'd like to toast my mother for putting up so long with my father, a law-breaking jerk."

I put a repair patch on one of the tubes, remembering the definition of madness is when one faced with repeated failure keeps repeating the same actions which brought said failure. That also defines stupidity and lack of imagination. Thinking the patch might hold, the adage clearly covered me.

Dusk came and went and still no Djina and Yonah. At 9:00 two bicycle lights appeared. We checked into a hotel and ate in the attached diner. I spoke about something that had been on my mind. I wanted Yonah to take more of a leadership role. After all, this was his trip.

"Like what," he asked, not happy with the conversation's direction.

"You know, like being the leader for the day. Wake us up, organize breakfast, be the navigator. Kind of like what Mom and I do."

"Do I have to?"

"It would be part of your rite of passage. You know, build self-confidence and leadership."

"Isn't riding across America enough?" he pleaded.

I said nothing, but wondered what other father would tell his thirteen-year-old son that sixteen hours spent riding eighty-three miles by bicycle, lugging twenty-five pounds of gear, and bucking twenty-mile-per-hour headwinds and triple-digit temperatures, wasn't enough?

Solomon was right. I was a jerk.

<hr/>

I woke early to check the tire, hoping to find air. Sort of like hoping the Chicago Cubs will win the World Series. The tire was—no drum roll necessary—flat. The hardware store had no new tires or tubes. I trudged to the train station to see about catching a train to Cedar City.

"Only freight trains here," the station manager said.

"Any buses?" He looked at me as if I had asked whether their ionic transporter was operational. "Car rental?"

"There's one in Cedar City. Your best bet is to go to the edge of town and hitch."

Solomon would walk the fifty-five miles first. The last option was to inspect the tubes in the sober light of morning to see if there was a common failure point. And there was. All the seals on the no-glue patches leaked. Maybe it was too hot. Maybe they were too old. Maybe I did a crappy job putting them on. So with slightly more attention to detail than a newly minted neurosurgeon employs, I repaired the two best-looking tubes with old-school glue patches and—*voilà*—they held air.

Though Cedar City was a mere five-hundred-foot elevation gain from Milford, we averaged 8 miles per hour, for as our path pivoted south so did the headwinds. These southern winds weren't content to keep us in Milford, they wanted to blow us past Polaris. Let me make this perfectly clear. If there is a choice between mountains and wind, mountains win. Mountains offer the satisfaction of accomplishment and then the downhill reward. Wind offers more wind. It is relentless. It dries you out. It enters your ears, nose, mouth, and pores. It is as if some uninvited, rude visitor climbs into your skin and vigorously rubs. When you see a mountain, you calculate what you need to do, steel yourself, and get the job done. You are in control. It is a finite problem. It can be conquered. Wind cannot be conquered. It has no form and you are powerless. Your only option is to pray for its demise. The mountain mantra is "Almost there, almost there," until you're there. For wind, it's "How long can this bastard blow?" If you're lucky, the wind shifts. The cyclometer jumps from 7 miles per hour to 28 miles per hour. You can finally hear yourself think. But don't get cocky. If Aeolus senses hubris, he will return with a vengeance, and you will weep.

The wind made me crabby until it blew the obvious thought into my head. If Nevada was the Saudi Arabia of solar energy, then Utah was the Iraq of wind energy. And Utah is a gentle breeze compared to the Dakotas. If our country's leadership had foresight, we'd build wind turbines. If wind can hold a three-hundred-pound load rolling down a 7 percent grade to 10 miles per hour, it can power more than a few refrigerators and laptops. China is already going big in wind. Why cede wind energy leadership (and profit) to them?

At Cedar City, we were thirteen days and eight hundred miles into the trip. Eight hundred miles is a significant ride; it is a great accomplishment. It is a round-trip from San Francisco to Los Angeles. It is two round-trips between New York and Washington, D.C. It is a distance greater than the width of France or the length of Italy.

It was one-fifth of our route.

Between the heat, the wind, and The Beast, we were beat. We needed a break, a shot of TLC. Lewis and Clark had Sacagawea to guide them through their tough times. Clara Barton nursed the

Union Army's wounds. We had Professor Ken Giles. He flew into Las Vegas, rented a minivan, drove to Cedar City, jumped on his bike, and met us twenty miles north of Cedar City. Had I ever been happier to see someone? Outside of watching my children's births, and outside of going to that party back in 1987 and realizing that my friend Djina was a babe, the answer was probably yes, but seeing that tiny fluorescent dot on the road grow bigger and bigger and turn into Ken was a moment of monumental joy. With his 25-mile-per-hour tailwind, he rocketed up the road like a dragster, grinning like George W. Bush after the Supreme Court awarded him the presidency. Ken's new pancreas jokes, sumptuous delicacies, and news from Davis were palliative to the weary family.

Someone once wrote that one's true religion is not Christianity, Islam, Buddhism, Wicca, Judaism, or even Atheism. Rather, it is what one focuses the majority of his thoughts, actions, and energy on. If this is the case, our true religious beliefs were defined by what the four of us chose to do upon arrival at the Best Western Cedar City. Solomon was a Cartoontarian, a devotee of *SpongeBob SquarePants*. Yonah, while he religiously denied any religious affiliation, was an adherent of Buffetism. He checked out the room where next morning's breakfast would be held. He praised the waffle iron and blessed the yogurt-filled glass refrigerator. Djina was a religious double-dipper. On one hand, she was an Epicurean. She went straight to the five brands of stinky cheese that Ken smuggled by airport security. After gorging, it was a hajj to the hotel computer, where she practiced Blogism. As for me, I was a disciple of Dionysus. After parking The Beast, the trauma of the windy ride melted into a single philosophical question: beer or wine? Why choose, spoketh my inner soul, and hence my chalice did overfloweth with both.

After our respective reveries, we found a Mexican restaurant and consumed an amount of calories equal to the three nearest tables combined. *Mis hijos los hablan con la waitress en Español.* She was so moved by these two cute gringos that she brought them a special dessert consisting of tortilla chips, sugar, and chocolate syrup. To an Epicurean, it might not sound gourmet, but between bites, Djina pronounced it holy.

We took two rest days. The first morning was dedicated to The Beast. At the bike shop, I jettisoned the patched tubes for new ones. The Beast also needed a new rear tire. The bike shop owner had difficulty finding a tire because The Beast's wheels were—surprise—outdated. By the mid-1990s, bike wheels went metric, twenty-seven-inch wheels became 700 mm, and tire manufacturers recalibrated their products. His only twenty-seven-inch tire was an ancient Schwinn designed for short urban commuting. Its heavy weight was balanced by its proneness for blowouts. Nevertheless, it was better than what I had. I sat in his shop and switched tires.

The entire time in the store, the radio was blaring the voice of Middle America: Rush Limbaugh. I'd listened to Rush before and found him quite entertaining. Entertaining in the same sense of watching eight-year-olds play Little League baseball. The kids in their immaculate uniforms are serious. The coaches with their clipboards and shouts of strategies are serious. The twenty walks and eighteen errors render the game ridiculous. And so with Rush. He tries to come across as a serious, well-informed political commentator, but his obvious half-truths and outright fabrications are so ridiculous, one can only grin. The question I grappled with as I worked was: Should I bring out the petition? On the "of course" side, he owned a bike shop and was a super nice guy. On the "are you kidding" side, he was a Dittohead, an acolyte of Rush Limbaugh, a man who claimed that global warming was a conspiracy cooked up by Al Gore and his ilk because they hated America.

"Uh, do you want to look at a . . . uh . . . petition we're bringing across America on global climate change?"

"I'll take a look."

For a full minute he studied the document. I was nervous he'd find a misplaced comma or some grammatical faux pas. (I may teach high school English, but "who" or "whom" isn't any easier for me.) I worried that he'd shout, "Ha! A split infinitive! I'd never sign such drivel! Get Rush on the phone! I got me an ignorant liberal elite here!" But he finished reading, picked up a pen, and said, "We need to do something about this."

I floated out of the shop on a new tire and the realization that if a guy who listens to Rush thinks we've got to do something about global warming, maybe, just maybe, we've got a chance.

O▬O▪O▬O▪O▬O▪O▬O▪O▬O▪O▬O▪O▬O▪O▬O▪O▬O▪O▬O▪O▬O

Imagine that a giant the size of the Empire State Building built a Manhattan-sized sand castle and then glazed it with paint made from the orange of wispy clouds at sunrise. Now imagine that a windy rain came and knocked three-quarters of it down. That's Bryce Canyon. Still can't picture it? Google it. All of us but Yonah hiked the canyon. Normally we would have dragged him along, but a rite of passage has to involve freedom of choice. Without freedom, he'd remain a kid. Though I wasn't ambivalent about giving him the freedom to stay behind, I was saddened. Hiking the canyon was a hot fudge sundae for the eyes and freshly baked bread for the soul. One of the tougher elements of parenting is when you let your child make what you believe is a mistake and not stop him. Following the hike, I told him about all the cool sights in order to show him what he missed, so next time he'd come along. I've used this ploy before. One day it's bound to work.

Later we stopped for ice cream. Solomon ordered a hot fudge sundae. His eyes sparkled with delight as the huge bowl was set down before him. By the time he knocked the spoon against the empty glass, the sparkle was a dull glaze. Clearly you can eat too much of a good thing. Does the same go with nature? Can you take in too much beauty? Does it ever become dull? For me, the answer is an emphatic No. I'd like to imagine that this is a universal truth. That's why I didn't say anything to my older son.

O▬O▪O▬O▪O▬O▪O▬O▪O▬O▪O▬O▪O▬O▪O▬O▪O▬O▪O▬O▪O▬O

Ken doled out one more gift before heading home. He hauled our gear to our next destination, Panguitch, so we could do the five-thousand-foot climb out of Cedar City unencumbered. The climb had the same orangey rock of Bryce Canyon. We looked down on long vistas of forests. The Nevada deserts were a memory of the past. It was no longer the Battan Death Ride. Today we were the Von Trapps out for a mountain picnic. Solomon and I sang up the mountain and came upon a 10 percent grade.

"Ready to kick it in?"

"Ready!"

We attacked the mountain. "We own this sucker!" I yelled.

"Yeah!" Solomon hollered.

The Beast begged to differ. There was a sharp snap accompanied by a spin of the pedals as if there were no load on them. The snap and the spin led to a sudden stop. I looked down. The chain was gone. Forty-two years of riding bicycles and my first chain break.

Checkmark.

Luckily we had the chain tool I had with great foresight purchased but hardly knew how to use. Turning to Djina, I proclaimed, "Don't worry. I can fix it." A pin holding two chain links together had failed, destroying the links. The two bad links needed to be removed and replaced with a special repair link. The operation was straightforward but tricky. The trick was to remove enough of a pin, so a bad link could slide out. Remove too little pin, and the link can't slide out. Remove too much, and the pin falls out. Once the pin is out, it is impossible to insert it back in. The solution then is stick out your thumb. I managed to slip out the bad links, but the repair link demanded fine motor skill and patience—two qualities I am not genetically wired for. After I dropped a critical piece in the high grass, Djina volunteered to take over as relief mechanic. I don't have any hang-ups about gender roles and insisting on doing the man's job, so after dropping that critical piece in the tall grass twice more, I offered, "Want to try?" She snapped the links together like a pair of Lego pieces, and The Beast was again whole. Djina didn't lord her successful operation over me. She didn't have to, for at that moment I knew who wore the mechanic overalls in the family.

THE BAR MITZVAH AND THE BEAST

In rural America, art is created by what's at hand. Hence, the dollar bill wallpaper and the shoe tree. But what about the rancher? What is his art? He hunts, and after eating the venison and tanning the leather, he's got antlers. What if you're not Georgia O'Keefe? What if you don't know how to scrimshaw? Ranchers make art by nailing antlers to gates, fences, and the sides of houses. Until this particular installation, none of us were particularly impressed with antler art. But this was different. A good quarter-mile from a lone ranch on a steep climb were sets of antlers spaced a couple of feet apart all the way to the gate. In terms of numbers, the average deer antler is about three feet wide. Fill four hundred yards of fence with one set of antlers every five feet and you come up with, well, a lot. But the jaw dropping was reserved for the gateway made of two posts planted in the ground twenty feet apart rising twenty feet in the air. A crossbar connected them at the top. Now imagine a colony of army ants attacking a hotdog. That's how tightly packed the antlers were on the gate. It seemed as if every deer antler in the entire country came to rest in peace here. It was art of abundance.

If The Beast were to give up the ghost right then, I'd request that the rancher allow me to nail it along his fence.

Two cyclists coming the other way stopped to chat. Like most people, they looked at the boys with gaping mouths. At the mention of this ride being a kind of bar mitzvah, the two volunteered that they were Mormons. I have nothing against Mormons. As I mentioned earlier, I respect their toughness and work ethic. Some of my best students are Mormons. But Mormon theology seems a bit silly with the gold hieroglyphics written in "reformed Egyptian." In addition are the white-shirted, tie-wearing, young missionaries possessing a toxic mix of naïveté and sanctimony. Add it together, and you see why I've never taken Mormonism too seriously. That's what passion gets you, I thought, and realized that I was beginning to think like Yonah.

But these two cyclists were not wearing their religion on their name tags. They were interesting and intelligent. They had graduate degrees. They understood the importance of combating global climate change. Again I was forced to rethink my prejudices. The beauty of traveling is that during our "regular" lives, we stereo-type in order to get through our busy days when we don't have time to meet people as they really are. But here, the only items on the "to-do" list were riding bikes and meeting people. You auto-matically become friendlier to everyone and discover you have more in common with other members of your species than you originally thought. You discover how once you become friendlier, everyone mirrors the friendliness back. You vow to hold on to this new way of being upon returning home.

Unfortunately, prejudices are impossible to extinguish. When they return, it's time to hit the road again.

Following the five-thousand-foot climb, I let go of The Beast's reins and plummeted down the mountain. If Solomon and I had gone any faster, time would have stopped.

The town of Panguitch was nestled in a picturesque green val-ley. Adding to the color were two festivals: a gathering of hot air balloons and a Harley-Davidson rally. Ken guided us to the KOA campground. While we set up tents, Ken scoured the town and, given the hard-partying balloonists, was lucky to find a six-pack. Ha-ha. The balloonists were strictly a two-glasses-of-Zinfandel crowd since they needed to rise before dawn and fire up their balloons for the "Mass Ascension at Dawn." Though it sounded like a title from the *Left Behind* books, the lifting off of over fifty colorful hot air balloons in the dawn sky was striking.

Ken scored a six-pack of "Polygamy Porter." Its slogan: *Why Have Just One?* It's Utah, remember? Alas, Ken had to ascend on a plane to California and invent a better almond harvester. So we were left at the campground, surrounded by the Harley crowd. At about midnight, they yelled at us to stop partying so they could get some sleep.

○━○┊○━○┊○━○┊○━○┊○━○┊○━○┊○━○┊○━○┊○━○┊○━○┊○━○

Though I'm a vegetarian, I have a genetically induced belief that I should teach my sons manly skills such as hunting and fishing. If I were a *real* father, I'd teach them basic construction or plumb-ing, so they could at least build a picnic table or replace a broken toilet. In the old days, fathers taught their sons trades. Of course, technology is infinitely more complex now, and you need a fifty-thousand-dollar computer to tune a car.

Although I haven't taught my boys very many useful skills, back in Davis, I did teach Yonah how to fix a flat. Now his front tire was flat, and it was time for him to demonstrate his expertise. Though he knew what to do, he was tentative with his hands. You can't massage a tire from its rim, you need to yank it off. It's the difference between tapping the bathroom door to see if it's occupied versus breaking it down when your two-year-old is in the bathtub behind a locked door. Yonah is a tapper. Eventually, after realizing that his father wasn't going to help, he got it. I can't say if competency in tire changing lifted his self-esteem, but if his life depended on his fixing a flat, he would live. It was a relatively tough day. Mostly desert, heat, wind, and elevation gain. Late in the afternoon was an ascent. Our destination, Escalante, stood on the other side.

"The summit!" If there are sweeter words after mashing your knees all day, I know them not. And there is no sharper knife to the heart than "Sorry, one more," when you reach the false summit and another, steeper one looms ahead. From our false summit rose a short, but extraordinarily steep mountain with a fire road at the top. While I scanned the mountain to find the regular road that would take us over the mountain's saddle, a car appeared on the fire road. First I thought, what the heck's a car doing on a fire road? Then the ol' heart skipped a beat when it realized the truth: That was no fire road—it was ours.

"No checkmarking way," tumbled out of my suddenly bone-dry mouth. A goat would need ropes to scale this grade.

"Can we do it?" Solomon asked.

For our children we attempt the impossible. "Yeah, we can do it. Slow and steady. Deep breaths. We can make it." The cyclometer dipped below 3 miles per hour and continued falling. At 2.3 miles per hour, the thigh muscles burn unnaturally. And so it went, foot after excruciating foot. At 2.2 miles per hour, you can actually see which spokes are not perfectly straight. At 2.1 miles per hour, you're ready to yank your feet out of the cleats, in case you don't have enough forward momentum to keep the bike upright. If we had breathed any deeper, our lungs would have burst out our toes—but we were *not* going to walk The Beast.

"Don't give up. We can do it."

It didn't seem possible that our legs could keep moving. We weren't inching up the grade, we were centimetering up it. I wasn't sure if my aorta or knees would be the first to blow.

And with a final grunt/grimace/pull/push, we were on top. Did Hillary feel prouder when he summited Everest? Of course. But we felt pretty darn good as we caught our breaths and took in the Powell Promontory. As we stood gazing, a motorcyclist pulled up.

"Which direction did you come from?" he asked.

"Same as you."

"No way." "Incredulous" can't describe the look he gave us. It verged on horror.

"Yep," piped up Solomon. Yonah, too tired to do anything but grin, was proud. This was tougher than anything thrown at him yet. And he had done it. Words were not necessary; his accomplishment said it all. That is pride.

From the summit was an easy descent to the Escalante Reservoir campground. We arrived at 4:45 PM. There was an excellent camping spot near the showers. However, a sign reserved the spot for handicapped patrons until 5:00 PM, after which it was fair game. I knew no one would claim it in the next fifteen minutes, so we set up camp. Solomon didn't talk to me because his outlaw father was again breaking the law. At 5:00 he forgave me because by then we were swimming in the reservoir, and it is impossible to be mad when you're splashing in the water. If there is a heaven, you can take your halos, harps, and wings, and give me a jump into a lake on a hot day after a long ride. I could do that forever.

7

AN ATHEIST
COVERS HIS BASES

AT THE END OF EVERY DAY, I'd say something like, "This was the toughest day yet." The boys knew that after the Baker–Milford fiasco of flats, I was just saying it to say it. But the ride from Escalante to Torrey was the toughest. How tough? It started in the cool dawn air of 5:30 AM and ended in the cool twilight of 8:50 PM. In between the cameo appearances of cool was a heap of hot with a five-thousand-foot climb and another grade where gravity needed defying.

Day Eighteen marked Yonah's first day as mapman. Though initially against it, he came to relish the job because it bestowed power on him. He was good, keeping us informed much better than I had. The day began with a steep downhill to the Escalante River. The river valley is a breathtaking piece of natural art made of enormous, smooth, naked rocks. As we dropped closer to the river, the light gray rocks turned terra-cotta red and were covered with lush green flora.

After crossing the river, there was a 14 percent pitch, which Yonah climbed with nary a bead of sweat. Solomon, too, looked relatively fresh at the top. Djina and me?

"Honey, which pannier has the oxygen?"

"Front left. While you're down there, could you grab me a couple Vicodins?"

Yonah informed us that the dreaded Hogback was just around the bend. Yonah first noticed this particularly nasty bit of pavement while poring over the maps a half-year earlier. Following every challenging moment, he'd remind us, "This was tough, but it's no Hogback." The following description is lifted directly from the ACA map: "The highlight (or terror) on this section is The

Hogback. It is a three-mile stretch of narrow two-lane road along a ridge spine with no shoulders or guardrails and has drops on both sides."

And then we were on it. Yes, it was narrow. Yes, if you ran off the road, you would slide significantly farther than Ricky Henderson stealing a base before a tree trunk or large boulder arrested your fall. But the wide-open vistas from Hogback were exquisite, the road itself was relatively flat, and the wind light. I think I speak for the entire nation of bicyclists when I say we would gladly ride a road flanked by rivers of fifteen-molar hydrochloric acid as long as there were no headwinds.

Into Boulder, Utah (population 180). Not for the first time did a town's size belie its character. The Hills and Hollows Market was more than Gatorade, Doritos, cheap beer, and racks of breakfast pastries with "January 07, 2018" expiration dates. There were homemade breads, granola, and real chocolate chip cookies. The store sold Persian carpets, locally found seashell fossils, and gasoline. We bought a feast and took it outside under the shade structure. We chugged quarts of Berry Rain Gatorade, and thirty seconds later, returned to purchase quarts of Tangerine Rain. Only I returned a third time.

Boulder was at 6,800 feet. The 9,600-foot summit was ten miles away. In other words, it was steep. Thankfully, there was a tailwind. If not, the 3.6 miles per hour average speed would have suffered. No steep climb was ever complete without a couple of chain-wedgies on The Beast. All in all, the climb built character.

One highlight was being passed by a car club of Volkswagen Things. VW built their Edsel in the early 1970s. Following on the wheels of their perennial success, the Beetle, they launched this vehicle that was so indescribable, they called it the Thing. Think proto–sports utility vehicle with a lawn mower–sized engine, surrounded by metal the thickness of a coffee can. That's the Thing. Probably the last twenty that escaped the scrap yard passed us. They sounded like small planes with asthma as they crept by. Truth is, they weren't going significantly faster than we were, and they had the advantage of sag vehicles hauling their gear.

There was an overlook with a stunning vista of a valley filled with huge red rock obelisks and a snaking river. In the foreground, wildflowers swayed in a large meadow. Trees sang in the wind. The world was alive. The entirety of Creation was dancing, and we were fortunate enough to be invited. Taking in the vista, it was easy to understand why the Transcendentalists saw the natural world as the real church/synagogue/mosque. The Hassidic rabbi Shneur Zalman said, "All that we see, the heavens, the Earth, and all that fills it, all these things are the outer garments of God."

I thought of Anne Frank, whose only access to the natural world while hiding from the Nazis was an attic window, and recalled the young girl's words: "The best remedy for those who are afraid, lonely, or unhappy is to go outside, somewhere where they can be quite alone with the heavens, nature, and God. Because only then does one feel that all is as it should be and that God wishes to see people happy, amidst the simple beauty of nature. As long as this exists, and it certainly always will, I know that then there will always be comfort for every sorrow. . . . And I firmly believe that nature brings solace in all troubles."

I paraphrased Anne Frank and asked Yonah, "What do you think?" I knew I had him, for how could he argue against the noble thoughts of this articulate fourteen-year-old girl?

"It's the grass is greener. She was inside a house for over a year. Of course she's going to think nature is great. I'm in nature all day, every day. It doesn't give me comfort. We should get going. It's still almost a thousand feet to the top."

I wanted to argue, but he was right, not about nature or God, but about the climb ahead. We came upon a forest of quaking aspen and participated in the running of the cows. A herd of free-range cattle grazed along the road. Wanting to initiate cross-species communication, we mooed. They raised their heads at our poor accents, and as soon as we passed the first cow, they ran alongside us with reckless abandon until we reached the day's last serious climb. One look and I knew we were cooked.

(Dear reader, I know you are thinking that I say this all the time and somehow we'll summon our strength to get the job done, as always. Perhaps you think I exaggerate in order to build tension. But this time it was real. It was the end of our most difficult day, I had serious lactic acid buildup, and the grade was scary steep.)

Desperation is the mother of invention. While we couldn't get The Beast to the top with both of us on, maybe if . . .

"Solomon, do you want to get off the bike and race me to the top?"

"Sure!" He couldn't jump off fast enough. He beat me convincingly, and we didn't have to push The Beast. Victories for all.

It was early evening and still no Torrey, our destination. Yonah was on top of the map, but the map was mistaken. First, Torrey was farther than advertised; and second, the eleven miles from the summit was supposed to be all downhill, but it wasn't. I had used up all my strength on the summit climb thinking we'd coast the final segment. Each subsequent uphill was a personal affront. The veneer of good, responsible dad peeled off, revealing a cranky kid in the back seat of his parents' car. "When are we going to get there?" I barked at Yonah. Since he had the map, it was *his* fault.

Instead of taking the easy parental action of turning to his son in the back seat and yelling, "Quit yelling or I'm pulling over!" Yonah calmly said, "It's just a little farther. We can do it." Give a kid a little responsibility and he grows up on you.

We pulled into Torrey's campground at 8:50 PM, fifteen hours after shoving off in Escalante. Pulling the panniers off The Beast, my arms couldn't bear the weight, so the bags tumbled to the ground. Every few years, I undertake a particular piece of extreme bicycle masochism. The Davis Double is a one-day, two-hundred-mile ride. It takes twelve to fifteen hours to complete, and for the next few days, I lie around the house mainlining ibuprofen while tending sore knees and muscles. The Davis Double has absolutely nothing on Escalante to Torrey except being easier, having multiple rest stops stocked with food, and much cooler weather.

To replenish calories, we went to a place called "Family Dining." Its name (like "Good Eats," "Mom's," or "Kountry Kitchen") did not inspire high gastronomical hopes, so we weren't particularly disappointed by the fare. That night, Djina made a rule never to enter another restaurant of this ilk. But she was just sore because of the flying cockroach that attacked her as we stepped out of the restaurant into the night air.

THE BAR MITZVAH AND THE BEAST

A good omen at dawn: the campground flags snapped in a stiff west wind. The map indicated a two-thousand-foot descent to look forward to. Yesterday's arduous ride would be evened out today.

Unfortunately, either the gods didn't log onto Djina's blog to learn of our trying day, or we had inadvertently upset them, because by the time we ate, broke camp, and mounted our steeds, the good west wind had pivoted into the Wicked Wind of the East. I was perplexed. "We gave the Family Dining waitress a decent tip, were friendly to the campground owner, and all the campers signed the petition. What did we do wrong?"

"Do you think God changed the wind because he was mad?" Yonah asked.

"Of course not," I laughed. "I was joking."

Yes, I am a rational man and know that God doesn't change weather based on a person's or a nation's merits or faults. I know that the righteous suffer and the wicked thrive. And prayer goes unheeded. Yet I pray to God on a regular basis, for better weather, for better health, for better everything. Even though this kind of prayer is delusional, I still do it. Many of us do. Why? We want to believe that there is something bigger than us who is in charge. We want to believe that there is an omnipotent entity that cares. Yonah, on the other hand, has the guts to say the universe is a purposeless accident.

"Do you think the universe or life has any meaning?" I asked.

"No."

"That's what the existentialists say. Their answer to a meaningless universe is for individuals to create their own meanings. Whether existentialist or true believer, they both have the same goal, to imbue life with meaning. What do you think gives your life meaning?"

Silence. I asked differently. "What is your life about?"

"Finding happiness."

I mulled this over and thought about Rabbi Hillel's famous answer to a heathen who two thousand years ago challenged, "I will convert if you can explain Judaism while standing on one foot." Hillel lifted a foot and replied, "What is hateful to you, do not do to others." The Golden Rule. Perhaps Yonah's answer to the meaning of life implied the Golden Rule's twin, "What brings happiness to you, give to others."

Rather than being the championship team breezing toward Paris on the last day of the Tour de France, we were an exhausted family of four struggling against a wind carrying the combined smelters of US Steel on its back. It was at moments such as this, when the wind was pounding my ears like an incessant bass drum and myriad tiny sweat wasps were stinging my eyes, that I struggled with my inner Zen. The truth is, I know nothing about Zen except for the adage "eat when hungry, sleep when tired." The bicycling equivalent must be "pedal when going." The idea is to focus on the pedaling and let all other thoughts wash over you like water over the proverbial duck's back. But—alas—hopes for a wind change were the only neural pathways firing, and more bitterness piled on with each new gust. Hoping for change that you can't control leads to disappointment. I tried recalling my friend Chris Kelsch's mantra, "It's all good." No problem when you're on a 40-mile-per-hour descent. When it's all good during a 6.7-mile-per-hour descent into a 25-mile-per-hour headwind, then you've found your inner Buddha.

The winds attenuated in Capital Reef National Park, a hundred-mile-long "wrinkle" in the earth's surface that created a narrow canyon with towering cliffs and hoodoos. (*Hoodoos* are the rock spires that are left behind when a cliff erodes.) We stopped at a scenic overlook and stared at a pair of gigantic hoodoos that were taller, asymmetrical versions of the Twin Towers. Their beauty stole my breath. Why does beauty have a hold on us? From an evolutionary standpoint, we choose mates we think are healthy enough to produce offspring. This evolutionary health is defined as beauty. At least that's the theory. But what of a hoodoo, a Mozart concerto, or a solitary red rosebud covered in morning dew? Why do we think these are beautiful?

Once I was teaching Solomon's baseball team the finer points of sliding, and a rainbow appeared. An entire team of eight-year-olds, whose holy trinity was baseball, pizza, and Gameboy, stopped and stared. I couldn't imagine an evolutionary reason for that kind of response. As I gazed at the hoodoos, understanding struck.

"Beauty is ambrosia for the soul," I pontificated to Yonah.

"I agree they're cool to look at, but I don't think they're ambrosia for the soul."

"Do you think there's an evolutionary reason to think hoodoos are cool?"

"Maybe. I don't know. But the reason I doubt they're ambrosia for the soul is because I don't believe in a soul."

"If there's no soul, then what are we? Is a person just the electrons jumping across our brains' neural synapses? Is being alive solely the evolutionary drive to go forth and replicate DNA?"

"I don't see evidence for anything else. Believing in a soul is like believing in the Tooth Fairy."

"That can't be right. I can't prove the soul exists through mathematical proof or empirical experiment, but there are too many stories, coincidences, and déjà vus to dismiss the nonmaterial world out of hand. If we are simply the sum total of neurons firing, how do you account for goose bumps when you hear a beautiful song?"

"I don't get goose bumps."

"You've never read a passage in a book or saw a movie that made you feel something in your body? I've read *To Kill a Mockingbird* with my English classes over twenty times, and I still get choked up when Scout figures out that Boo saved her life."

"Sure, I get feelings, but why say it's the soul?"

"What else can it be?"

"I don't know. I'm only thirteen years old."

We left it at that.

At the overlook stood a couple in their late fifties. He wore a long, gray ponytail atop a heavily tattooed body. Crosses and the visage of Jesus shared his living canvas with an image of his granddaughter. He introduced himself as a prison minister. He had been a motorcycle mechanic and drug addict until one morning he arose and heard Jesus call him to minister to prisoners. He customized his Harley by welding on bullets, handcuffs, and nightsticks. For the next seventeen years, he and his wife visited prisons spreading the gospel. This is religion at its best, when it can save a person and motivate him to bring peace and a feeling of self-worth to others. Soul or no soul, this man was doing holy work.

"What you're doing, riding across the country on bicycles, is noble. I'd like to pray with you, if you don't mind." We held hands in a circle and he offered a prayer, ending with, "Please, Lord, may they cycle no faster than angels fly." Nothing to worry about there unless the angel needed ambrosia-flavored ibuprofen for its arthritic wings.

Back on the road, I asked the resident atheist what he thought of participating in a religious event. I expected cynicism mixed with scorn.

"Actually, it wasn't bad. Maybe we should get more religions to pray for us."

"What?"

"It can't hurt to cover all bases."

Either his spirit was growing, the hot wind had short-circuited his cerebral wiring, or my son was more complicated than I thought.

O━O⫶O━O⫶O━O⫶O━O⫶O━O⫶O━O⫶O━O⫶O━O⫶O━O⫶O━O

Djina bemoaned the fact that we inadvertently passed the "famous" Gifford House in Fruita. In the late 1800s, a group of hearty Mormons settled in that area and grew fruit trees. Djina's interest wasn't in Mormon history. It was in the pies sold by the Gifford House.

"Want to go back?" I asked with a please-say-no voice. Backtracking was almost as dispiriting as wind.

"That's all right," she replied with a why-don't-you-be-a-good-husband-and-just-do-it voice.

"God," Solomon uttered from the back seat, "could you send us some pie? Please."

Everyone laughed and soon a minivan pulled alongside Djina. A guy yelled, "Hey, lady, got any water?"

Ha-ha. A real comedian. Turned out the comedian was an old friend, Jonathan Ferris. He and his wife were traveling through Capital Reef. They knew of a swimming hole nearby, where we luxuriated in cool water filled with millions of fingerlings trying to jump a thirty-foot waterfall.

The Ferrises gave us a cherry-blackberry pie they had purchased at Fruita. I would have exclaimed, "There is a God!" But I was speechless, for to speak would have meant taking a break from devouring the pie, and Yonah's, Djina's, and Solomon's forks were moving faster than the wings of a hummingbird-sized angel.

"My prayer worked," Solomon exclaimed after finishing.

Yonah bristled. "The Ferrises would have been there whether or not you prayed. It didn't mean anything." I don't know whether or not Solomon's impromptu prayer was efficacious; however, I know this: But for the love of friends, it would be a lonelier world.

We still had twenty-five miles to Hanksville. But it took over an hour to get Solomon out of the water. The air temperature was 102 degrees; we weren't trying that hard.

In a dry sauna the temperature is so high, it hurts to take a deep breath. Hanksville was the same. The grocery store provided sanctuary, and we did quart shots of Gatorade (Frost Glacier Freeze). The grocer suggested we call ahead to the next day's stop at the Hite Recreation Area on Lake Powell because its store was sometimes closed. Cell phone reception was bad, but there was no need to worry. A National Recreation Area would at least stock Gatorade and Doritos.

The winds had abated and stars blanketed the sky, making the Hanksville campground a pleasant stay. The campground owner was a man in his seventies with a face not so different from the Utah rock—chiseled, hard, and craggy. He built the campground in the early 1960s and had been living there since. If anyone knew weather, it was this guy.

"Think the wind is over?" I asked.

"She done blown herself out sure. Tomorrow'll be good for y'all."

O═O▪O═O▪O═O▪O═O▪O═O▪O═O▪O═O▪O═O▪O═O▪O═O▪O═O▪O═O

The road to Hite crossed a low summit into Glen Canyon, and then followed thirty twisty, downhill miles to the Colorado River and Hite Ranger Station. At every turn there were beautiful red rocks and hoodoos. We could examine every unique and spectacular rock in great detail because, even though it was downhill, we were riding in our lowest gears; the headwinds funneling up the canyon were Aeolus unleashed.

Eight hours after waving goodbye to the Hanksville weatherman, four haggard bodies rolled into Hite needing quarts of Gatorade and buckets of food. The grocery store's handmade sign read "Open Noon to Two." It was 3:05. Not only was the store closed, but so was the Lake Powell Visitor Center. Picture me screaming "Aarrgghh!!" and pulling out tufts of hair. We were up the Colorado River without a paddle. Thank God there was no need to pull a Donner Party and eat Solomon, for there was a working water pump, and we broke out the emergency stash of ramen.

As official navigator, Yonah pointed out the next day's seventy-two-mile ride to Blanding had no services and a three-thousand-foot climb.

"No way," I said. When I was mapman, I ascertained that Milford was the last no-water day. "Let me see that map."

He handed it over and advised, "We should do the beginning climb tonight after dinner. There won't be any wind or heat. We can ride at night, camp somewhere, and tomorrow have a shorter day."

I was aghast. How could I be so wrong and my son so right? Had the gods played me for a fool and hid this day from my eyes or was it simply early-onset Alzheimer's?

The boys voted Alzheimer's. Djina picked "Other." "I'm sure you rushed through the maps like you do everything. No news here."

We went with Yonah's sage recommendation. The air cooled in the late afternoon, making the thousand-foot ascent tolerable. The sunset and twilight created one Sierra Club calendar page after another. The landscape was soundless as if God had pressed the cosmic mute button. The moon was up and there was absolutely no one on the road, save one king snake. We rode three abreast and stopped atop a bridge to gaze down five hundred feet into a narrow canyon. The solitude, beauty, and quiet mixing together with the notion that we were experiencing this together as a family created a transcendent moment. It was sacred. If the ride were suddenly to end on the bridge, I would have been content.

Somewhere in the distance a large rock exfoliated, and the crash reverberated throughout the land and our bodies. A reminder of the impermanence of that which seemed permanent, like the bridge we were standing on. We didn't sprint off the bridge, but we departed. The ride was so enjoyable that Yonah suggested we cycle through the night and arrive in Blanding by morning. But by 10:30 PM, we were beat and pulled over to a flat spot in thin sagebrush.

As we settled into our sleeping bags, Djina said, "Remember that sappy Eagles' song about sleeping in the desert with a billion stars?"

"The one that goes, 'I want to sleep with you in the desert tonight'?"

"Oh, is that in it too?" Long moment of silence. "Just kidding. There's no one I'd rather sleep in the desert with. Night."

8

DIARY: DAY TWENTY-ONE, HITE TO BLANDING

5:00 AM   Woke up.

5:15 AM   Finished granola and dried fruit. Remaining
           food: two-week-old containers of peanut butter
           and jelly stuffed inside three leaky plastic bags.
           Gross. Half block of semi-solid cheddar cheese
           smothered with oozing cheese oil. Really gross.
           Stale, crumbly stuff in bread bag could be called
           many things. Word "bread" did not come to mind.

5:30 AM   Stuffed sleeping bags, loaded bikes.

5:49 AM   On the road.

5:51 AM   Headwinds. Not small breezes but ha-ha-ha-try-
           to-get-past-me cyclones. Already exhausted.
           Water situation, not yet dire.

5:59 AM   Epiphany that we wouldn't make Blanding by
           bike. Sixty-five miles uphill against wind. No way.

8:15 AM   Maximum morning speed attained: 5.9 miles per
           hour.

8:20 AM   Started to doze. Experienced sudden jerky feeling
           similar to falling asleep at the wheel. Micro-
           adrenalin rushes jarred me awake for thirty
           seconds before returning to doze. Only thing
           preventing me from completely sleep-cycling was
           Solomon chanting, "Jet packs, jet packs," when-
           ever he gave it the gas.

8:30 AM	Whined to Djina about not making it.
8:30:04 AM	"Buck up!" she retorted. "We're going to make it."
8:30:10 AM	Wondered how I married a woman oblivious to reality.
8:31 AM	Looked for trucks to hitchhike on.
8:59 AM	Not a single vehicle passed.
9:00 AM	Honda Civic going the other way honked and waved.
9:01 AM	"Let's take a break. I'm falling asleep."
	"Take a Clif Shot," Djina commanded. "They've got caffeine."
	Muttered "It won't help," but sucked one down.
9:03 AM	Caffeine molecules crawled into brain and slapped pathways awake.
9:15 AM	Hit 10 miles per hour.
10:20 AM	Above huge promontory stood a large rock called Jacob's Chair. Boys and I spoke about Jacob's Ladder, his dream, and other related topics.
11:30 AM	Wind died.
12:30 PM	Thought, with luck and more water, fifty-fifty chance of making it.
12:35 PM	Down to quart of water. Map showed Natural Bridges National Monument five miles away. Probable water at visitor center. Yonah downgraded "probable" to "possible."
1:05 PM	Arrived at Natural Bridges turn off. Car coming from monument confirmed water at visitors' center two miles away. I commandeered Yonah's bike, attached trailer, threw in nine empty water bottles, three one-gallon jugs, and left Djina and boys. All downhill, but not happy. Thirty miles per hour downhill with empty water jugs meant uphill return with over forty pounds of water.

1:14 PM	Two miles were actually four-and-a-half.
1:18 PM	Found water pump outside visitor center.
1:22 PM	Loaded water bottles and jugs.
1:22:05 PM	Decided to hitch to junction.
1:25 PM	Older couple with pickup gave me a lift.
1:30 PM	They dropped me off, conversed with Djina and boys, signed petition, and left us four pints of Gatorade (assorted flavors).
1:31 PM	If not for kindness of strangers . . .
1:33 PM	Four Harleys took turnoff onto Natural Bridges road. One slid on loose gravel and toppled over. Helmet strapped to back of motorcycle. Woman on back scraped up arm. Djina bandaged it.
1:40 PM	Harleys left. Helmet strapped to back of motorcycle.
1:55 PM	Solomon's new ritual question: Friendly or unfriendly honk? Friendly honk is a light tap or two, often accompanied with wave. Every honker from opposite direction was friendly. Vehicles overtaking us divided, one-third to two-thirds, unfriendly to friendly. Friendly: light tap timed so honk occurred immediately after passing to avoid startling us. Two varietals of unfriendly: Number 1: "I'm in a hurry! Get out of my way!" Warning honk begins half-mile away. They don't swerve to hit cyclist as long as cyclist knows his place to right of white line. Number 2: Dickheads. They wait until two yards behind cyclist, then let loose single long honk hoping sound waves will blast cyclist from bike. To avoid misinterpretation of intention, honk accompanied by expletive and/or middle finger. Man in mild coma can differentiate friendly from unfriendly. Yet be it solar-powered Prius flashing peace signs as they tooted or misanthrope aiming heavily-dented

1974 Pontiac Le Mans as if in a demolition derby, Solomon needed honk verification. Rising from the gravel that the Le Mans forced us into, he'd ask, "Friendly or unfriendly?"

"What do you think?"

"Unfriendly?"

"Right. You knew it. You didn't even need to ask."

2:05 PM   Car blasted us with its horn. Teenage passenger screamed profanity.

"Unfriendly?"

I ignored the question."Daddy, unfriendly?"

"You already know."

"But tell me, okay?"

"Unfriendly."

"I was right. Jet packs, jet packs."

2:07 PM   Solomon held court about his top five cartoons.

2:15 PM   Yonah opined that *SpongeBob* was the stupidest cartoon in the history of the world.

2:15:04 PM   Solomon let loose unfriendly scream at Yonah.

2:15:06–

2:17:52 PM   Dueling screams.

2:20 PM   Yonah chanted, "Jet packs, jet packs," after someone farted.

2:21 PM   Boys fought about whether or not Yonah was allowed to say "jet packs."

2:46 PM   Solomon regaled me with tortures from the Middle Ages.

"You never heard of the Spanish Donkey?" he asked in disbelief.

"Do I *want* to know?"

"The person sits on this sharp piece of wood, his

legs on each side like he's riding a donkey. They attach heavy weights to both legs. The weights pull him down, and the wood cuts him in half."

"Did you learn this in school, on the Cartoon Network, or from the CIA?"

"Gruesome, huh?"

3:15 PM	Solomon complained of boredom. I wanted to say, "There's nothing wrong with being bored. It's part of life and the entrance to self-discovery." I bit my tongue because he would hear, "Blah-blah-blah, part of life, blah, blah." We plugged in his iPod.
4:15 PM	Boredom complaints renewed
6:30 PM	Djina, Solomon, and I complained about never getting there. Yonah replied, "Seven more miles. We can do it."
7:25 PM	Arrived at gas station/mini-mart west of Blanding. Gatorade (X-Factor Lemon-Lime + Strawberry) and ice cream.
7:45 PM	Checked into hotel.
8:12 PM	Ate at only pizza joint in North America that didn't sell beer.
9:05 PM	Watched *SpongeBob*, *Court TV*, clips from Tour de France.
10:02 PM	Fell asleep.

SEABISCUIT TAKES CHARGE

9

FRIDAY NIGHT IS THE BEGINNING of Shabbat. At home we make a nice meal; when on the road, we improvise. Candles were tea lights. Wine was fruit juice, and challah, a twisted, glazed donut. During the middle of blessings, an RV pulled into the campground in Monticello, Utah. This particular RV was larger than most in the same way a blue whale is larger than a guppy. Besides its size, the other striking feature was that it idled in front of our table while the driver spent ten minutes in the campground office. The RV was an Alfa brand with a large American flag painted across its side. I am tempted to say that this symbolized the worst of America, a way-bigger-than-needed vehicle spewing an overly large carbon dioxide footprint without regard for the rest of the world's citizens, both human and non-human. But I won't take that cheap shot. Solomon, however, gave it a checkmark.

Every day Djina and I rose earlier than the boys. She did yoga. So did I. She claimed I didn't because yoga involves less farting. Harrumph. Around 6:00 we'd wake the boys. Yonah was always up first unless there was a television. Breakfast was cereal, yogurt, fruit, and milk. Tents were laid on their sides to dry, sleeping bags stuffed, ensolite pads rolled, water bottles filled, teeth brushed, dried tents folded up, and panniers loaded onto bikes. We mounted the bikes and the day officially began with Djina's rendition of "On the Road Again" and Solomon's *"Gracias, Gallina"* shout out. Yonah and I provided harmonizing groans.

A light tailwind pushed us out of Utah. After all those tough days, Utah wanted to make nice. Djina asked if her butt was hard enough to ricochet a pebble. The secret of a happy marriage is to know the right answer to such questions without needing to examine said body part. Into Colorado and our water woes were over. We cycled through miles of cropland where what looked like alfalfa seedlings pushed up through rich, reddish-brown soil.

Rabbits were the primary roadkill in Nevada. In Utah it was deer. Deer continued to be cadavers of record in Colorado. On an average day we'd see at least a dozen dead animals. Be it deer, toad, rabbit, or snake, Solomon developed a ritualized eulogy. The animal deaths took a toll on him, and he needed a sacred space to mourn.

Solomon: "Was that [species of animal] killed by a car?"

Me: "Yes."

Solomon: "That's sad." Eight seconds of respectful silence. This service was as scrupulously followed as a Catholic mass. If instead of "Yes," I replied, "What do you think?" Solomon would begin anew. "Was that [species of animal] killed by a car?"

In addition to the billions of alfalfa seedlings, we saw a number of storage facilities for beans, with their accompanying billboards toting the area as "Pinto Bean Capital of the World." The faded billboards, however, looked as though they were last touched-up prior to World War II and the rusting bean elevators looked as though their happiest days were during the first season of *Happy Days*. We chalked it up to another sign of the demise of America's rural economy. How many broken lives and destroyed families did these abandoned bean elevators represent? Perhaps we could donate something to a rural assistance nonprofit.

At a convenience store where we stopped to buy Cool Blue Gatorade, I commented to the clerk, "Sure are a lot of rundown bean elevators. They still grow beans?"

"Yes, sir. That's all we grow around here. Pinto Bean Capital of the World. They just finished planting. Can't miss the seedlings coming up."

Think of my constant misreading of people and situations as a motif. Am I unique? No. We all do it, all the time. Here my misinterpretations are mildly amusing; unfortunately many of our misinterpretations, both political and personal, occur on issues that matter.

○━○┄○━○┄○━○┄○━○┄○━○┄○━○┄○━○┄○━○┄○━○┄○━○

At Dolores, Colorado, we completed the third map. Thirteen hundred miles, one-third of the way. *Dolores* is Spanish for pain or grief, but who would describe a town nestled in the foothills of the Rocky Mountains that has its own brewery as depressing? We camped at an RV park and spoke with members of that growing subgroup, people who live in their RVs. I know I badmouthed that one RV a few pages back, but here we gained a new perspective. The residents of this RV park were mostly retirees. Like the million or so other Americans living in their RVs, they didn't pay mortgages, rents, or property taxes. They had no worries about heating a three-thousand-square-foot house. And when they tired of where they were, they removed the tire covers, rolled up the Astroturf, and went somewhere new: a subset of the American Dream.

One of the problems of aging is the feeling of isolation. No more interaction with people at work. The kids are gone. Marriages end. Friends die. There is little to do but watch TV and leaf through photo albums of better times. With their built-in communities, RV parks are an antidote. The RVers were kind and watched over each other like members in a nondenominational church. And though the RVs themselves are gas monsters when driven, the RVers total carbon footprint is miniscule compared to the average suburban household.

Onto the brewery! Pizza out of a brick oven, organic salad greens, homemade berry cheesecake, and fresh local beer. We sat on a patio with thirty other patrons and struck up a conversation with the folks at the table next to us. Before you could say, "What do you think about global warming?" petitions flew between tables, and people volunteered to sag our gear up Lizard Head Pass. I was half-expecting to be given the key to the town, but I doubt they locked their doors.

The Dolores River snakes through a lush valley. In Nevada "lush" meant tumbleweeds with soft thorns. Here in the Rockies, it was grass, trees, flowers, streams, the works. Fifteen miles into the day, we came to the provocatively named town of Stoner. Stoner consisted of a hotel and the Stoner Creek Café, where we ate Second Breakfast. "Second Breakfast" was an eating strategy pioneered by Djina. First Breakfast was not a sit-down meal. It was a quick gobble of cereal and yogurt and then onto the road to get miles in while still cool. Second Breakfast took place once the temperature warmed.

The Stoner Café introduced us to the ubiquitous Midwest and Southern delicacy: biscuits. In California cafés, there is choice: bagels, muffins, rolls, or multigrain toast. Starting in the Rockies, it's biscuits to the Atlantic. Our friend Ken, being from Georgia, had earlier prepped Djina, so she ordered a side of biscuits and could hardly contain her anticipation. The biscuits arrived with a small tin cup filled with white stuff that resembled lard congealed with butter and milk. It looked like a viscous fluid that one usually expels from the body rather than ingests. Djina, the most adventurous gastronome in the family, was not quite sure what to make of it. "Excuse me," she flagged down the waitress. "What is this?"

The waitress looked to see if she was serious. Then in an exasperated tone, "It's gravy. If you don't like it, I'll take it away."

What Djina failed to realize was that biscuits always arrive with gravy. One would more likely drive a car without engine oil than eat a biscuit without gravy. The biscuits were good, but a lick of gravy was all any of us felt comfortable stomaching. Ken later explained, "There are essentially two types of gravy. Morning gravy is a white, pseudo-plastic, non-Newtonian emulsion, not unlike 90-weight gear oil. Lunch and dinner gravy is brown and flammable, more like 10W30 engine oil. Both will get you a bypass soon enough."

We continued to the town of Rico, where there was a rumor of natural hot tubs. Djina enjoys soaking with the enthusiasm of a fraternity boy at an open keg. The fact that we had missed the Austin, Nevada, tubs intensified her desire to soak. Built on the edge of the Dolores River, in one more Sierra Club calendar setting, was the beautifully painted, yellow-orange tub.

I would like to say that we stripped off our sweaty clothing and jumped in. But that is not what happened. The ambient temperature was 98 degrees; the hot tub was 108 degrees. Why would we jump into this scalding water? I can think of only one reason. To escape the battalion of biting flies who were hungry for their daily blood meal. I got into the tub and for about thirty seconds, sat there with visions of Edgar Allan Poe's "The Pit and the Pendulum" running through my brain. I could either stay in and become fondue or perch on the side and die through massive blood loss. Djina put in her hand. That was enough. It was too hot even for the lover of soaking. Yonah never took off his bike gear. He hates all hot tubs. Solomon happily played with the frogs in a nearby cool pond that the flies hated. Had the tub been in Dolores, they would have had a faucet of cold water to regulate the temperature along with mosquito netting and bar service.

We camped at the 9,500-foot Barlow Creek Campground, so the next day's climb over Lizard Head Pass wouldn't be overly tough. The campground was in the midst of an alpine paradise. Ragged peaks stood as sentinels above the river canyon. A rainbow of wildflowers colored the meadow. Songbirds symphonized. The temperature cooled to 70 degrees.

Guess what the boys were doing? Huddled inside their tent around the two-square-inch screen of Solomon's iPod, they were playing a micro-video game called "Brick." Parents reading this are nodding: "Yep. Exactly what my kids do. Kids today live in a virtual world. Got no appreciation for nature." Kids reading this are shaking their heads: "Poor kids. Stranded in a dirty tent with only 'Brick.' I'm going to get their email and upload them a real game."

Eventually, hunger forced the boys from their nylon sanctuary. During dinner, a red, wren-type bird visited. Sure he wanted grub, but it seemed more like he wanted to hang out with us. He alighted not only on Yonah's hand but on Djina's back when she bent over. He politely stood on the table as we ate.

"Clearly, this bird has been fed by too many humans," Djina said.

"What if it's only like this with us?" I ventured. "What if it's really Old Gramps?"

Old Gramps was Djina's deceased father, who had always accompanied us on vacations. We all laughed, but Djina said, "I've never seen a bird act like this. And Old Gramps loved red. If he were alive, he would have bought a train ticket and met us at every stop along the way. Maybe it really is Old Gramps."

A minute later the bird landed on Djina's arm; she looked it in the eye and asked, "Are you my dad?" The bird cocked his head at Djina and flew into a nearby tree.

Postscript: After Djina posted this story on the blog, our friend Laura wrote: "My mom loved cardinals, and the morning after she died, the first thing I saw upon waking was a cardinal right outside my window, which immediately flew off after I said, 'Hi, Mom.'" Now that I've heard a number of anecdotes about strange coincidences following the deaths of loved ones, I no longer dismiss these after-death occurrences out of hand. I told Yonah about a few of these strange instances. "So what do you think? Is it possible that there is something to these after-death experiences?"

"I guess it's possible, but it seems more like Occam's Razor, where 99 percent of the time the right answer is the one that's most plausible. I'd say that it's way more plausible that these things are coincidences instead of after-death experiences. Weird things happen all the time. I mean, do you *really* think Old Gramps came back as a bird and landed on Mom's butt?"

○■○¡○■○¡○■○¡○■○¡○■○¡○■○¡○■○¡○■○¡○■○¡○■○

The 13,156-foot Lizard Head Peak is a protuberance rising 450 vertical feet above a ridge in Colorado's San Juan Mountains. In 1932, the United States Forest Service proclaimed the sheer rock "unclimbable." In 1920, Albert Ellingwood and Barton Hoag took pictures of themselves on the summit. Do the math.

Though we were simply attempting the 10,220-foot Lizard Head Pass, we approached the climb with apprehension. The air might be too thin, the grade too steep, an angry yeti might lie in wait around a turn. Alas, our worries were unfounded. The air was fresh and invigorating, the grade only 6 percent, and not only were there no yetis, but the traffic wasn't bad. None of the roads in the Rockies would be much over 6 percent because the roads were originally railroad tracks. For a cyclist, a 6 percent grade is relatively easy. An 8 percent grade is hard, but doable. Gritting one's teeth is necessary for a 10 percent, and a 14 percent grade can be conquered only if it is short and accompanied by a checkmark or two.

Yonah, now referred to as Seabiscuit, waited at the top for a good five minutes while the rest of us huffed and puffed up. He said, "That was sort of anticlimactic." The Biscuit needed a handicap; I put the peanut butter in his panniers.

The engineering of these roads was impressive. In order to keep the grades acceptable, the builders constructed bridges over impossibly deep ravines and backed the tracks over miles and miles of rough mountains. And this was done with the nineteenth-century technology of steam-powered equipment, dynamite, and elbow grease. No matter how tough we thought ourselves, cycling cross-country, those guys were a quantum leap tougher. While not belittling our trek, we had many amenities to ease it: at least one decent meal a day, ibuprofen and Gatorade, showers every few days. The two amenities those guys had were alcohol and the Telluride bordellos, though there was a good chance that the latter amenity might leave one with a liability.

From Lizard Head Pass it was downhill to Telluride, a beautiful resort town nestled in a bowl at the end of a deep canyon. Telluride is home to music festivals, multimillion-dollar vacation getaways, upscale restaurants, and excellent skiing. One hundred years ago, it was not supported by jet-setters but by twenty-six saloons and twelve bordellos. It garnered a bit of notoriety as a town where Butch Cassidy made a large, unauthorized bank withdrawal. We rode into town casing the place for food rather than easy money. We settled on a Mexican restaurant.

It would be hyperbolic to say the service moved with geologic speed, but Djina did have time to order food, walk down the street to a bike shop, buy and install new cleats on her bike shoes, deliver a baby, write a dissertation, and return before our food arrived. Not only was the service slow, but there were no chips. This was a clear violation of the international ordinance requiring Mexican restaurants to provide an endless chip bowl. A Mexican restaurant without chips is akin to a sushi bar sans rice or an Italian bistro running out of tomato sauce. And to pour salsa into our wounds, the table next to us had chips.

"I'm sorry, but that was the last basket. The woman who makes them is not here yet."

Chipotles, our local burrito bar franchise, can whip out four burritos in less than one minute, thirty seconds. Here in Telluride, they assembled their $10.99 burritos one black bean at a time. Thirty minutes passed and there were no burritos to go with the no chips. I was tempted to take the half-eaten basket at the vacated table next to us, but Solomon would have called 9-1-1 on me. My bloodstream experienced a surge in the surliness hormone. All that Zen crap and being in the moment flew right over those fourteen-thousand-foot peaks because I was hungry. Luckily, I was able to channel my inner gurus, the Marx Brothers, and we made the obvious jokes of how they were planting the corn for the chips and milking the cows for the cheese.

And then, suddenly, inspiration poured down like manna from the heavens, and the three of us came up with an advertising idea to compete with the wildly successful Got Milk? campaign of painting milk moustaches on famous celebrities. It was Solomon who set the course with his *"Gracias, Gallina!"* morning salutation. In addition to his morning chant, he often saluted his food, be it French fries, cereal, or milkshake, and announce, *"Gracias, Gallina!"* Woe to he who mocked, giggled, or pointed out that there was nary a chicken element in a milkshake, for the salute would begin anew, with more vigor. If it was hamburger, however, he altered the blessing to, *"Gracias, Carne!"*

While we joked about how the cooks were drilling for natural gas to fuel their oven, the *"Gracias, Carne!"* campaign was hatched. A thirteen-year-old cyclist crosses the finish line at the top of a mountain pass, lifts his trophy, and announces, *"Gracias, Carne!"* Election night. The winning candidate faces a wildly enthusiastic crowd, pumps his arms, and hollers, *"Gracias, Carne!"* A high school senior gets her report card. Straight As. She tilts her head and coyly whispers straight into the camera, *"Gracias, Carne."*

Sure, everybody needs milk. But if you want to win, to succeed, to be champion, ya gotta eat meat. It was a beautiful concept. We were poised to call Madison Avenue when Yonah pointed out that he and I were vegetarians. "And," he added, "beef production is carbon dioxide heavy, and that's without adding cow fart methane." We considered shunting our moral quandaries aside with carbon offsets. We toyed with *"Gracias, Tofu!"* as a compromise slogan, but in the end tabled it, for the burritos arrived, and, face it, *"Gracias, Tofu!"* would never work.

Later, when the waiter came with our bill in his left hand, he held a basket of chips in his right, destined for another table. His tip was the size of our chip basket.

After lunch, the boys and I had ice cream while Djina found the library and blogged. We met up with her there. The spa at a high-end Manhattan hotel had nothing on the restrooms at the Telluride Public Library. Thanks to the good tax base, this was the handsomest and most well-appointed library I had ever walked into. Too bad I had to hurry Djina out.

"But you can blog too," she said, fingers flying across the keyboard, "and so can the boys. We can all blog."

"We've got forty miles and a two-thousand-foot climb ahead."

That in a nutshell is the conflict of our marriage. She doesn't like to be hurried. I don't like to wait. Neither of us was overly happy as we rode out of Telluride. Within two hundred yards of leaving town, there was a thirty-minute road construction hold up. I did not look at her during the wait, but her telepathy was clear: "For *this* you made me stop blogging. Jerk."

Colorado's roads were under constant repair, so Yonah dubbed it "The Construction State." Djina gave it a different nickname—"The Land of Shitty Drivers." True, Solomon counted significantly more unfriendly honks, and we were forced onto a few road shoulders, but I argued that this was simply a product of raw numbers and not the innate nature of Coloradoans. More drivers equal more jerks. Unlike the vast majority of Nevada and Utah, Colorado is actually occupied with people, and hence, more bad drivers. Djina didn't buy it, and held to a "something's rotten in Colorado" theory.

After a gentle two-thousand-foot climb accompanied by exhaust gases and drivers who were grouchy due to the delay, it was ten miles of downhill averaging 35 miles per hour. All good things come to an end, and the thrilling descent was dampened when a sheriff pulled us over, saying we were driving on the wrong side of the white line that separated the shoulder from the road. Though bicycles have the same rights as motorized vehicles and are allowed in the roadway, and given the fact that the shoulder was filled with loose gravel and sharp pieces of metal sloughed off assorted cars and trucks, I thanked him for concerning himself with our safety. But as he drove off, Djina's "something's rotten" theory sounded less ridiculous.

We arrived in Ridgeway at 8:00 PM. There was no official camping in town, and we were too tired to pitch tents in the park; it was a hotel night. But of the two hotels, the first was full and the second had only the Presidential Suite at $260 per night. Solomon, anticipating a multiplex-sized plasma screen, was upset when we declined the room. It was 10:00. We were exhausted, hungry, and cranky, though not in that order. It wasn't a life-threatening situation, but we were stuck and needed either a stroke of luck or a small act of God. And we got one. A desk clerk told us about a real campground at the reservoir three short miles away along a bonafide bicycle path.

With Venus and a million stars above, we strapped on lights and sailed along the bike path that paralleled the Uncompahgre River. Except for Solomon's bellyaching about the Presidential Suite, it was another perfect moment of night riding. I, for one, don't gaze at stars nearly enough. Besides their beauty, stars are the passageway into the fourth dimension. The Big Dipper might appear to be seven stars in a two-dimensional plane. But they are not. The closest star is seventy light-years from Earth and the farthest over two hundred. Since the lights in the night sky are all different ages, gazing at them allows us a glimpse back into time, the fourth dimension. I like that. Looking into the night sky also creates a feeling of humility and smallness. In the face of millions or billions of galaxies, each with billions or trillions of stars, one cannot help but feel like a tiny grain on a Mount Everest of sand. I don't like that.

The reservoir was dark and large. We couldn't locate the camping sites, only day-use spots. At the fifth one, I decided,

"This is good enough." Solomon, still traumatized from our earlier run-in with the sheriff and light-years beyond tired and hunger, started bawling.

"Solly," I reasoned, "we don't have a choice, and it's not *really* illegal because the regular campground is closed. We are allowed to camp here. It's called the necessity defense."

"I've heard of that," said Yonah.

"Yeah, it's totally legal. We'll eat, go to bed, and before the sun is up, we'll be out of here. No one will know."

Solomon insisted on returning to the Presidential Suite. He was inconsolable. We made a quick dinner, which he ate between sobs, and then we sent him into his tent. I climbed into my sleeping bag and read by flashlight.

"You should turn off your light," Djina warned.

"Are you kidding," I chuckled. "There isn't anyone around for miles." And it was true. We were fronted by a large lake on one side, and all around us there wasn't a single light or auto until three miles back in Ridgeway. It was silent and peaceful.

Fifteen minutes later, the sheriff arrived. "Shit, we're busted," was not my initial thought; rather, "Solomon will never forgive me until well into his next life." Poor Solomon. Petrified in his tent, his absolute worst nightmare had come to fruition. An innocent boy caught in the snares of a criminal family. I explained the situation to the sheriff, and he let us camp.

"*Gracias, Policía!*"

○━○▪○━○▪○━○▪○━○▪○━○▪○━○▪○━○▪○━○▪○━○▪○━○

The plan was to skedaddle out early. Instead of crawling out of his sleeping bag following the fourth wake-up call, Solomon was up and dressed before I opened my eyes. He would never again see the business end of the law.

During the twenty-five-mile jaunt to Montrose and breakfast, Djina stopped at a store advertising, "World's Best Jerky." After a month of grilled cheese, buffalo jerky looked particularly tasty, but pride in my moral superiority held me back until later that day when Djina was out of sight and I snuck a piece.

In Montrose we ate Second Breakfast at a cute café. When finished, we asked the waitress for a baggie of sugar. A few days prior, we had ran out of brown sugar. We had avoided buying more because we didn't need much, and I didn't want to haul a pound of sugar up the monster Monarch Pass we would be climbing later in the week. A small baggie would tide us over. But rather than spooning a few tablespoons in a sandwich-sized baggie, the waitress brought a filled-to-the-seal liter baggie, easily two pounds of sweetener.

"Tell her we don't want that much," I said.

"It'll embarrass her."

"You're kidding, right?"

"We'll use it."

It wasn't an argument worth pursuing, so I wedged the baggie in a pannier. We climbed on The Beast only to realize that it was sick. Its middle chain ring was way out of alignment, and I had no idea how to fix it. We consulted the ACA map for bike shops. Along a ninety-five-mile stretch of road, there were only three. One was twenty-five miles back in Ridgeway. Even if we wanted to backtrack, we couldn't. Solomon was convinced "wanted" posters were plastered in the post office, and the four desperadoes were featured on the evening news. Seventy miles ahead was a shop in Gunnison. The third was . . .

"Hey, I think I see it," Yonah said.

Sure enough, like the grandfather who lives long enough to see his granddaughter's wedding, The Beast had miraculously kept itself together until six buildings from Cascade Bicycles. Coincidence or the hand of Providence?

"And this time I'm not making it up!" I crowed as we walked the bikes toward the shop.

"It's a coincidence," said Yonah. "Did The Beast get flats next to a bike shop or in the middle of the desert? Where did the chain break?"

"Those were character builders!"

"Dad, you can't have it both ways. It's not logical."

"Logic isn't everything," I muttered feebly as I grappled with the possibility that my teenager might have more insight into the world than I had. I was happy to walk into Cascade Bicycles and end the discussion.

The fix was easy. It wasn't the bicycle equivalent of a heart transplant, only a tooth pull, an outpatient procedure. The Beast had broken one of the bolts that held the chain rings together. The proprietor extracted it and inserted a new one for free. Less than thirty minutes from walking out of the café, we were on the road again. Though I was finished with the earlier conversation about The Beast's breakdown, Yonah wanted the last word.

"Saying those flats in the desert were character builders but a breakdown in front of a bicycle store is Providence isn't consistent. It would be like saying gravity works most of the time. If we always broke down in front of a bike shop, then maybe you could say it was God. But we don't, so it has to be coincidence."

"I was only joking about Providence."

"Whatever," he said, and accelerated to leave me behind.

<hr/>

Cimarron was a gas station/market/campground. However, instead of a mini-mart dominated by efficient rows of Hostess products, items looked as if they had been organized by a toddler who had just polished off a pint of Ben & Jerry's. Yonah, Djina, and I started with Gatorade (two Lemon-Limes, one Tangerine), but Solomon continued with his new passion: Sprite. For a solid week, Solomon had regaled us with stories of the wonders of Sprite. He sang an ode to Sprite that went, "Sprite, Sprite, Sprite, Sprite, Sprite, Sprite, Sprite, Sprite, wonderful Sprite, glorious Sprite," repeated to infinity and beyond. If Solomon were a drink, he would be Sprite. He insisted we call him that.

For dinner we walked down to the river, sat at a table, made pasta and salad, and topped it off with a couple slices of Cimarron apple pie. The meal was a perfect ending to the day. It was 6:30 and Cimarron's mayor/pie maker/gas station attendant had informed us that the next campsite was seventeen miles away and had no services. I was tired and wanted to spend the night in Cimarron. But Yonah laid out the options. We could camp in Cimarron and take hot showers, but the next day would be seventy-seven miles, beginning with a fifteen-hundred-foot climb. Or we could continue seventeen miles to the Blue Mesa Reservoir and shorten the next day to sixty miles.

The vote was three to one, and I grew sentimental for the time when children were seen and not heard, and the husband's word was law. At 6:37 PM I reluctantly bid goodbye to the mayor, who, with a headshake, stood with me in solidarity.

The twilight ride was littered with the highest concentration of deer carcasses to date. If Sprite didn't see the deer, he'd smell it—strong and tangy but not repulsive. For each and every dead deer (or skunk, snake, rabbit, or toad), it was the same drill: "Daddy, was that deer killed by a car?" "Yes." "That's sad." Respectful eight seconds of silence.

We saved one life. It was dark and our lights were on. In the middle of the road stood a deer, looking exactly like a deer paralyzed by headlights.

"Get off the road!" we shrieked. He nonchalantly chewed, then moseyed off. Given this one's reaction time, it was surprising there wasn't more road venison.

○━○┄○━○┄○━○┄○━○┄○━○┄○━○┄○━○┄○━○┄○━○┄○━○┄○━○

In the town of Gunnison, we bought cycling gloves at Tomichi Cycle. Like the guys at all the bike shops, they were great and gave us complimentary bike inspections. Lo and behold, Yonah's rear tire had worn through the rubber. A micron of nylon now separated the fragile inner tube from the pavement. Hadn't we just replaced it two weeks back? We were going through rubber faster than a prostitute. The guys put on a new tire and threw in a free spare.

The terrain to Sargents was relatively flat, but in places the wind was wicked. At one point, a stretch of road was cut through a hill, creating fifty-foot walls on either side. The walls funneled headwinds strong enough to pick up road grit and sandblast us. I couldn't see a thing.

Apparently, Djina, who was two feet away on my side, screamed, "Let's go back to Gunnison and do this later!" I never heard her. Actually, the sandblasting was kind of a relief from the heat. (Unfortunately it didn't clean our clothes.)

Sargents is located at the foot of Monarch Pass. At 11,312 feet, it would be the highest point on the route. By the time we sat down in Sargents's restaurant, the grill and oven were closed. The fryer, however, was still on, so dinner consisted of fried fish, fried mushrooms, fried mozzarella cheese, fried chicken, and a Rocky Mountain–sized platter of French fries. Thirty minutes later we had Rocky Mountain–sized tummy aches.

SLAUGHTERING
SACRED COWS

10

DAY TWENTY-EIGHT. Monarch Pass. The Continental Divide. Once over, we'd join the water flowing east downhill all the way to the steps of Congress. To summit the pass, a ten-mile, three-thousand-foot climb of 7 percent grade needed to be spanked. As usual, it took a mighty heave to break Earth's gravitational pull on The Beast. Solomon, aka Sprite, saddled up on the back, ready with chants, songs, and observations to motivate us. Less than 150 yards from the initial pedal, on flat ground, my right knee hissed, "One more push and I buckle faster than a San Francisco brick building during an earthquake. And then there's the pain, Matt. Don't forget the pain."

"Checkmark! Checkmark! Checkmark!"

I yelled to Djina, "How many ibuprofens can you take without liver damage?" I swallowed seven but also needed to shed ballast. Solomon proved too bulky to strap onto the trailer, so Djina took the baggie of sugar.

Magical describes "Vitamin I." Within five minutes, my knee wanted to dance up the mountain, albeit a long, slow dance, since ten miles at 4 miles per hour equaled two-and-a-half hours to the Divide. On the other hand, Yonah, aka Seabiscuit, was a cheetah pursuing an antelope. By the time Sprite and I were two miles into the climb, The Biscuit had summited and was nearing the Kansas border. Up and up we pushed. Four miles, six miles, eight miles. (For Yonah read: Missouri, Kentucky, Virginia.) And then, just as

Yonah was delivering the petitions to a joint session of Congress, Sprite and I reached the top of Monarch Pass seconds in front of Djina. We posed in front of the Monarch Pass, Continental Divide sign. I tried convincing Solomon to straddle the Divide and let loose a stream of pee in both directions. "C'mon! Half of it will go to the Atlantic, half to the Pacific. Won't that be cool?" He pretended we were not related.

A ten-thousand-square-foot gift shop/snack emporium stood in the middle of a humongous parking lot. We leaned our bikes against the building and strutted to the front door. I hoped we had enough petitions for the ensuing mobs dying to greet the heroic family who had just conquered the indomitable Monarch Pass. One was more than enough. No one gave us a second glance. They could have cared less about us. It was all about them.

"You better get a postcard for your mother."

"Can I have an ice cream?"

"Only after you finish your corn dog."

Fortunately, the indignity was short-lived due to a hailstorm. This wasn't the "Look, honey, I think that's hail" brand of hail. This was the stuff that Yahweh sent to kill Pharaoh's cattle. While we hoped the hail would dent a Hummer hood, up came a cyclist from the other side. He saw my duct tape pencil sticking from a pannier and said, "I had a tire blow out 150 miles from a bike shop. I patched it with duct tape and it held."

"Duct tape can fix anything," I concurred.

When the hail slowed, we started the long-anticipated forty-mile downhill. We were cautious the first mile because of the wet road. But then, suddenly, the hail disappeared, and it was dry pavement. For the next thirty-nine miles, we outraced the storm, thanks to a generous tailwind blowing through the narrow Arkansas River Canyon. Any stronger wind and I would have unzipped my jersey to use as a spinnaker.

We wound up in the village of Howard and rented a cabin. Over dinner, Solomon announced he would climb Mount Everest for his rite of passage trip. We wished him luck.

Bighorn sheep lived along the Arkansas River, so Solomon and I rode slowly, searching the canyon walls. It's a different experience to ride without incessantly checking your speed. Every spiritual awakening book and every religion contain the same lesson about slowing down, so I'll spare you the multiple benefits of an unhurried life. I will say this: In 1953, Ray Bradbury published *Fahrenheit 451*. In it a character comments that people go so rapidly through life that they never notice anything. Two generations before the internet, cell phones, and airport hubs, someone noted that civilization moves too damn fast. While most adults and many of my students agree with Bradbury, our individual and collective lead feet push ever harder on the accelerator. Yonah, as per usual, disagreed with the diagnosis.

"You want to live in the time before electricity?"

"That's not what I'm saying."

"I bet you wouldn't give up your computer."

"That's not my point."

"You don't like going fast, but you like the things that let you go fast."

"I like my computer, and I think we should slow down."

"I doubt you can do both."

"Why not? I've got a cyclometer and I rode slowly. It's free will."

In truth, bicycling had slowed us all down, even Yonah. And while not at the bodhisattva level, we were sort of living in the moment. Yet Yonah had a point. If we want to live in the moment, live a life in sync with the pace of life we were evolved to live, we may need to reconsider the conveniences and lifestyles that prevent such living. It would be a twofer because the world's carbon footprint would shrink if our species chose to slow down.

Who am I kidding? Not only am I never going to give up my computer, but I'm going to drive when I need—nay—when I want to. So will everyone else. We've opened a Pandora's Box of ever-faster, time-saving technologies, and the most likely scenario is that we are not going to slow down but will continue to speed up until we crash. Only hope remains to prevent me from sinking into utter despondency over the present trajectory of the world's environmental condition. Hope that global climate change will be recognized as *the* issue facing our species. Hope that everyone will recognize that his or her actions matter. Hope that governments and business leaders will look beyond the next election cycle or quarterly economic reports in order to arrest carbon dioxide emissions.

These hopes encapsulate the energy transformation that we need to undergo. Yonah would never have set out on his rite of passage had Djina and I not insisted. Unfortunately, there is no power to insist that humanity embark on an energy rite of passage. The movement to a sustainable energy future will depend on the evolution of our free will.

We stopped at a grocery store in the town of Cotopaxi for Second Breakfast. "Sorry, Solly, nine-thirty in the morning is too early for a Sprite."

A weathered-looking, sixtyish man with leather chaps, leather vest, and bandana leaned against his Harley smoking a cigarette while we sat on the porch chugging strawberry yogurts. He was a Vietnam vet from Cotopaxi and a novelty, for he wore a motorcycle helmet. "Never wore one. But I busted my leg in an accident. Figured it was dumb luck I didn't crack my head open. After I got out of the cast, I got me one. I didn't like it much. Couldn't feel the wind as good. Got hot. My buddies laughed. That stopped after one of 'em cracked *his* head open. Now he's in a wheelchair. My accident was the best thing ever happen' to me. Made me grow up. You understand?"

I understood. What the country needs is a broken leg that could be pinned to global climate change. Unfortunately, Hurricane Katrina is barely viewed as a sprained finger, the Midwest floods and tornadoes of 2011 don't even register as earaches. We need to stop misinterpreting these climatic aberrations. Since that doesn't look like it's going to happen, we need something bigger—say, Ecological Armageddon Lite—to rouse us.

The ACA map flummoxed us a bit, but our new friend showed us the route, south along a wide, green plain. Ten miles west stood the eastern edge of the snow-capped Rockies. The town of Hillside was populated by a single building that served as market/post office/library. Sprite got his Sprite and the rest of us, Lemon-Lime Gatorade quarts. At this point, being in a library

THE BAR MITZVAH AND THE BEAST

and all, it might be of interest to learn the history of Gatorade straight from their website.

In early summer of 1965, a University of Florida assistant coach sat down with a team of university physicians and asked them to determine why so many of his players were affected by heat and heat-related illnesses. The researchers soon discovered two key factors that were causing the Gator players to 'wilt': the fluids and electrolytes the players lost through sweat were not being replaced, and the large amounts of carbohydrates the players' bodies used for energy were not being replenished.

The researchers then took their findings into the lab, and scientifically formulated a new, precisely balanced carbohydrate-electrolyte beverage that would adequately replace the key components lost by Gator players through sweating and exercise. They called their concoction 'Gatorade'. Soon after the researchers introduced their Gatorade formula to the team, the Gators began winning . . . outlasting a number of heavily favored opponents in the withering heat and finishing the season at 7–4.

The team's success progressed even more during the 1966 season, with the Gators finishing at 9–2 and winning the Orange Bowl for the first time ever in the history of the school. Word about Gatorade began to spread outside the state of Florida, and both the University of Richmond and Miami of Ohio began ordering batches of Gatorade for their football teams.

The rest is—as they say—marketing.

While we thumbed through the library books, the egg lady entered with eight dozen eggs. She asked, "What brings you out this way?"

"We're riding cross-country to deliver a petition on global warming to Congress."

"Good for you. I heard Al Gore speak on TV last night. Makes a lot of sense."

Everyone in the small crowd nodded and signed. It wasn't too long ago that global warming was discussed only by the quixotic Green Party and the effeminate Europeans. Now it was on the minds of Mr. and Mrs. Middle America. Hope sprang forth from Hillside. We took our drinks to the lawn outside and sat in the shade of a large tree to eat PB&J sandwiches. The birds were chirping, the boys were smiling, another perfect moment. Djina announced: "There's an Arabic saying, *mara assal o mara bassal*, that means 'sometimes honey, sometimes onions.' These last few days have been honey, honey, honey."

We met a cyclist in Westcliff, our day's destination. He claimed to have reached 56 miles per hour on his bike. This meant Sprite and I were no longer the dragsters we thought we were. Luckily, I had a handy rationalization. It would have been an irresponsible father to go faster than 45 with his son. Now if it were just me . . .

A campground was two miles off-route, but the extra two miles didn't matter. The next day was an easy sixty-mile jaunt with a four-thousand-foot drop, and I was planning on doing the descents particularly fast. The campground faced the Rockies. The sunset was a mandarin-orange sun topped by pink cotton-candy clouds. Whether you're a Republican or Democrat, an evangelical or atheist, we can all agree that we live on one spectacular planet. Here's a thought exercise: Imagine Earth to be two feet in diameter, and you are standing next to it watching it revolve and do all its earthly things: rivers, storms, animals, plants, volcanoes, the works. Wouldn't this globe be miraculous? Wouldn't you treat it with the same care you'd hold a newborn? (In my case, perhaps with more.) But because we live on Earth, we don't see the miracle. This is the lesson of the sunset. It allows one to momentarily see the magic and reaffirm the desire to care for Earth. Do you need a Rocky Mountain sunset to feel it? No, but it helps.

A local couple sent us to a rarely traveled shortcut. There wasn't a single car on it, so we rode three abreast while Solomon and Yonah sang the UC Berkeley drinking song in alternating lines:

Oh, they had a little party down in Newport;
There was Harry, there was Mary, there was Grace.
Oh, they had a little party down in Newport,
And they had to carry Harry from the place . . .

And when the game is over, we will buy a keg or two,
And drink to California till we wobble in our shoes.
So drink, tra la la,
Drink, tra la la,
Drink, drank, drunk last night,
Drunk the night before;
Gonna get drunk tonight like I never got drunk before . . .

It is a sad statement that the only knowledge I've retained during four years at the flagship school of the prestigious University of California system is a single ditty.

After ten miles, the pavement ended and the shortcut continued as dirt and gravel. "This shortcut seems to be taking a long time," said Djina after five miles of bouncing along. "I don't think it's any shorter."

"You're confused by the gravel because it takes longer," I said. "It's definitely shorter." We passed a "Covenant Community" sign. It wasn't clear what that meant until Benediction Street and Good Hope Lane appeared. Everyone was friendly and waved. Clearly, they were unaware that an atheist had breached the community's walls. Solomon made friends with a dog who jogged with us for a few miles. The paved main route finally appeared, and Yonah calculated the shortcut saved us minus 2.3 miles. "I told you," Djina crowed. I pretended to be engrossed in the map and did not respond.

Despite the four-thousand-foot descent, a slight headwind held us to 40 miles per hour. (Rats!) During the final two-thousand feet, humidity joined the ride, and the Great Plains replaced the Rockies. At Pueblo, map four and the entire Western Express route were finished. Since San Francisco, we had logged 1,589 miles over thirty-one days. Finding a hotel proved challenging, for Pueblo seemed to be a dead and dirty Rust Belt city, only much hotter. We checked into the least dingy hotel and found a Japanese restaurant. I was wary of eating sushi prepared by non-Japanese chefs at a restaurant 1,600 miles from the nearest ocean. Happily, no one took ill.

Onto the Great Plains, that large swath of grasslands bordered by the Rockies on one side and the Mississippi Valley on the other. Though grass does not inspire awe the way Utah's red rocks or Colorado's Rockies do, it is far more crucial to civilization. It was the domestication of two grasses in Mesopotamia, wheat and barley, that created the free time necessary to build culture. Unlike Mesopotamia, Great Plains grasses were not domesticated, but they fed the buffalo, which in turn fueled nomadic Indian nations. It is no secret that the plan of the United States during the nineteenth century was to destroy the Indian nations in order to take their land. Though the US Army led an ongoing war against these nations, it was the wholesale slaughter of the buffalo that ultimately defeated them. General Philip Sheridan, the man appointed to "pacify" Plains Indians, said of bison hunters, "[They] . . . will do more in the next year to settle the vexed Indian question than the entire regular army has done in the last thirty years. They are destroying the Indian's commissary." By 1880, the buffalo and the Indians were gone, replaced by cattle and corn.

Though our nation spends trillions of dollars on defense against terrorism, our destruction will more likely come by spending so little on combating global climate change, for climate change may destroy our commissary.

We flew across the plains at 14 miles per hour. A poky pace for an unburdened bicyclist, but for us, it was warp factor two. A tailwind pushed us along our new route, the TransAmerica Bicycle Trail. At Pueblo, we linked into this granddaddy of cross-country routes established by intrepid cyclists who wanted to celebrate America's bicentennial in 1976 with a bikecentennial. The prevailing winds in the Great Plains are generally west or southwest. If this day was a portent for the rest of the trip, we would be happy cyclists.

After five weeks of cycling, we were fit. To an upcoming day of seventy miles, the boys would sing out, "Bring it on!" My legs were beginning to resemble those of a frog's. I truthfully could ricochet a pebble off Djina's butt. Our days followed a familiar rhythm, beginning with the breaking of camp with no less efficiency than a homeless encampment dispersing on word of an impending police sweep. We ended each evening in our sleeping bags reviewing the day past, previewing the day to come.

Though we tackled the ride like a well-oiled machine, being together 24/7 without respite led to the fabric of familial relationships sporadically unraveling. The boys' fighting increased. They fought over which songs to sing. They fought over who was funnier. They fought over:

"Red is the best color."

"Blue is."

"Red."

"Blue is better."

"Red is better."

"Don't be stupid. Red's for Republicans."

"I like red."

"Stupid."

"Shut up."

"You shut up."

My role resembled that of the pro-wrestling referee who, though he is in the ring, is utterly ignored. Djina was lucky. Whenever the boys went at it, she could ride by herself. While I screamed, "Stop fighting!" until white foam sprayed from my mouth, Djina listened to Mozart concertos on her iPod. Though I did not wish my wife a flat, justice should have mandated it.

The Hotel Ordway's lobby resembled my Grandma Dora's apartment circa 1967. Lots of comfortable, mismatched chairs and couches, plants growing on end tables, and books and magazines flopped hither and yon like a pride of lazy house cats. True, Grandma Dora didn't have an old AT&T phone booth to the left of her front door, but if one had been available . . .

Ordway's Main Street was lined with beautiful stone buildings from the 1800s, built to outlast the pyramids. Unfortunately, the majority of them were boarded up or closed. Ordway was the first of many eastern Colorado towns that suffered a double-punch: loss of the railroad and loss of water. Farmers sold their water rights to the burgeoning cities of Denver and Colorado Springs, so this once perennial grassland, transformed to productive farmland, had now morphed into a high-elevation desert. Though one could argue that this demonstrated how progress often goes the wrong way, Ordway did have a Dairy King. Djina called it a downscale Dairy Queen, but the only food that mattered, the milkshakes, were excellent. For dinner, nothing on Main Street was open, so we cooked in the hotel room. Fuel was running low, but we'd pick some up in Hutchinson, Kansas, the next large city.

Djina was blogger-in-chief. At every internet connection, she stopped to write anecdotes, download pictures, and respond to readers' comments. I was surprised to find so many people following the blog. If Djina skipped a few days, there would be comments such as, "Thank God, you're all right! We were beginning to worry." Okay, so that one came from my mother, but complete strangers were logging on. Djina blogged to stay connected to her circle of friends, which is wide and deep, because outside of our nuclear family, her friends are her family. As for me, I mostly I logged on to check the weather. I didn't bother with the rain forecast; outside of the hail on Monarch Pass, it was always dry. I never checked the temperature; it was always hot. I wanted wind knowledge: tail, head, or cross. Smiles or frowns depended on the letters: N, E, W, or S. The July 10 prediction for "light, variable winds" was slightly disappointing because of the prevailing westerlies, but at least we wouldn't fight headwinds.

Unfortunately, Aeolus didn't log onto to the National Weather Service to see which direction he should blow because by dawn an east wind was tossing leaves, dirt, and untethered toddlers through the air. We slogged six miles to Sugar City and stopped to regroup at a café. Damn it. Hadn't we conquered the Sierras, the Great Basin, and the Rockies? Weren't we entitled to rest on our laurels?

"You said the winds went west to east," Djina said, insinuating this was my doing.

"Maybe God's telling us we haven't suffered enough," I offered.

"Wind is air from a high pressure area going into a low pressure area," Yonah explained. "I doubt God's got anything to do with it."

"Can I get a Sprite?" asked Sprite. But 8:30 AM was too early for a sugary drink. Instead, we ordered a round of cinnamon buns and looked out the window. I'd never ride in wind like this back home. We had expected a different day and weren't prepared to handle this one. But there wasn't any choice.

"It's a character-builder day," I said. "Sometimes you just have to saddle up and go."

Yonah was silent. Solomon replied, "I'd rather take out the recycling a hundred times."

"Three dollars," the waitress said when I went to pay for the buns.

"Per bun?" They were good, but New York City prices in Sugar City?

"That's for all of them, hon." We should have bought a dozen more, if not for energy, then at least for ballast against the crosswinds. Though the headwinds punished, the crosswinds were the danger. We leaned into them and held on tight to prevent being swept off the road. At one point, a whopper grabbed Djina's and Yonah's lighter bikes and threw them onto the gravel shoulder. It was good that we weren't going east to west because these gusts could throw someone into a semi.

If Solomon joins the armed service, he'll laugh through boot camp.

"A hundred push-ups! Five hundred crunches! Run around the base! Twice! Go! What are you smirking at, Private Sprite?"

"Sir! Comparing this to biking across eastern Colorado, Sir!"

There were more cyclists on the TransAmerica route than on the Western Express. When our paths crossed, we'd have a short chat and exchange information such as, "The road's flooded fifty miles ahead. We took such-and-such instead." We met a sixtyish man who made Eeyore look like a starry-eyed optimist. The winds and gathering thunderclouds appeared bright and cheerful in his presence. He called the petition silly and stupid.

"The climate's always changing!" he lectured with pseudo-professorial authority. "We're going to be extinct in ten thousand years, so it doesn't much matter, does it?" We learned how he hated camping. The ride was too long. His wife was mad. He was lonely. We quickly escaped to avoid committing the sin of curmudgeonicide.

On the other hand was Josh. We met him later in the day in Eads. Djina thought this twenty-something guy so cute that she took his picture and blogged about how she was going to make a pinup calendar: Hot Guys of the TransAm. Josh would be Mr. January. She told her readers that these other two young bucks, Cole and Simon, would be Mr. February and Mr. March. She liked Cole because he volunteered to work with underprivileged children and just broke up with his girlfriend because she spent too much time modeling for a Paris fashion magazine. Simon impressed her because he was an eighteen-year-old blond from Switzerland.

"What about me?" I asked.

"You can be Mr. May 10, your birthday."

Djina theorized about single men riding cross-country. Guys under thirty equaled "cute, cool, and funny." Guys over thirty meant "wacko, eccentric." Remember Dave, the guy we met in Middlegate, who schlepped electric hair clippers? Though her sample size was only five, the hypothesis had some merit. For the under-thirty crowd, their lives filled with possibilities, this was the big adventure before settling into school or career. It was an exotic physical challenge, something they could share on Facebook to impress babes. They were optimistic and bright-eyed. The world was their oyster. For the post-thirty (actually, it was post-forty) cyclists, nothing was working. They were trying to reboot their lives. They rode solo because, well, no one could stand going with them.

Josh was finishing a PhD in some science engineering discipline way beyond the comprehension of my Cal drinking song-sized brain. He wasn't dogmatic about anything, but looked coolly at costs and benefits. Regarding nuclear energy, he said, "It's carbon neutral, and if we are ever to wean ourselves from fossil fuels, we'll need all the energy we can get to keep up with the ever-increasing worldwide demand."

Because Josh was intelligent and reasonable, I didn't attack his idea with my Pavlovian anti-nuke responses of, "What about storage? What about terrorism?" Even with the latest nuclear disaster at Fukushima, it would be a mistake to say that nuclear energy has no future. We are a species that hungers for energy, especially now with China and India demanding their places on the world economic stage. There isn't a magic energy bullet, so I won't be surprised if the United States builds new nuclear energy plants. It's tough when your sacred cow gets slaughtered, but when you're hungry, you need to look at all your options, even if you're a vegetarian.

Mid-morning, the desert gave way to a carpet of foot-tall corn genuflecting to the ground in the wrong direction. The wind made communication too much of a chore, so for six-and-a-half hours, we were alone with our thoughts, with the exception of, "Daddy, was that [dead animal] killed by a car?" With no one to talk with, I tried the meditation technique of focusing on breathing to empty the mind. Once in a while, I achieved something, some transcendence, I guess. Then in the midst of reverie, my eyes, without permission, would steal a glance at the cyclometer, and the moment of grace disappeared.

On average, I looked at the cyclometer twice a minute. That's one-hundred-twenty times an hour, or about a thousand times a day. This constant glancing was the curse of knowledge. Cyclometers report speed, average speed, maximum speed (best avoid this function on headwind days), elapsed cycling time, actual time, total mileage for trip, and cadence (leg rpms). The more functions the cyclometer, the stronger the curse. Rather than a tool to help, it enslaves the cyclist. Instead of using the hours in the saddle to watch raptors soar on thermals into the heavens or think about ways to establish peace between humans and the other creatures that occupy this wondrous planet, he pants, "If I go a little harder, I'll average 18 miles per hour." He'll stare at the two-inch screen and calculate what time he'll reach the next town for Gatorade. During the calculation, he'll miss the eagle's nest. My single small victory vis-à-vis the cyclometer was that when the wire attaching the cadence magnet broke, I didn't fix it.

Late afternoon we pulled into Eads (average speed: 9.4 miles per hour; elapsed time: nine hours, thirty-seven minutes, forty-eight seconds; maximum speed: 15.2 miles per hour). The public pool was open ten more minutes. We were in the water before our unpeopled bicycles toppled to the ground. The local kids thought me weird as I repeatedly told them what an awesome pool they had and how lucky they were to live in Eads.

"Think he's over forty?"

"Yeah."

"Thought so."

The truth was, except for the pool, Eads was another Ordway. It was difficult picturing the town reviving. Of course, some venture capitalist might invest in wind turbines and turn the town around, but more likely Ordway, Sugar City, and Eads will continue fading away. Could these towns be microcosms of how global climate change will render vast areas of the planet? Will low-lying cities and countries, such as New York City and Bangladesh, be inundated with rising sea levels? What about the Southwest that relies on far-flung water imports? Will L.A. dry up and thousands of palatial mansions be abandoned for lack of a glass of water?

We slept in the city park along with six other cyclists. Three of them boasted they had cycled 150 miles that day going west. Big whoop. With 25-to 30-mile-per-hour tailwinds, a unicycle could manage that. There was also a pair of mysterious cyclists—two fit young men who had a middle-aged man sag their gear in a minivan. Unlike the other cyclists, they kept to themselves and slept in the van. They appeared to be a pair of troubled youth with their counselor. The difficulty of a cross-country ride would straighten them out. Tough love.

***

To describe the day after Eads, simply copy and paste the previous twenty-four hours here. The only difference is to replace the 9.4-miles-per-hour average with 8.8 miles per hour. My Zen continued to suffer as I kept praying that the winds would blow in the direction they were supposed to blow. My inner Obi-Wan Kenobi taught, "Young Windrider, accept that which you cannot change and absorb the wind, do not fight it." I told him where he could stick his Force. My life is more than halfway over, and instead of gathering more power and wisdom with age, my spiritual strength is lessening. Creature comforts meant little to me as a youth. I contentedly spent three months in India on a lentils and rice diet. It wasn't about the food. The discovery of Truth was the grail. Now if given a choice between Truth and an all-you-can-eat sushi buffet surrounded by an assortment of tasty beers, I say, "Pass the chopsticks."

I've let my spiritual seeker card lapse because I no longer have the surety that there is Truth to be found and am cynical of most who claim to walk the spiritual path. Though I lament the sapping of my spiritual strength, I do practice one spiritual/religious ritual on a more or less daily basis: the silent recitation of the traditional Jewish morning prayer service, the *Shachrit*. I recite it on my morning work commute and continued the practice across America. I pray because you don't need to be a Bible thumper or even "religious" to gain from prayer. If the goal of religion is to create meaning in life, prayer is one path to this goal, perhaps religion's most traveled road. The Hebrew word for prayer, *tefilah*, comes from the verb "to self-reflect." One can self-reflect with or without a deity. I do, however, invoke God in my practice.

Shachrit begins by thanking God for returning the soul to the body. In traditional Judaism, sleep is equivalent to being one-fortieth dead. This prayer gives thanks for another day of life because sometimes (read: practically every waking second) I forget the awesome miracle of being alive. The next prayer comes from the Bible when the pagan prophet Balaam was hired to curse the Hebrew nation. As he stood on a cliff overlooking the Hebrew tents, he was moved to bless them instead. Most rabbis interpret *tents* to mean *synagogues*. (Welcome to the world of rabbinic exegesis.) I interpret *tents* to mean the *natural world*, for this is where I feel a spiritual presence. (Welcome to Matt's world of exegesis.)

Now a prayer that gives praise for bodily functions to work properly. A prayer for a good dump in the morning might seem sacrilegious, but if your body isn't working right, nothing else matters (see the Book of Job). Next comes Psalm 150, the beautiful song of praises all creatures sing to God. The tradition translates the songs of the lark into Psalm 150 as, "How wondrous are your works, Great God of Creation!" While I'd love to believe the birds are singing hymns to God, more accurate translations are probably, "Here I am, Baby!" and "This tree is mine! Get lost!" The next prayer, *Yotzer Or*, is dedicated to God renewing Creation each day. *Yotzer Or* is a prayer of boundless optimism that every day holds the possibility of shedding one's dross and reinventing oneself. It may be delusional to think that after twenty-five years of repeating this same prayer—with more or less the same dross to exculpate—I will actually change. But as Alexander Pope wrote, "Hope springs eternal . . . "

The prayers climax at the *Shema*, Judaism's core statement of belief. It is a scant six words in Hebrew translated as "Listen, Israel, *Adonai* is our God, *Adonai* is one." Like most prayers, it sounds better in the Hebrew for two reasons. First, prayer language and conversational language have different uses. Conversational language is to exchange ideas while prayer language is an attempt to create holy space. Using a separate language is helpful. Since Hebrew is not my mother tongue, it adds to the mystery of prayer and somewhat avoids Yonah's problem that the majority of Jewish prayers focus on God's greatness. Prayer as mantra. The second reason has to do with Hebrew's ambiguity and multiple levels of meaning. The *Shema's* word for God, *Adonai*, is the most mysterious and interesting word in the Hebrew language. The four-letter word is actually not *Adonai*, but *YHVH*. *Adonai*, which means "My Lord," is a substitute word because *YHVH* is considered too holy to utter. In the time when the Jewish temples in Jerusalem stood, on the holiest day of the year, Yom Kippur, the High Priest would enter the inner sanctum, the Holiest of Holies, and pronounce God's actual name. The name was considered so powerful that if the High Priest was not of sufficient purity, he would die (or so goes the story). Though no one is certain how this name was pronounced, many think it *Yahweh*. The etymology of *YHVH*, known as the tetragrammaton, seems to be a melding of the past, present, and future tenses of "to be." In other words, the proper name of the Hebrew God might be translated as, "He was, He is, He will be." ("She was, She is, She will be" also works.)

The word "Israel" also has multiple meanings. It is the name of the nation of Jews. The first time it appears in the Bible is when the Patriarch Jacob wrestles a divine being and is given the name Israel, which translates to "He who wrestles with God." It turns out that questioning God is one of the most holy endeavors a Jew can engage in.

"So in that sense, Yonah, you're a terrific Jew."

"Great, Dad."

The *Shema's* basic proclamation is that *Yahweh* is one. The word here is clear, though the meaning is not. Does it mean that there is only one God? Maybe it is saying that *Yahweh* is a single entity versus—say—a trinity? Could it mean that all the gods—Allah, Jesus, Krishna, Zeus, The Flying Spaghetti Monster, and *Yahweh*, to name but a few—are simply different names for the same God? Perhaps it points to the notion that we are all part of a great unity. All I know is that the *Shema's* ambiguity imbues it with a majesty, for it allows each individual to decide what it means.

After a few more prayers I'm finished and even if I didn't reach transcendence, at least I chipped away thirty minutes of a windy ride.

O━O┇O━O┇O━O┇O━O┇O━O┇O━O┇O━O┇O━O┇O━O┇O━O┇O━O

The winds finally attenuated. Maybe my prayers worked. I beseeched God to do something about the rising humidity, but here I was even less cheery about prayer's efficacy. To pass the time, Yonah and Solomon played many matches of "Who Will Laugh First?" Yonah won 100 percent of the matches because of big brother advantage. Their humor of choice involved some form of cannibalism, such as eating a person, a body part, or a particular body product. If you can't guess the product, think brown. I'm sure if we had girls, the trip's conversations would have been different.

We rode by George Washington Carver's homestead. He's the guy who reputedly invented peanut butter. Thorough Wikipedia research, however, disproves that claim. But Carver did come up with some three hundred uses for peanuts and championed crop rotations. He was a teacher, poet, and painter. Perhaps the greatest achievement of "the Black Leonardo" was exposing the canard that blacks were intellectually inferior. I tried to impress upon the boys what one person with an inquisitive mind could do.

"What did Daddy say?" asked Solomon.

"George Washington Carver blah-blah-blah peanuts blah-blah-blah inquisitive something or other," Yonah said.

"I thought he said he drank his pee," Solomon replied and then broke out in uncontrollable laughter.

The only campground in Dighton was the city park, so we found a hotel. After exiting the Rockies, we had found no real campgrounds. If you are young and broke, city parks suffice. One cross-country cyclist claimed he had not spent a dime on housing. But Djina and I were neither young nor broke, so it was the Heritage Hotel followed by Dighton's solitary restaurant, The B and B Sports Bar. The menu consisted of grilled cheese, beer-battered fish, and eighteen varieties of burgers. I didn't think my taste buds could stomach another grilled cheese. However, the thought of eating a fish caught in the mid-1990s, stored ten years in a Kansas freezer, then deep fried—well, I took the grilled cheese. With fried onions and peppers, the burgers were tempting, but I wasn't quite ready to relinquish my vegetarian superiority complex.

Our rain luck continued to hold. It rained and thundered all night in Dighton, but we were safely ensconced at the Heritage Hotel watching a televised debate on global warming between Robert Kennedy Jr. and Glen Beck. I thought Kennedy would annihilate the guy, but Beck proved a worthy opponent, agreeing with much of Kennedy's position and essentially tongue-tying the man. Yonah and I spoke about the finer points of debating. As in chess, it's not enough to see your move; you have to get into your opponent's head to predict his. Beck was proficient at this. It didn't matter that the facts were not on his side. This is the whole problem with the global climate debate. It is easy to imbue doubt into anyone who can't examine data with a critical eye. Recently I found myself unable prove to a group of skeptical eleventh-grade students that President Obama was born in Hawaii and not Kenya. Whatever evidence I brought to bear was met with disbelief and scorn. Why? Because what people want to believe is more important than truth. Ideology trumps reality. A foreign-born Muslim is our president. Global warming is a hoax. It's all the same.

The skies cleared and we cycled through swamped fields. Crickets and frogs sang and croaked. Ethanol signs appeared in the corn-fields. Besides being grown for corn syrup, feedstock, and tortilla chips, corn is now a controversial renewable fuel. Yes, ethanol has the potential to decrease oil imports. Yes, it is more carbon friendly than petroleum. Yes, it is renewable. And yes, it is a boon to corn-producing states. But by the time all the fertilizers and other energy inputs are added up, there is barely any energy gain when the Btus of corn are measured. And critics claim that by allotting so much cropland to fuel, the quantity of corn available for food decreases, increasing its price. Turning corn into ethanol to help wean us off of oil is like using methadone to get a junkie off heroin.

The only break from corn were the humongous soybean farms. Miles and miles of soy protein and not a block of tofu to eat. Sigh. Food was increasingly becoming problematic, especially for Djina. In Ness City the boys and I went into a café. Djina passed. Her sustenance now came from Gatorade, yogurt, energy bars, and blogging. So while she spied out the library, we gorged on shakes, fries, and grilled cheese. As Yonah and Solomon argued about whether or not fries were better with or without ketchup, in walked the two emotionally disturbed and/or mentally deranged teen bicyclists. When all the other young riders were averaging ninety to 120 miles a day, these two were mirroring our moderate sixty to seventy miles. I love talking to weird people, so I approached their table using the voice I reserve for my on-the-edge students so not to set them off on a violent tirade.

The "patients," Roger and Evan, had just graduated high school. They would both be attending college in the fall. Their "counselor" was Evan's uncle. They rode sixty miles because they had all summer, and as teens they were obligated to remain in bed until 10:00 AM. In other words, they were completely normal. Those of you laughing at my inept psychological diagnosis, listen to this: In 1973, Stanford psychologist Dr. David Rosenhan played a hoax on a few mental hospitals. He and eleven others voluntarily gained entrance to the hospitals by faking a single symptom, hearing voices that said "hollow" and "thud." The twelve were admitted, eleven with the diagnostic label of "schizophrenia."

Once in, they acted completely normal, but none of the hospital staff caught on.

If those who seem mad are normal, what then of those who appear normal? Here's what Emily Dickinson had to say about this in her poem "Much Madness Is Divinest Sense":

Much madness is divinest sense
To a discerning eye;
Much sense the starkest madness.
'Tis the majority
In this, as all, prevails.
Assent, and you are sane;
Demur,—you're straightway dangerous,
And handled with a chain.

Prior to our trip, we had no surer confirmation that what we were doing was right than the warnings delivered by well-meaning colleagues and friends about biking across country with children being insanity. Here's to less assenting and more demurring.

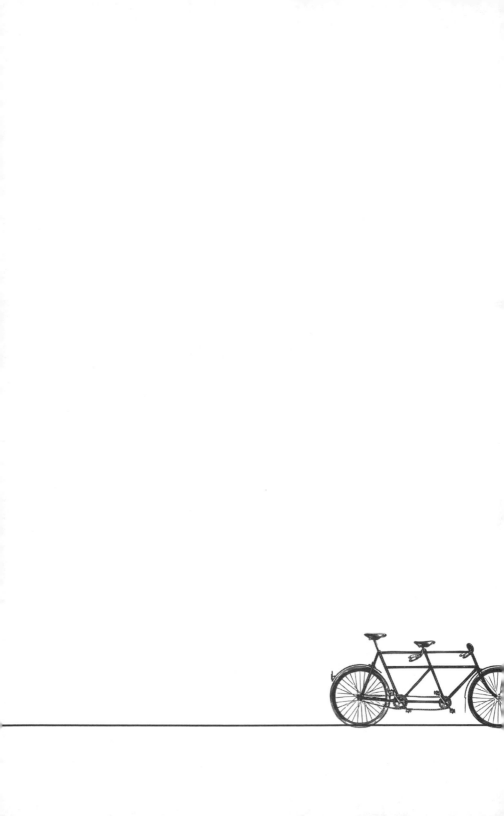

SARAH VS. YONAH

11

EVERYONE SAID THAT KANSAS had the nicest people. Everyone was right. Not a single unfriendly honk in the entire state. If passing was unsafe, cars lined up behind us and patiently waited. When they passed, they'd wave. Djina observed that going from Colorado to Kansas was akin to leaving *South Park* for *Mr. Rogers' Neighborhood*. Say what you will about Kansas and their attempt to teach Intelligent Design (read: Creationism) as science—I have never found such nice people anywhere I've ever lived. Because of the preponderance of churches, and the fact that in many of the towns, the church was the only public building in good repair, the Kansas attitude appeared to be fueled by a love for Jesus and taking the command of loving thy neighbor to heart. I said to Yonah that this was what religion was really about, to get beyond the notion that religion was simply theological dogma antithetical to rationality and to see how religion builds compassion and community; it has the ability to shape someone into a better person.

"Religion isn't brain food, it's heart medicine."

"If you need Jesus to be nice, are you really being nice?" he countered.

"It's better than not being nice."

"But it's not free will."

"What do you mean?"

"Remember the Garden of Eden? Adam and Eve had everything. It was perfect. Then they got knowledge of good and evil and lost their innocence. The goal of humanity is to return to the Garden of Eden by using free will, and live in a perfect world again but have wisdom too."

"Where did you learn that?"

"You. The point is: religion tells you to be nice. That's not free will. Free will is when you're nice without anyone telling you."

"So without a church or synagogue, how do you exercise your free will to be nice?"

"When I want to kill Solomon, I don't."

"I think there is a commandment about that, Mr. I'm-Exercising-My-Free-Will. Maybe you can freely laugh at one of his jokes."

"Are you kidding?"

Alongside the churches forming the character of Kansas drivers stood billboards such as the one with a close-up of Jesus and the message: *Christ Pilot Me.*

I petitioned the Savior, "We've got good enough maps, but if you could watch over the bad drivers, that'd be great."

Yonah amended the Cal drinking song to, "Oh, they had a little party up in Heaven. There was Jesus, there was Mary, there was God . . . "

We passed a coyote squashed flatter than a bear rug.

"Daddy, do you think that coyote was killed by a car?"

"Yes."

"That's sad."

I don't know what possessed me, but instead of recognizing the eight seconds of silence, I temporarily lost my mind and replied, "Maybe not. Maybe it's in coyote heaven."

"NO!" he shrieked and then calmly, "Do you think that coyote was killed by a car?"

"Yes."

"That's sad."

Yonah, exercising his free will offered, "The coyote was flat as a pancake."

"NO!" Tears welled and Solomon sobbed. "Do you think it was killed by a car?"

"Yes," I repeated and glared at evil son.

"That's sad."

"That's scrambled eggs and salsa!"

"NO!!!"

The cycle repeated. Each time Yonah created a new breakfast metaphor: waffle with jam, spilled cereal and strawberries, granola guts. Each time Solomon became more hysterical. After waiting far too long, I banished Yonah, and Solomon composed himself. Like a tire rolling over pavement, anger did not stick to him.

"Do you think that coyote was killed by a car?"

"Yes."

"That's sad."

Eight seconds of respectful mourning.

○━○━○━○━○━○━○━○━○━○━○━○━○━○━○

On Day Thirty-Six we crossed the halfway point at Rush Center. There is a possibility that you are fatigued by this memoir and have flipped to the end to see how many more pages. What about the promising books piling up on your nightstand? How many more metaphors can you read describing heat? If "fatigued" describes your state of mind, then you have the slightest inkling of how the boys felt. Nineteen hundred miles on a bike. Nineteen hundred to go. The trip was no longer a novelty. The food was abominable. The scenery was one ocean of corn followed by another. Every mile was getting muggier.

For Yonah, The Ride had morphed into The Chore. Something to get through as quickly as possible. If it was up to him, we would have found the nearest interstate and ridden a hundred miles a day for nineteen straight days. I, on the other hand, was reveling in the journey. Not to discount the harsh conditions, I loved the whole thing and wanted to celebrate halfway across the country with a good beer. As in many tiny rural towns, a gas station mini-mart was the hub of Rush Center. And, as in many of America's rural mini-marts, two-thirds of its stock was beer. Unfortunately, the beer was available only by case unless you wanted "Milwaukee's Finest," whose thirty-pack went for $10.99. A farmer walked out with two of them, enough to irrigate a small plot of corn seedlings, and why not? The swill was half the price of bottled water.

Not only were there no single beers to be found in Rush Center's only market, but no Gatorade. I stared long at the refrigerators refusing to believe a single Lemon-Lime Original was not lurking behind cases of Coors and Coors Light. In the end, I celebrated with a Mountain Dew. At forty-three grams of sugar mixed with enough caffeine to pull an all-nighter to research and write an essay on Proust, the drink had my stomach doing tricks a contortionist could only dream of, and the decibels coming from my backside were equivalent to a Boeing 757 at take off.

There was no hotel, so we camped at the city park. We were about to cook dinner when we realized we were out of fuel. Those special MSR fuel canisters promised by the REI salesman to be ubiquitous throughout the States did not include the Central Time zone. Here, Coleman was king. Not at one, not at two, but at three different stores I tried screwing a green metal Coleman propane bottle onto our MSR Pocket Rocket. Alas, the Rocket was grounded. There was as much chance of finding MSR fuel in Kansas as finding a copy of the *Hindustan Times*. Luckily, the "deranged" teen cyclists, Evan and Roger, and their uncle showed up and bequeathed us a spare fuel bottle. The dinner to mark halfway across the country consisted of spaghetti with powdered pesto sauce, chicken noodle soup, and chips. Celebratory tootsie rolls for dessert.

If Rush Center at two buildings was no city, its park also struggled to live up to the word. It was a plot of grass about the size of a Little League infield, equipped with one trashcan, two picnic tables, two benches, and a hose. We turned the hose on each other to shower off the day's accumulation of dried sunscreen, sweat, and road grit. A 1977 Ford Galaxy drove up. Uh-oh, I thought. The map was wrong. The park wasn't really a park; it was someone's backyard. And if it was a park, it certainly wasn't intended for camping; there wasn't even an outhouse. Before the man stepped out of his car, I was already employing traveler's charm, a mix of enthusiasm and diffidence coupled with a friendliness that doesn't go overboard so as not to appear crazy. An elderly man wearing dirty overalls and a huge smile greeted us.

"Is it okay that we're camping here?"

"That's what we made it for. To make a place for you cyclists to camp. You need anything?"

"No, we're fine. The park's a lifesaver."

His smile widened. "I see you got your dinner cooking. I won't keep you."

"It's no problem."

He was a seventy-seven-year-old farmer. Like all the other Kansans, he was the epitome of friendliness. Even though he had never taken a bike ride in his life, he and the town fathers felt bad about cyclists having no place to sleep as they passed through the town, so they built the park. And I, the ungrateful boor, disparaged it a few paragraphs earlier by saying it wasn't even a park.

Mensch is a Yiddish word for a decent person, a good guy, a man you'd be pleased to have as a relation. This old farmer was a *mensch*. He taught me a valuable lesson about thankfulness. I vowed to be more thankful and to take nothing for granted. After all, a small swath of grass is better than none. If only the mini-mart stocked single bottles of beer, it would have been a perfect evening.

Our route through the Midwest had been light on historical attractions. So when we arrived at Fort Larned, an outpost on the Santa Fe Trail reconstructed as a National Historical Site, I wanted to stop. Unfortunately, the fort was four hundred yards off-route, and the boys would not take a single pedal stroke that did not bring us closer to D.C., so we pressed on. However, a few miles farther, we ducked into the Santa Fe Trail Museum— partly because it was right on the road, mostly because we needed water. The museum was terrific due to its refrigerated water fountain and excellent air-conditioning. There were also exhibits where both Indian and pioneer artifacts lived peacefully side by side. In real life there was often antipathy between the cultures, yet the Indians had quickly embraced American material life. They not only coveted guns and other weaponry, but soon after meeting traders and pioneers, much of their cloth came from East Coast factories, and traditional cooking baskets and ceramics gave way to iron pots and pans. The Native Americans had complex emotions toward the new immigrants. On the one hand, they desired the white men's material culture. On the other hand, they resented the fact that these light-skinned people wanted their land.

The artifacts told many stories, such as how long nineteenth-century food preparation took. For us, putting food into our mouths can be as fast as pulling up to a McDonald's drive-through and deciding whether or not to supersize. For them, every meal was a slow meal; their daily caloric intake was significantly less than ours. A large map of the 1860 United States dominated one museum wall. It was fascinating to see which cities and areas would grow and which would fade over the next 150 years. Anyone who bet the long odds that the Los Angeles pueblo would become the nation's second largest metropolis would have struck gold.

What will be in the museums of 2150? Primitive computers that had to be manually operated with fingers instead of brain waves? Gasoline-powered vehicles? A portfolio of fertility goddesses: the Victoria's Secret catalog?

O═O¹O═O¹O═O¹O═O¹O═O¹O═O¹O═O¹O═O¹O═O¹O═O¹O═O

In Larned, we stopped to blog at the town library. I struck up a conversation with the librarian, a pleasant woman interested in our trip. In instances such as this, it was usually easier getting people to sign the petition than shooting buffalo from a train circa 1870. They signed so fast, the only worry was the pen might rip the paper. But here . . .

"I probably won't sign it," she smiled. "I don't believe in global warming."

Though taken aback that a woman whose career focused on providing knowledge could utter such blather, I seized the educational moment and replied in my least patronizing voice, "You might not be aware of it, but the Intergovernmental Panel on Climate Change, made up of the top atmospheric scientists in the world, just issued a report saying that not only is global warming real, but it has anthropogenic causes. I'm wondering what your information source is?"

Point, Matt.

The librarian's smile did not fade, and she replied in a superior nonpatronizing voice, "God controls everything. If He wants to make it warmer, He will. Besides, my husband and I vacationed in Alaska where we spoke with people who told us that the glaciers are advancing, not retreating."

Point and match, librarian, for not only did she have real people, not egghead scientists, prove to her that global warming was a liberal conspiracy designed to take away our freedoms, but she threw out the God trump card. What could I say to that? God is wrong? I scooped up our godless petition and stuffed it into its pannier.

"See," said Yonah, "this is why I hate religion."

"But," I countered, "not all religious people think like that. In fact, a lot of religious people see global warming as a threat to Creation, and that's their reason to fight it."

"Yeah, but you don't need religion to be against global warming. If no one was religious, everyone would see it was a problem and do something without using God as an excuse to do nothing."

"There are plenty of apathetic atheists in the world."

"Apathetic atheists cause fewer problems than passionate believers."

"No, that's wrong. Passion is what moves the world forward."

"What about suicide bombers?"

"What about the women in Afghanistan who risk their lives to educate girls? Passion cuts both ways. Unless people get passionate about global warming, we are cooked."

"You're right about that."

For the first time, Yonah and I had a conversation involving religion in which we wound up agreeing. The question that neither of us could answer was how to get Americans as passionate about global warming as they are about the Super Bowl.

○━○ː○━○ː○━○ː○━○ː○━○ː○━○ː○━○ː○━○ː○━○ː○━○

Before we left California, *The Hutchinson* [Kansas] *News* wrote a story about our upcoming trip, and I received an email from a couple offering to put us up for the night. Daniel Wallach and Catherine Hart lived off the TransAmerica route, so they picked us up in Hudson. Hudson was also slightly off-route, and we got slightly lost. After flagging down a few trucks for directions, Djina observed, "When you ask for directions in Kansas, there's an 80-percent chance the driver will be a shirtless Brad Pitt look-alike (albeit with a big ol' wad of chew between his cheek and gum). The other 20 percent, it's the same guy twenty years later devolved into John Goodman."

Daniel and Catherine arrived with a pickup truck, a sedan, and quarts of ice-cold Recharge, the organic food community's answer to Gatorade. Daniel filled and refilled six-ounce Dixie cups for us from one of the bottles. It was one of the most thirst-quenching liquids that had ever passed my lips, and my evil self yearned to rip the bottle from Daniel and chug. Thankfully, I exercised free will. We put the bikes in the back of the truck, and Djina and the boys went into the sedan with Catherine. Before climbing into the cab with Daniel, I noticed the front vanity license plate on the pickup read, "Jesus," and I had a moment of panicked cognitive dissonance. Hadn't Catherine included in her email the fact that Daniel was the only Jew in Stafford County? Was something amiss with this seemingly sweet couple? Were they Jews for Jesus? ("Jesus was a rabbi, for goodness sakes. But he was also the Son of God, making him the Messiah. Once every Jew recognizes Jesus's divinity, he will return in flesh and blood. What do you say? Can you give Jesus a chance?")

I was sweating in the air-conditioned cab. We would be at their mercy for the entire night. That's the potential problem with staying with people you've never met. It's a blind date for both host and guest, but you can't ditch the boor or religious wacko after a quick dinner. You're stuck at a slumber party. To reach their farm, we drove a circuitous route that mirrored Theseus's trek through the Labyrinth. Without a string to find our way out, we were further at their mercy while they attempted to brainwash us. That was a best-case scenario. The worst case was their ritual murder of Solomon and using his blood to make their wafers. (I noted that Daniel's key chain was from Remy's Gun Shop . . . real Jews do not hunt.)

As we drove, Daniel didn't mention Jesus once but explained that he borrowed his truck from his neighbor. (Phew!) He and

Catherine were transplants from Colorado who worked on the reconstruction of the nearby town of Greensburg, which had been destroyed by a tornado in early 2007. Their idea was to rebuild it as a green, sustainable community. Here, in the middle of Kansas, where global warming was taking as long to become accepted as did the notion that the Earth circles the sun, a town was reinventing itself to live more in tune with the environment. A more hopeful sign was difficult to conjure.

After settling in, Catherine put out a Mexican dinner buffet complete with sautéed tofu and Corona beer. I lingered around the bowls to polish off everything. Not Solomon. He wolfed down his food and ran out into the pristine wetland prairie surrounding their house to play with the toads. (All day long, Solomon had hollered at the toads on the road to hop out of harm's way. Once he witnessed a truck squish one. It took him hours to recover from the trauma.)

What finally brought him inside was Daniel's Holy Grail, a binder of classic baseball cards. Daniel let Solomon keep a Hank Aaron. Between the toads and baseball cards, Solomon at the ripe age of nine had glimpsed eternity through a perfect moment and achieved nirvana. This is not hyperbole. Children naturally access the full range of emotions easier than adults. For an adult to have an I-Thou moment might take years of spiritual practice. For a kid, a toad might do the trick.

Daniel, a liberal Jewish urbanite plopped into the middle of rural Kansas, taught me that the most right-wing, Bible-thumping, gun-toting, pro-lifer is not an Other, a person to laugh smugly at for his ignorance. When you scratch the surface of the person holding polar opposite views, you see someone who is looking for the same things in life: connections with others, a feeling of purpose, happiness. The Jesus pickup was his next-door neighbor's, but their relationship extended beyond borrowing a vehicle or a cup of sugar. By listening to each other's stories, they became ambassadors who bridged the gap between two groups that reviled each other out of ignorance. For us to reach beyond the surface of those we think we hate might give us the glimpse into eternity that the toads gave Solomon.

The next morning as Daniel drove us back to Hudson, he pointed out copse after copse and said, "Without hunters there'd be no wilderness area in Kansas. The whole state would have gone under the plow." Catherine and Daniel learned about the good that hunters do. In return, they taught their hunter neighbors that going green in Greensburg was how Jesus would rebuild.

○■○■○■○■○■○■○■○■○■○■○■○■○■○

We arrived in Hutchinson for a date with *The Hutchinson News* reporter who wanted to do a follow-up story. The reporter was unable to meet us, so he handed us off to a colleague. The interview was scheduled for three o'clock. At two we pulled into a Hutchinson gas station. While we were lingering in the cool mini-market chugging Gatorades and Sprite, a petite, older woman walked in to check her lottery tickets. She tossed the losing tickets into the trash, looked at me looking at her, and said, "You're that bike-riding family from California."

"Uh, yeah."

"I'm the reporter who's going to interview you."

"Oh," I said, thinking this city was a lot smaller than the map indicated.

"My name is Sarah Firestone. I'm a retired English teacher turned reporter. If you like, we can do the interview early. My office is just two blocks away."

"We were thinking of eating first," Djina said.

"I promise I'll have you out in thirty minutes."

We followed her to the newsroom and rolled four chairs into a semicircle around her cubicle. The thirty-minute interview was not memorable except for looking over her shoulder as she typed and silently chuckling at the English teachers' occassional mispellings. We were anxious to go because of our aforementioned hunger, so when she typed the last period and swiveled her chair to face us, I stood up ready to thank her. But she wasn't quite finished. Sarah fixated on Yonah and said, "You say you're an atheist."

Now that the formalities of the newspaper interview had ended, the inquisition began. For the next forty-five minutes, Yonah, and by association the rest of us, were on the receiving end of Sarah's attempt to get him to embrace God.

"Why don't you think there's a God?"

"Well," Yonah replied, "I don't see any evidence."

"Hasn't being around nature changed your mind?"

"No."

"What about the diversity of species? Aren't all the different species evidence of God?"

"I'd say evolution can explain that."

And so it went. Djina and I sat speechless. On the one hand, I had a hard time believing how a nice human interest story could morph into the Features Section equivalent to waterboarding. It was as if I were at the theater watching a one-act play between Sarah and Yonah. On the other hand, this Torquemada was grilling my son. As a parent, I should have protected him. On the third hand, Yonah was more than holding his own, so why intervene?

"Do you know how God works?" she jabbed.

"If God exists," Yonah parried, "I have no clue how he works."

Sarah changed tactics. She told a long anecdote about how God saved her when she had breast cancer. Her story in summary: She got breast cancer. She prayed. Her congregation prayed. She received medical treatment. The cancer did not respond. She discovered an experimental drug in Texas. The drug's regimen required her to fly down monthly. She did not have the resources. She prayed, and an airline offered her free flights. She received the experimental drug. Her cancer went into full remission.

"Now after hearing what happened to me, don't you tell me, young man, that there is no God. Have you no soul?"

There was silence. I didn't say anything but thought: "You might think God saved you, but if it wasn't for some medical researcher, more likely than not a Jewish atheist, you'd be dead." Djina's thought bubble was easy to decipher due to the exclamation points: "You pathetic lunatic! How dare you! You are talking to one of the most ethical, compassionate, and honest people you'll ever meet! You're the soulless one, you old bat!" Yonah, calm and respectful in the face of a tirade of personal attacks, had a very Zen thought bubble: "I am hungry for a grilled cheese, fries, and a milkshake."

Realizing that Yonah was destined to Hell—no doubt in the company of his parents—and there was nothing she could do to arrest his descent, Sarah released us from the darkened newsroom into the brilliant sunshine of downtown Hutchinson. Djina and I felt abashed for making Yonah deal with Sarah on his own. Sprite lifted our spirits by telling Yonah, "You should have stood up and sang, 'Manchester, England, England/ Across the Atlantic Sea/ And I'm a genius, genius/ And I believe that God, believes in Claude/ That's me.'"

"Yeah," Djina took it up. "We should have ripped off our clothes, danced around the newsroom, and sang, 'Let the Sunshine In!'"

"Next time," I said, "we tell them that when our kids get sick, we behead a rooster and sprinkle the blood on them. Then we have them eat dried lizard tail, give them a course of antibiotics, and in seven days, good as new."

Yonah said, "I think Sarah's story backfired. Now I believe even less in God and more in chemo drugs."

"But," I said, "prayer probably does help if you think it works. It can't hurt, and all that positive energy must do some good."

"Maybe," Yonah reluctantly conceded.

O━O:O━O:O━O:O━O:O━O:O━O:O━O:O━O:O━O:O━O:O━O:O━O

After years of bashing Walmart's hegemony over retail sales in America, it wasn't until July of 2007 that any of us had ever been inside one. We were not disappointed. Everything was there. Hutchinson's Main Street might have been deserted, but Walmart's aisles were packed. Besides low prices, Walmart provided an important community resource: cool air. Though Walmart may be in cahoots with Lucifer to destroy rural America, for the first time all trip there were soy products to be had. With garden burgers in hand, I trekked to the camping section for fuel. It was a camping bonanza with tents, sleeping bags, stoves, and half an aisle of fuel bottles. Alas, it was all Coleman, not a single canister of MSR. Borrowing a leaf from Sarah, I prayed. I prayed that a certain REI salesman would be blessed with hemorrhoids. But even without fuel, Walmart provided an exquisite gastronomical evening as we had a fresh salad to go with garden burgers, which we microwaved at the hotel. While this meal was not evidence of Providence's hand, it was a welcome relief from grilled cheese and fries.

Anxious to flee Hutchinson before being tarred and feathered and run out on a rail, we were on the road by 6:30 AM. At the Newton library, we read *The Hutchinson News*. Sarah's article was well-written with neither spelling errors nor a mention of the "A" word; thereupon, I did not write the excoriating letter to the editor that I'd spent the entire morning constructing in my head. The whole God-responding-to-personal-prayer thing left a bitter taste. If God responds to prayer, then She/He/It has a lot of 'splaining to do about the myriad times God has not responded. The one million innocent children murdered during the Holocaust is just one of God's more egregious oversights.

Djina checked the blog, which had a lot of activity. The night before, she had written about the interview, and readers had responded. Some told us we should have walked out. Others commended us for letting Yonah deal with the situation. One friend expressed umbrage at Sarah's ethics and sent us the web address of a site that reports such behavior. Bottom line: If it hadn't been for Sarah Firestone, there wouldn't be much to say about Hutchinson besides, "It was hot and muggy, and we had no fuel."

HARRY POTTER, SAVE US!

12

ON THE EDGE OF CASSODAY, Kansas, towered a bill-board announcing the town as the prairie chicken capital of the world. Once abundant on the prairies, these large grouses were decimated through hunting and habitat loss. If Cassoday is prairie chicken ground zero, they are heading for imminent extinction because other than the enormous bird on the bill-board, we saw none. Cassoday's restaurants and hotels were closed, so we camped in the city park: a large lawn interspersed with shade trees surrounding a raised gazebo, an idyllic setting for a July Fourth oompah-pah band. Hundreds of fireflies enter-tained us, but a quadrillion mosquitoes harassed us. A cacophony of cicadas chirped as loudly as a rock concert, and then as if on cue, stopped. How do they do that? Is it the same gene that con-trols flocks of small birds to turn at the same instant midflight? I imagine it's a defensive maneuver for a mass of animals to act in unison. As a species it seems that we humans have either lost or suppressed the gene to work together harmoniously. If ever there was a time for civilization to stop our direction of travel and together redirect our flight, it is now. How else can climate change be arrested? If not, our species may likely follow the prairie chicken.

To seek heat and humidity relief, we poured water bottles over ourselves. Ten minutes later, we were sweating. Cassoday's popu-lation was 92. With this climate, it was surprising the number was that high. We were out of fuel, so dinner was option one:

PB&Js; or option two: oily cheese sandwiches. There weren't even milkshakes. We sat miserably in the tents de sauna to escape the mosquitoes that had launched the insect equivalent of Operation Overlord. We zipped up the tents and hunted down the little bitches who had parachuted behind enemy lines. Yonah announced he was ready to be done with the trip.

"Do you want to quit?"

"No."

"Think you can make it?"

"Any more nights like this, then no. This is torture."

Sweating atop my sleeping bag, I gave Yonah's let's-ride-on-the-interstate idea a little thought, but mostly I felt nostalgic for the Nevada desert.

We ate a luxurious breakfast of instant oatmeal, hot chocolate, and coffee at Cassoday's gas station. "Luxurious?" you smirk. "Oatmeal in a gas station? C'mon." When you've got no fuel and have provided an all-night, all-you-can-eat buffet for mosquitoes because you are the only large, furless animals not ensconced behind closed doors within a hundred-mile radius, then sitting at a gas station, slurping a bowl of microwaveable oatmeal, and sipping a cup of coffee brewed the night before isn't less enjoyable than crumpets and high tea with the Queen of England. Like time, food and ambiance are relative.

One of the ride's joys was conversing with each other. Unfortunately, I often forgot what I had earlier told the boys, so regularly they'd say, "We know. You already told us." More than once Solomon has related an event from my life in such detail that I would swear it was his story—except that it occurred thirty years before his birth.

"Remember when you were with your friend Walt and climbed the fence to get into Vandenberg Air Force Base to protest those missiles, and it started to rain? And then when they looked for you, you hid inside a culvert because your poncho was bright orange. And they arrested you and you knew the policeman who arrested you."

"I knew the policeman?"

"He went to high school with you."

"Oh, yeah, right."

At some point Solomon will change the "you" to "I," and I'll be amazed at what a rich life he has led. Perhaps I'll say, "I know. You already told me."

This particular morning we compared the Civil and Revolutionary Wars. Why did the Colonists win but the Confederates lose? Yonah, with his emeritus insight, explained that it boiled down to the fact that the Revolutionary War wasn't an existential crisis for Britain. They could lose their colonies, but retain their country. It was simply a cost–benefit analysis. It was too costly to keep America. But each side in the Civil War needed victory. Even though the vast majority of fighting was on Southern soil, the North also felt it was fighting for its life. In the end, the manpower and industrial advantage of the North proved decisive. Victory in the war on global climate change will hinge on whether our species will perceive carbon dioxide buildup as an existential threat.

○━○━○━○━○━○━○━○━○━○━○━○━○━○━○

The roads of eastern Kansas were punctuated with hundreds of dead armadillos. With their silvery bodies and bony armor, they looked like flattened shoulder pieces of knights' mail. There were many seconds of silence. A local blamed the victims themselves for armadillocide. Eons ago, armadillos perfected a variety of defensive maneuvers. You may have heard of armadillos curling into bowling balls. That kind doesn't live in the United States. We have the nine-banded armadillo whose defense is to jump in the air and startle the predator. Imagine a nocturnal armadillo standing on the road enjoying fresh carrion. Suddenly, two bright eyes of a large cat appear on the horizon. The cat emits an awful growl that becomes unbearably louder as it rapidly approaches. As the cat is ready to pounce, our armadillo startles it by jumping up and striking the front grill of the 2005 Ford Explorer.

"More evidence for evolution," said Yonah. "In a hundred years, armadillos haven't had time to evolve a better survival tactic." Playing dead would be a much more effective defense because the tires might miss. Perhaps the bowling ball brand can be moved north to breed with its cousin. Short of that, a kind-hearted geneticist could splice in a few opossum genes. Or the species might simply hold out until the price of oil gets too high.

For a recreational rider, a hundred-mile (or century) day is a lifelong goal to strive for, the biking equivalent to a marathon. We managed a 102-mile day, but not because tailwinds blew us across the state and not because we were feeling particularly strong. The itinerary called for fifty-seven miles and camping at a city park, which meant another water-bottle shower and cold dinner while providing mosquito blood meal. Yonah's amendment of an additional forty-five miles to Chanute, Kansas, and a hotel was unanimously approved.

A century bike ride is a major accomplishment for anyone; for a thirteen-year-old, it verges on heroic. Had this been his first, it would have been enough (or as we say in Hebrew at the Passover table, *Dayenu*). Had he ridden the century in a hot and humid sauna, *Dayenu*. Had he ridden in said sauna hauling twenty-five pounds of Clif Bars, peanut butter jars, and a cooking set, *Dayenu*.

Seabiscuit rode a century with his back brake on. I discovered this the next day. During the routine bicycle check and lubrication, I could barely get his rear tire to spin; it was wedged against the brake pad. The culprit was a broken spoke.

"Aha!" I exclaimed. And I removed it. But what was this? A second broken spoke? And a third? Incredulously, Yonah had not noticed. The repair was not a thing of beauty. I don't have the graceful hands of a real mechanic. I am, after all, an English teacher. By the time I muscled the replacement spokes in, they resembled the paths drunks make when trying to walk a sobriety line. But the spokes were sturdy and the wheel was true—more or less.

O━O⋮O━O⋮O━O⋮O━O⋮O━O⋮O━O⋮O━O⋮O━O⋮O━O⋮O━O

In Kansas it was difficult bringing out the petition. First, it was hard enough just to ride. When we stopped, it was to get Gatorade, cool down, and rest. The petition was an extra expenditure of energy that we didn't have. Two, after the librarian and Sarah

Firestone, we were a bit shy asking people to take a stand on global warming. I entered Chanute's gun/pawn shop to buy pepper spray. Every westbound cyclist warned us that the Ozark dogs love the taste of lycra. One cyclist claimed that as he passed one residence, a man lifted his head from under the hood of his car and commanded his dogs, "Sic 'em!"

Two middle-aged guys worked the shop. One wore a USMC shirt and sported a USMC tattoo on his upper arm. His arms and torso were big in that Marine-way, though the years had relaxed the muscle tautness. The other was lanky, his face the lightest shade of pallor this side of a corpse. Give him a black suit and top hat and you've got the stereotypical undertaker. Guns lined the walls. Pistols coexisted with gold rings and watches in a display case. My favorite was a hot pink rifle. ("Happy Valentine's Day, honey.") I didn't count how many firearms were there, but had the South had access to two or three more armories such as this one, the Civil War might have ended differently.

"Whatcha need?" the Marine asked.

"You have pepper spray?"

"Second aisle, halfway down, top shelf, right side."

I took two of the small cylindrical bottles. It had also been suggested to bring whistles, so I grabbed a couple. Djina and I would handle the pepper spray; the boys the whistles. While I was paying for my weaponry, the Marine asked, "Whatcha doing with these?"

"They're for Missouri's dogs. Me and my family are riding our bikes east."

The undertaker tapped a long cigarette ash into a Rotary Club ashtray and offered, "Better to pack a pistol."

The Marine asked, "Where d'you start?" I gave him the California to D.C. spiel but paused before going into the petition. I wasn't in the mood to talk to a couple of flat-earthers. But they knew I was withholding and stood behind the counter waiting. Avoiding their eyes, I mumbled, "And we're bringing a petition to Congress about global warming."

The undertaker stubbed out his cancer stick and proclaimed, "This damn place is getting so goddamn hot. Ain't I been saying it for ten years?"

The Marine added, "Tell them boneheads in Washington that they got to make those idiots in Detroit make hybrids like the Japs."

"Hell, I read how there's this guy who invented this car that runs on water. Them bastards from GM bought the goddamn patent and are sittin' on it. I'll show you." He went to his computer.

The Marine added, "And tell 'em to lower the goddamn speed limit back to fifty-five. It'll save gas, and we won't have to invade any more goddamn Iraqs."

"So, uh, you want to sign this?"

"You got it."

They signed and their friend walked in. They browbeat him into signing too. I stepped onto a small soapbox to suggest that the government needed to take the lead on global warming. The undertaker, still looking for the water-fueled vehicle, said, "No, sir. It's us gotta change. You can't depend on ol' Bushy to do shit. Just like the Constitution says, 'We the people of the United States.' Don't say nothin' 'bout the guvmint. Now where's that goddamn car? It can go two hundert mile on a gallon of water. I don't see it, but Google it. It's there."

I left the store confused and bemused about Kansas. Confused because you had two well-educated women, a librarian and an ex-English teacher, spouting drivel. Bemused because you had a pair of gun shop owners, who between the two of them probably equaled one high school diploma, yet they understood.

While I was telling Djina the gun shop story, she said, "If I hear anyone say, 'Sic 'em,' I'm getting off my bike, spraying the dog, marching over to the guy, spraying him, and then making him sign the petition." I love this woman.

There were dogs. While each attack was an open-the-carburetor adrenalin surge, the dogs never caught us unprepared. Either they sat patiently in their front yards evaluating whose thighs had the most meat before giving chase, or they heard us coming and started their I'm-gonna-rip-out-yer-throat barking early enough for us to have whistles and pepper sprays out while stepping up the pace. At the first sign of a canine charge, Solomon and Yonah blew the whistles, and the dogs usually stopped. Once the intrepid ones who still advanced saw what Djina and I held in our hands, they suddenly needed to stop and scratch. Clearly, we had reaped the benefits of earlier TransAmerica cyclists who had taught the dogs Pavlovian lessons.

Solomon rescued his third turtle, but it was a close call. Like chickens, turtles have a thing about getting to the other side of the road. Only way slower. The drill for the first two was Solomon would pick them up, whisper a few words about jaywalking, and place them far from the pavement. But by the time we saw this one, a semi was bearing down. I waved the trucks into the other lane, saving the turtle from turtle heaven and Solomon from eternal turtle nightmares.

My knees were screeching. Earlier, I had vowed that if God got my knees to D.C., and then never allowed me to pedal another stroke, I'd be content. I renewed the vow and meant it, mostly. Though the intention of every "God get me through this and . . . " is to carve the vow in granite, in truth our vows are written in wet sand on the ocean's edge. As soon as my vow to never do something is tested, ninety-nine out of a hundred times I will break it, for I am all too human (read: weak). I knew it would be no different with the bike. Upon returning home, if I could no longer ride a bicycle, contentment would not be my state of mind. The most honest thing to do would be to make one last vow: never make another vow.

To pass the time, the boys and I spoke about *kashrut*, the Jewish dietary laws. I explained how the biblical injunction against boiling a young goat in its mother's milk expanded over time to include prohibitions against the eating of any dairy product in the company of meat—for example, cheeseburgers. The tradition speaks about compassion and how the source of life—milk—shouldn't be used as the agent of death.

Yonah replied, "They kill the cow for the burger. With or without cheese, that's not compassionate. But why can't you have milk with chicken? They aren't mammals."

"The rabbis said, 'What if a person walking down the street looks into your house and sees a glass of milk next to a platter of chicken? From that distance, the chicken could easily be mistaken for lamb chops, and the neighbor would think you're breaking the law.'"

"That's stupid."

"It's tradition. And *kashrut* has done more than just about anything to keep the Jews together for over 2,500 years."

"If a tradition is stupid, they should get rid of it."

"The people who keep kosher don't think it's stupid."

From *kashrut* we went to the historicity of the Bible and the first extra-biblical evidence of the ancient Israelite kingdom: a small, ivory pomegranate inscribed with "Of the House of David" dated around 750 BCE. Yonah asked, "Since David was the big Jewish hero and had lots of wives, what's wrong with polygamy?"

I couldn't give him a biblical answer, for many biblical figures were polygamous. I gave him the standard Jewish response about how each person is half a soul. One finds his other half-soul and they become whole. I also gave him a sociological answer about keeping the masses happy. If powerful men could keep harems, then those who didn't have the economic means would rise up and society would crumble.

I said, "The sexual needs men once sated through multiple wives are now met through prostitutes, pornography, and extramarital affairs, none of which are condoned by American society."

Yonah replied, "Do you think an atheist could be president if he ran against an adulterer?"

❧

The first building in Pittsburg, Kansas, was a humongous sporting goods store. Five aisles of fishing lures, two aisles of camouflage clothing from boots to hats, elk urine up the wazoo, and over two hundred green containers of Coleman fuel. Hoping I had missed the MSR bottles, I asked the proprietor who was price-stamping a gross of camouflaged socks. "Sorry," he said, and then upon reflection offered, "You know, a lot of you bike fellows ask for it." Then he returned to his socks.

The day had taken out two more of Yonah's spokes, so we got a diagnosis at the bike shop.

"You need a rebuild," Roger, the owner/mechanic, told us.

"How long will it take?"

"Well, I'm going to close soon. It's about a two-hour job."

"Tomorrow morning then?"

"Well, I'm going to a funeral tomorrow morning."

"Oh, I'm sorry. [Eight seconds of mourning] Noon?"

"Let's see. I could take it apart tonight and probably have you on the road by noon."

[Brainstorm!] "Hey, you don't have any already built wheels?" [Every bike shop I've ever been in does!]

"No."

"What if I just bought a bunch of spokes and replaced them as necessary?"

"It's up to you, but I wouldn't. You bust a spoke on the cassette side and that's it. There isn't another bike shop for three hundred miles."

Had I been a mature man, I would have smiled the smile when you realize no matter how hard you try, you are not in control. Besides, in eighty years of life, what's a half-day delay? At least it wasn't my funeral he was attending. But I wasn't mature; I was antsy and resentful. Though biking had slowed me down, I still hurtled through life at a pace considerably faster than we were created or evolved to travel.

We left the bike with Roger and found a hotel where the East Indian desk clerk was reading the *Hindustan Times*. Later we had a family debate over the soon-to-be-released last book in the *Harry Potter* series. The proposition was: The Biers-Ariel family should purchase the book. Arguing for the affirmative were Yonah, Solomon, and Djina. Their case was pure pathos: "Are you kidding? *Of course* we're getting it!"

I countered with facts and logic. "Djina, if you remember when we shopped for equipment at REI, you insisted on the titanium pots in order to save two grams of weight. We paid a hundred and twenty dollars more for a tent when you said, and I quote, 'You laugh, Matt, but every ounce counts.' And now you have no problem getting a nine-hundred-page, eleven-pound book because it will be me who will carry it. Ha!" Following the great American tradition, when reason faces emotion at the line of scrimmage, reason gets knocked to the ground and trampled on.

The next morning was spent killing time, waiting for the bicycle shop to open. We arrived at 11:45 thinking conscientious Roger would be there early, finishing the wheel. By 12:15 I was pacing the parking lot sending out strong telepathic messages to Roger to get his butt to work. Solomon didn't resort to telepathy to let me know that he could have stayed at the hotel to watch two more episodes of *SpongeBob*. Roger arrived at 12:30, but the hub, spokes, and rim, instead of congregating together in one happy wheel, were splayed over his work bench.

Roger, reading my clenched jaw, assured me it wouldn't be long. But I knew better. Whenever a preacher opens with, "I've only a word or two to say," it's time to slip off the shoes. Had I needed a knee replacement, we would have been on the road faster. To be fair, Roger was an excellent mechanic but easily distracted. Though there appeared to be three employees on payroll, he personally attended to each customer.

"Roger, I can't decide if I want a mountain or road bike."

"Well, there are advantages and disadvantages to both. Here let me get out the catalogs and we can look through together . . . "

A young boy came to buy an inner tube. Fifteen minutes later, he left with a new tube and a list of five things to prevent future flats.

Instead of salivating, I cringed when the front doorbell sounded. "Roger," I said at 4:00, while he was painstakingly truing the wheel, "don't worry about making the wheel perfect. He's not racing." For almost four hours, Roger the Zen master tried to teach his surly and stupid student patience. Finally, he gave up and put the tire on the wheel. Theoretically, there was enough light to get in forty miles to flee Pittsburg and enter Missouri. Alas, the lesson in patience was not finished. God needed to add a tutorial. Between the time Roger took the bike from the work stand and wheeled it to my outstretched fingers, the heavens opened up and—behold—there was rain. A great quantity of rain. Another-night-in-Pittsburg rain.

"The rain is the heavens crying with laughter at us," I announced.

"Right, Dad," scoffed Yonah.

"Well, at me anyway."

○■○:○■○:○■○:○■○:○■○:○■○:○■○:○■○:○■○:○■○:○■○

July 21, 2007, will be forever remembered as the day when the last installment of *Harry Potter* was available to purchase, and author J. K. Rowling overtook Germany as the world's fourth largest economy. A better question than how many books were sold would be: Who *didn't* buy one? Reporters parachuted deep into the Amazon to witness a blow-gun fight between elders of the last remaining pygmy tribes about whether or not Snape would ultimately be a good or bad guy. Tea houses throughout Nepal's Himalayan region received books via yak express, and the space shuttle *Discovery* made a hastily planned trip to the International Space Station to deliver them. The only place on Earth, or in low orbit around Earth, where one was hard-pressed to find a copy of *Harry Potter and the Deathly Hallows* was in western Missouri. Towns on the route weren't large enough to support bookstores, so books, like pretty much everything else, could be purchased only at Walmart. And these particular Walmarts ordered books only for people who had preordered them. Sprite bubbled less and less with each passing Walmart.

As always, there was plenty of time to fill as we rode through endless cornfields. We played sports trivia. I always lost because my sports trivia knowledge ended in 1980. Question: "Which Hall of Fame Dodger pitcher refused to pitch the first game of the 1965 World Series because of Yom Kippur?"

Answer: "Dad, you asked that yesterday."

"He asks it every day."

We spoke at length about ethics and morals; specifically, should Barry Bonds be inducted into baseball's Hall of Fame. It was a split decision. Yonah—yes; Solomon—no.

"He's a great player," Yonah said. "Steroids weren't illegal when he took them. They shouldn't even be illegal."

"He cheated and lied," Solomon replied.

At 5:30 PM we arrived in Ash Grove, Missouri, after a respectable day of seventy-two miles. The beginning of the Ozarks were ahead, but the tyranny of the majority forced me into thirty more miles of steep grades on what the ACA maps euphemistically call "self-propelled roller coasters." The grades were the steep 3-mile-per-hour kind, but they were short. Usually no more than a few hundred yards up, then 40 miles per hour down. Then back up. Then back down. Curses. Cheers. Curses. Cheers. Repeat for miles. We only needed two gears: first and twenty-first.

Solomon felt the need to practice using his dog whistle. I didn't mind except when we were doing one tough, muscles-bulging, veins-popping, sweat-cascading climb, and then one-foot-behind-me Solomon cheerfully kept time to our cadence with his whistle, like a coxswain urging his oarsmen. I prayed for a prehensile tail to burst forth from my tailbone and slap the whistle from his lips.

Yet another unanswered prayer.

At mile eighty, Solomon invented a new annoyance. He debated with himself about which TV shows were the best versus which had the best theme songs. Here is an almost verbatim transcript of the final twenty miles:

"*The Simpsons* is the best show followed by *SpongeBob* and *Fairly Odd Parents*. But *Fairly Odd Parents* has the best theme song. The question is can *Fairly Odd Parents* overtake *SpongeBob* for number two show. Best shows are number one *The Simpsons*, number two *SpongeBob*, number three *Fairly Odd Parents*, number four *Camp Laslo* . . . " Repeat until father numbed into semi-coma swerves into oncoming semi-tractor.

By now the sun had set, bike lights were on, and I was exhausted from the unrelenting Ozarks, whose motto is: "Our elevations never exceed eight hundred feet, but there ain't a single graded road in the whole darn range." There was no such thing as a road going around a mountain or over a saddle. All that was missing was a road sign proclaiming, "No dynamite was used in the production of this road." At this moment, Solomon, for the one-hundred-thirtieth time (extremely conservative estimate), exclaimed the superiority of the *Fairly Odd Parents* theme song. Without consulting me, my hand reached into my back pocket, found the pepper spray, and switched off the safety. Luckily, my free will was able to stop the terrorist digits before anyone was hurt.

"Daddy?"

"What?"

"What do you think?"

"I'm thinking about the 10-percent grade just ahead."

"*Fairly Odd Parents* has the best theme song, right?"

"Sprite, if you mention another TV show, I . . . will . . . kill . . . you."

It's amazing how you think your kids never listen to you, but when it counts, they do.

O▬O:O▬O:O▬O:O▬O:O▬O:O▬O:O▬O:O▬O:O▬O:O▬O:O▬O

After being available for two days, the number of *Harry Potter and the Deathly Hallows* books sold had overtaken the number of stars in the Milky Way, but Missouri was still a black hole. Both boys bemoaned the fact that their friends knew Harry's fate after staying up forty-eight straight hours to read. During these two days, a silence descended across the globe as children turned their backs on Halo II and *The Simpsons* in favor of turning pages. I wasn't sad because we had yet to reach the tough stretch of the Ozarks. The longer I didn't haul a book whose heft made the Oxford Unabridged Dictionary look anorexic, the happier I'd be.

Missouri was lush with an artist's palette of wildflowers. Symphonic bird songs provided an endless concert. We even found a Mexican restaurant with chips. Missouri rocked! The map indicated camping at Bendavis. Turned out the campsite was a patch of grass behind a gas station that stood at a nondescript crossroad, perhaps a spot Robert Johnson might have met Lucifer. The gas station was closed for the night. We set up the tents ten feet from a very large, aboveground diesel tank. The liquid beneath the tank was iridescent. This, added to no bathroom, no water, and no food, made for a cranky evening. Yonah lost it when I asked him to do the dishes.

"I have no free time!" he bellowed.

I responded with Parent Lecture #17 on responsibility.

"Fine! Then I want privileges!"

"Okay. What do you want?" Eight seconds of thoughtful silence. "I want to be able to bug Solomon during his stupid dead animal ritual." Twenty-five hundred miles down. Thirteen hundred more to go. I was wrong. We desperately needed *Harry Potter*.

Red streaks of dawn illuminated the eastern sky when the first pickup truck pulled into the gas station. I felt vulnerable sleeping behind the gas station because we had not asked permission to camp, so we quickly packed the tents and leisurely strolled into the gas station pretending we'd been biking for an hour and had simply stopped for breakfast. If you've ever seen the nonchalance of a cat that falls off a chair and pretends nothing happened, that's how we entered, minus the crotch lick.

We got coffee and hot chocolate, and Djina ordered a plate of biscuits (without gravy). There were two booths adjacent to each other. The first was occupied by a quartet of cowboys, each with a large plate of biscuits smothered in gravy. We slid into the second. They paid us no mind and spoke about fence mending and cattle moving. The waitress set the plate of unadorned biscuits on our table. The animated cowboy talk stopped as suddenly as a lassoed calf hits the end of the rope. They surreptitiously glanced from Djina to her plate. "Gravy clogs my colostomy bag," she mumbled and dug in.

The Ozarks were different from what we had read in the blogs. True, the grades were steep, but they were short. True, the dogs were hungry for Spandex, but 95 percent of them were chained or locked up. True, there were run-down shacks and dilapidated mobile homes, but more often there were mowed lawns fronting well-kept houses. We expected the everyday sight of Clem rocking on his broken-down front porch, listening to "Dueling Banjos" out of his transistor radio, and shooting tin cans with his coon gun. Only once did we hear gunshots, and they appeared to be of small caliber and far away. On the whole, the blogs got the "Show-Me" State's mountains wrong.

Black oak and hickory provided some sun relief, though riding was still hot and humid. We arrived in Eminence, ground zero of the Ozarks. Being a popular tourist destination, Eminence had campgrounds; we found one that sat on Jack's Fork southern bank. It was twenty acres of lawn punctuated by majestic black oaks, melodious meadowlarks, and ubiquitous trash. Showers were fifty cents for four minutes. The shower heads had either been stolen or considered too much luxury, so it was warm water from a pipe in the wall. To prevent further theft, every roll of toilet paper was marked on the side with an "x" from a fat-tipped, permanent marker. Another aspect of the campground was the brigade of ATVs sporting large Confederate flags slaloming through the campsites.

So the campground wasn't Yosemite. So the most delicious food of the day was a dry biscuit breakfast. So we were traveling through an area where Abe Lincoln shared the same pantheon as Judas. None of this mattered because we found a copy of *Harry Potter* in Houston's Walmart! As with the other Walmarts, we burst in and breathlessly wrangled the first employee with "Do you have *Harry Potter*?" Bracing for the usual "Sorry," I was unprepared for, "There were a couple of copies when we opened." The boys didn't bother to hear their location. They took off like a pair of Jedi certain that if the book was somewhere in the multimillion-item Walmart, The Force would lead them to it. Within three minutes they returned holding it aloft like the Stanley Cup. It was heavier than I thought it would be.

"Weigh it?" the cashier asked, as if nobody had ever made such a request.

"Please."

Two pounds, six ounces. Heavier than a sleeping bag. Heavier than titanium pots and utensils wrapped in a sleeping bag. But at this point, the sleeping bag would be jettisoned first. (And if there was a vote, mine would have been voted off the trailer.) I shoehorned the book into a pannier and left the ibuprofen at the top for easy access.

BICYCLE MINISTRIES

13

IMAGINE YOU OWN a waterbed. Now imagine your best friend plays a prank and cracks open the valve while you're asleep. You sleep through it and wake to discover you're on a leaky raft. That was how dewy Day Forty-Eight in Eminence, Missouri, began. The tents collected enough water to fill water bottles. The sleeping bags were saturated sponges; our clothes were post-washer, pre-dryer damp. We wrung everything out, stuffed the wet tents and bags, and ate a cold breakfast. The boys wanted hot cocoa, but there was no fuel. Even Solomon cursed MSR and then gave himself a checkmark. A cool, wet morning without a hot beverage combined with a flat on the trailer made for perfect fighting conditions. Yonah made fun of one of Solomon's rituals, and soon Dueling Screams reverberated through the hills. I did some stupid, insensitive guy-thing (no idea what), and Djina and I went at it. The ATV guys peeked from their RVs to see if the ruckus called for rifles or only pistols.

The ACA map warned of steep hills for the first five miles out of Eminence. Since you are tired of me whining about steep grades, I'll only say that we were moving so slowly, the turtles were afraid *we'd* get squashed by the trucks and tried to move us out of harm's way. The hills somewhat eased, and we arrived at the 21 Diner for a midafternoon meal, spreading the morning's wet gear on the lawn before going in. A couple in their mid-sixties sat in the next booth. We exchanged pleasantries and they signed the petition. The guy was a rancher who came to the 21 Diner for its burgers.

"They must be good," I ventured.

"None better."

"I'm a tofu man myself," I started, "but if a rancher says the burgers are good, I'll try one." And just like that I was standing with Darth Vader on the dark side. True, I had snuck some of Djina's buffalo jerky, and I "helped out" Solomon when he couldn't finish a chicken burrito. But a hamburger is a different animal. It's the real deal. It's uber-American. Ingest one and you can no longer claim the mantel of "vegetarian."

The last burger I ate was in Reagan's first administration. But if you're going to sin, go big. "Make it a cheeseburger." Take that, *kashrut*. "And add a shake. Large. And fries. Don't bother draining the grease. Yonah, want to join me?"

"I'll have a grilled cheese."

For years I was a true believer in vegetarianism with a panoply of reasons: kindness to animals, meat uses significantly more resources to grow, and it is carbon dioxide heavy. (A pound of beef generates about a hundred times the amount of greenhouse gases as a pound of carrots. According to the United Nations, livestock raised for food cause more emissions than the total from cars, buses, and planes combined. Turns out one of the best things one can do to stop global climate change is to become a vegetarian.) There is even biblical precedent. God allowed Adam and Eve only a vegan diet. As a vegetarian, I smugly stood on the Mount Everest of moral ground.

When asked why he was a vegetarian, Yonah could barely articulate, "I don't know, eating meat just doesn't seem right." In the end, it was the atheist who stuck to his moral compass while the believer's needle lost its magnetism. At the very least, I should have felt guilty—but I didn't. The epicurean experience of ingesting that slab of ground-up steer covered by melted curdled sour milk was sublime.

Rejuvenated, we continued to County Line Campground and Bar. Registration for the campground was in the bar. Though smoke was present in every bar and restaurant outside of California, think Killer London Fog of 1952 when you think of County

Line. Imagine King Kong rolling an entire tobacco field into a huge spliff, taking a deep drag, and exhaling into the room. But by Missouri, none of us gave it a second thought.

"Have any campsites?"

"Got thirty-two spots 'n only one oc-cu-pied."

"Are there showers?"

"Yes, sir, but take 'em quick. Warm water runs out fast."

"Warm?"

"Yes, sir. 'Bout two years back the heater, she broke. Now we jus' run a line undergroun'. You got 'bout four minutes warm water."

"We'll take a spot, and I'd like a beer."

That Budweiser went down smooth and cold, a good 5 degrees cooler than the open-air showers. A hose from the ground led to two nozzles that dispensed cool water. Though the sun had set, the temperature was still above 90 degrees, and all we desired was the removal of the sweat, grime, and sunscreen paste. In situations like this, hot water is overrated.

●━○━○━○━○━○━○━○━○━○━○━○━○━○

Five miles west of Old Man River, the Ozarks ended, and we entered the Mississippi River Valley. A straight shot through corn and sorghum to the river was punctuated by a guy in a truck who blasted us with a handheld air horn as he passed us. I prayed the guy would get a flat, crash, or run out of gas. If any of the above happened and we were to somehow catch him, I wouldn't crow that he deserved what he got because he was a dickhead. Rather, I'd ask, "Did you suffer lack of parental love, or is it simply that you have a diminutive penis?"

Again God refused my entreaty.

Crossing the Mississippi, we entered Illinois and passed a coal train made up of hundreds of cars snaking through the corn-fields. It was a magnificent visual: the jet black cars through the emerald green fields under a cobalt blue sky. Magnificent until you thought about the carbon dioxide those cars represented. Sobering when you thought about how many wind farms would be needed to replace all that coal. There is no silver bullet to slay the carbon dioxide werewolf.

We found a large shade tree on the edge of a farmhouse lawn and ate lunch. Before our bread was out, the screen door swung open and an elderly woman stood with a plate of freshly cut tomatoes. Her husband followed and directed us to their well to fill our water bottles. He told us how God had blessed him all his life. God granted him healthy children and whenever he was troubled, God had answered his prayers.

Why had God answered him and not me? Obviously because I asked for stupid things. If I had asked for the important things in life—good job, great wife, wonderful kids—then God answered my prayers as well. I simply had the wrong expectations about prayer and took my actual blessings for granted. Yet even without speaking to him, the voice of Yonah entered my head: For every lucky person whom God has blessed, there is the person whose life God has cursed. If God is to be praised for the good, then it seems logical to curse God for the bad.

"Hold it right there," spoke my inner believer. "You can never understand God's mysterious ways. What *appears* bad often is not." This bromide is occasionally true but usually not. Even William Jennings Bryan would have difficulty making the case that the death of a child furthers God's plan. There is no reply a believer can give to an atheist about the capricious nature of God except that giving thanks for what is good in life feels good.

The religious couple invited us to their church for prayer and fellowship. Here was religion fueling goodness and providing meaning. It was an absolute in a world of relativism.

"Yonah," I asked after we respectfully declined and were on our way, "Wouldn't you like this kind of surety, to really believe in something?"

He thought a minute and then said, "Sure, I'd like to believe there is a God and the world has meaning. And I'd like to be the richest man in the world. But wishing for something doesn't make it true. It just gives false hope."

"For me," I said, "I would love to feel the comfort and surety of the believer, but I can't make that leap of faith."

"I guess we agree on something."

"In fact, I seem to have more and more doubt about religion. You might be partially responsible for that."

"You're welcome."

O═O⁗O═O⁗O═O⁗O═O⁗O═O⁗O═O⁗O═O⁗O═O⁗O═O⁗O═O⁗O═O

We stopped at a bar for cold drinks. Though it was early afternoon, there was not an empty stool at the bar, and they were not pounding down Sprite. But they were nice and interested in our trip. I prayed they'd stay at the bar long enough for us to get off that particular road. This time God was generous.

By spending 24/7 with your children, you learn a lot about them. I discovered that Sprite lies. One of my pet peeves was him not keeping his hands on the handlebars. If his hands were on the bars, there was a chance he'd be pedaling hard. But if his hands were fiddling with his iPod or stretched over his head, there wasn't much going into the power train. When the sun hit us from a perpendicular angle, I saw our shadow in profile. When his hands weren't where they were supposed to be, I'd tell him. He'd reply with incredulity and anger, "My hands are on!"

Unlike many of Solomon's rituals that faded away, his roadkill mourning ritual never abated. When I saw a dead animal first, I'd try to get it over quickly, "There's a dead armadillo run over by a car. That's sad." Usually he'd accept this abbreviated service as long as the eight seconds of silence was not compromised. When Yonah was nearby, the evil older brother would follow "That's sad" with "Breakfast!" and all hell would break loose. So much for the maturity that was supposed to come with my elder son's rite of passage.

Though there were still a thousand miles left, the Appalachian Mountains, reputed to be the toughest grades on the route, stood in our path. And it was hotter and muggier each day. And though *Harry Potter* helped, it wasn't enough. I felt we *could* physically make D.C. I wasn't sure mentally we *would*.

In Carbondale, Illinois, we stopped at a bicycle shop to get Djina a new tire and ask about a thirty-mile shortcut recommended by other cyclists. We wound up on a wide-shouldered highway, but it wasn't only Yonah who was ecstatic. We all needed a break from the grades before taking on the Appalachian Mountains. With a flat road and a strong tailwind supplemented by trucks passing at 80 miles per hour, we sailed along at over 13 miles per hour. Unfortunately, Djina's brand new tire found a shard of glass that cut out a hunk. Over 2,500 miles on her old tire, no problem. Fifteen miles on a new thirty-five-dollar tire and it's ruined. Random chance?

Yonah: "What else could it be?"

Me: "Maybe God doesn't want us to take shortcuts."

Sprite: "Dad, you should see a psychiatrist."

Me: "You should put your hands on the handlebars."

Sprite: "You're seeing a mirage. You need help."

After checking into a Harrisburg hotel, we ate at a Mexican restaurant. Unlike California, where smoking in a restaurant is a capital crime, most eateries along the route had smoking and nonsmoking sections. This particular restaurant was divided by a large sign *"Fumar/No Fumar."* Under the *no-fumar* half of the sign was a booth where a young mother and her two toddlers sat. Sharing one wall of the *no-fumar* booth was a second booth. This one was under the *fumar* half of the side. The four adults occupying it were *fumar*ing. A cloud of thick smoke engulfed both booths. Everyone happily ate.

At home, Shabbat dinner is an important family function. We are not like Orthodox Jews who, with songs, prayers, and Torah study, celebrate the finishing of Creation. We observe Shabbat partly because time is amorphous, and the marking of each week gives the happy illusion of order. Mostly Shabbat is a time for the family to be together. On this trip, Shabbat was not necessary for a gathering of the clan, but it gave us the opportunity to check off another four hundred miles and share stories of the week.

"The best part was the shortcut," Yonah said. "I want to stay on the highway the rest of the way." Though this was Yonah's rite of passage, and though he was the navigator, Djina and I wanted to follow the bike maps and take the back roads as planned. True, Yonah's idea was not without merit, but Djina and I laid down our trump card. We were the parents. Discussion over. Shabbat Shalom.

Not one but two toilets overflowed at this particularly bad hotel that I will refuse to name in order to prevent a libel suit. But if you are ever in Harrisburg, Illinois, think twice about the hotel that has a one-digit number on its yellow sign. Though we did eat a lot the night before, the double clogging was not our fault. The suction on the toilet in the hotel room sucked. No convenient plunger stood behind the bowl, so the front desk sent the maintenance man. He said, "Don't worry, this happens all the time. We're planning on fixing the plumbing soon." Great, I thought as my morning constitutional was revving its engine. I knew it would be another no go for the feeble toilet, so I hurried downstairs to the restroom adjacent to the office. Alas, the outcome was the same. I stupidly tried to flush a second time and was forced to evacuate as the flood waters breeched the levee.

Not to be outdone by the toilets was the SuperStart breakfast consisting of Wonderbread, fake butter, jam, weak coffee, and doughnuts with a coating the texture and taste of brown plastic.

It was Shawneetown for Second Breakfast. The thermometer outside the market read 91 degrees. Inside, cash registers were manned by clerks bundled in sweaters and hats. As with many American buildings, the difference between the exterior temperature and the air-conditioned interior was vast, in this instance, over 25 degrees. At the Harrisburg hotel, the room temperature more closely resembled an autumn day in North Dakota than July in Illinois. These air conditioners were the equivalent to hunting quail with one-ton bombs. Not only was it overkill, not only was it unhealthy, but had that cheapskate hotel turned its thermostat to 72, it could have fixed its toilets, installed a waffle iron, and still come out ahead. The amount of energy needed to cool American buildings to 62 degrees instead of to 72, when the ambient temperature is 91, is the equivalent Btus we import from a certain Middle Eastern country where we brought about a regime change in the not so distant past.

An erstwhile American vice president once remarked: "Conservation may be a sign of personal virtue, but it is not a sufficient basis for a sound, comprehensive energy policy." Hitler's belief that he could beat the Soviet Union in the winter was equally wrong, for conservation is the single best way for us to decrease our country's carbon footprint. Period. Exclamation point. Checkmark.

Conservation is more than just installing compact fluorescent lightbulbs and turning down the air. Those are no-brainers. Real conservation calls for behavior modification. For example, why drive a car three miles to the store when a bike could do the same? A bike takes longer, but in terms of energy usage, it's the mature option. Practically every summer day in Davis is over 90 degrees, yet one sees few laundry lines in this environmentally conscious city. People use the gas clothes dryer because they don't have time to hang the laundry. Perhaps that should be a litmus test. If one doesn't have time to hang clothing when it's 90 degrees, it's time to reexamine the schedule. Technology allows us to teleconference across the globe, so even though it is nice to travel to see old friends and colleagues, airplane travel for business or conferences should be discouraged.

Besides the inconvenience in shifting our lifestyles, there are two problems with conservation. First, it is voluntary. To capture conservation as an energy source, we need to tax carbon consumption. A lot. And before you know it, the July run on down parkas in Dallas will decline. Second, the conservation poster child is the tree-hugging, latte-drinking Sierra Cluber whom few want to emulate. Instead of posters of earnest-looking Al Gores in flannel shirts explaining how biking one mile prevents one pound of carbon dioxide from going into the atmosphere, print us posters of *Playboy* vixens pinning lingerie onto the clothesline and screwing in compact fluorescent lights.

As we ate breakfast, coal truck after coal truck rumbled by, dumping their loads onto a humongous barge docked on the Ohio River. Besides being America's largest domestically produced energy source, coal is king of carbon dioxide emissions. Yearly premature deaths attributed to coal emissions is in the neighborhood of thirty thousand. That's ten 9/11s every year. Where's the umbrage? Why no outrage? Shouldn't we invade West Virginia?

Over the Ohio River and into Kentucky. The map indicated a bicycle hostel at the Sebree First Baptist Church. When we pulled into the church driveway, the minister shepherded us into the youth lounge where hot showers and a fully-equipped kitchen awaited. There were canned foods and books for the taking. (Had there been MSR fuel bottles, I would have considered baptism.)

For the first few years of the TransAmerica route, bicyclists camped at the Sebree City Park. But one summer, the park was closed and cyclists unfurled their sleeping bags on the lawn of First Baptist. The minister and his wife not only welcomed these hungry, ripe-smelling travelers, but when they remodeled the church, they made sure to include a shower for cyclists and allowed them to sleep in unoccupied rooms. For thirty years they have been running their bicycle ministry.

The church youth set up a huge slip-and-slide and invited us to join them. A small posse of teenage girls surrounded Djina, sensing in her both empathy and a powerful, self-assured woman that they could aspire to be. They told her what it was like to be poor farm kids. They asked her about travel. They knew another world existed, and they wanted to live it, as the cyclists did. Djina empathized with them, sharing her own dissatisfaction with her teen life. She spoke about not accepting her fate and fighting to create a life that she was proud of. She challenged the girls, telling them that even if they lacked the resources, they could make the lives they wanted if they had the fire.

The Sebree First Baptist was the first church we saw up close. The well-tended church was community center, movie theater, day care, counseling provider, and pretty much everything else. The church was the town rock and source of pride. Even an atheist could recognize the beauty of this.

○■○:○■○:○■○:○■○:○■○:○■○:○■○:○■○:○■○:○■○:○■○

The Tooth Fairy, the Easter Bunny, Hanukkah Harry, Santa Claus, Ken Giles. Sensing our need for one more recharge, Ken flew to Kentucky with supplies. He called from the airport: "I'll meet you somewhere around Utica. I'll be driving a white Carbon Footprint." When he drove up, I experienced the cognitive dissonance of being joyful at seeing a large SUV. More miraculous than a magician pulling a rabbit out of a hat, Ken produced French bread, cheese, chocolate, a cooler of Gatorade, peaches, and—yes, Virginia, there is a Santa Claus—imported beer.

Ken loaded Solomon, Djina, Djina's bike, and the gear into the Footprint and drove to the Rough Falls campground. Yonah and I, now unencumbered by *Harry Potter* and peanut butter jars, flew for forty-five miles with a tailwind. I suggested to Yonah that some people might construe Ken's presence and the tailwind as evidence of divine intervention.

"If we chalk this up to God, should we blame Satan for the gas station at Bendavis?"

"I didn't say I believe it. I said some people."

"You used to believe it. Remember when The Beast broke down next to the bike store, and you said it was evidence of God?"

"I never said that."

Ken gifted us a backpacking stove that ran on unleaded gas, and the ill-fated MSR stove returned home with him. We made pasta primavera and had a dinner guest. A young woman in the adjacent campsite had been cycling alone for a month living off ramen and peanut butter. When she beheld the four-course meal of cheese, pasta, chocolate, and beer, she claimed divine intervention. "It's good to play Santa Claus to you folks who never get Santa," Ken said.

The only sore point of the day was that The Beast, who had behaved so well for so long, resented the attention Ken gave us, so it decided to go flat in the rear. After I changed tubes, it would not let me properly adjust the drum brake due to its increasingly fraying cable.

The next morning Yonah, Solomon, and I rode the bikes. Ken and Djina packed up the Carbon Footprint and headed for a town called Abraham Lincoln Birthplace. Djina needed a day to catch up on her blog, so she found a McDonald's with WiFi and spent the day sipping iced tea and blogging on Ken's laptop. A word on iced tea. The *habañero* is the hottest chile pepper, measuring about three hundred thousand on the Scoville heat scale. In comparison is *cayenne*, weighing in at forty thousand heat units, *jalapeño* a measly four thousand. In the South, you have two choices for iced tea: sweetened or unsweetened.

Sweetened tea is the *habañero* of sweet drinks. Mountain Dew with enough sugar to put Sprite in low orbit around Earth is a ninety-pound weakling compared to sweetened iced tea. "I grew up on the stuff," Ken said. "My advice is 70/30 mix, unsweetened to sweetened."

While Djina blogged, Ken backtracked on Djina's bike to meet us. The boys and I continued east past lawns sprouting plastic animals and statues of angels. Solomon was curious about two statues—one a man, the other a woman—which seemed to adorn every other lawn.

"That would be Jesus and Mary." Then it was "Look! There's Jesus!" and "Did you see Mary!" for every single Jesus and Mary statue in Kentucky. Solomon's rituals morphed in my subconscious and at random moments, thoughts such as, "Was that Mary killed by a car?" popped into my head.

Besides wanting to know about Jesus and Mary, Solomon wanted the facts on Satan. I gave him the Jewish version. Satan is not the Devil. He isn't even a fallen angel. He's God's adversary. Satan is in the book of Job. God was ecstatic with this guy Job because Job always praised God and sent up tasty sacrifices. God said, "What do you think of Job? He's the best."

Satan yawned. "He's rich. He's got seven sons and three daughters. Of course he praises you. Let me make things tough for him, and he'll curse you."

"No way."

"Way."

"Bet."

"Bet."

The wager was on, and after Satan gave Job a serious case of boils, Satan proved to be the better judge of human nature. The author(s) who redacted the Bible didn't think it proper that such an important book as Job would open the theodicy problem, so a final chapter was added wherein Job returns to his faith, and God returns Job's health, children, and possessions. It was a cheap theological shot that ruined a perfectly good story.

We later met up with Ken, rode to McDonald's, bought fries, 70/30 iced teas, and used surprisingly little local anesthesia during the surgery to remove Djina's fingers from Ken's laptop.

The Nancy Lincoln log cabins overlook the building housing the log cabin that Abe Lincoln was born in. Had Abe been born in one of the four Nancy Lincoln cabins, he would have been mighty happy, for these log cabins are equipped with electricity, running water, and soft sheets. From our porch, an expansive lawn swept downhill and back uphill to a mausoleum-like edifice of classical architecture. Inside the building stands Abe's reconstructed birthplace.

Well, actually, no. Two ironies here. One, the cabin is not the actual Lincoln cabin; it disappeared over a hundred years ago. Two, the history lesson about Honest Abe rising from humble origins to become president is utterly defeated by the marble edifice. Nevertheless, the cabin was worth seeing.

Next door is a museum that holds the Lincoln family's actual Bible on display. Or so we were told. Interesting note: While it is true that Lincoln was a voracious reader as a child, his reading list was quite short. There weren't any libraries at the edge of the frontier where he lived, and his internet only had dial-up access, which was way too slow to download books. What Lincoln read was the Bible, a smattering from The Bard, and *Aesop's Fables*. He read these books multiple times. One fable that remained with him was "The Lion and the Three Bulls." The lion wanted to eat a bull, but the three bulls stuck together and the lion couldn't attack. One day the bulls got in a fight and went their separate ways. The lion was then easily able to kill them one at time. The moral learned by the boy and repeated fifty years later by the president: "United we stand, divided we fall."

The landscape became more and more lush while the dawn and dusk bird-and-bug chorus sounded richer and richer. While Djina and I marveled at the beauty, Yonah pored over the maps looking for shortcuts. Rerouting had already saved us seventy-five miles—a full day—but Yonah wanted more.

"Don't you want to see the picturesque churches and rolling hills of forests?"asked Djina.

"Are you kidding? Look, if we take this road we can save ten miles."

"But it's a highway."

"If we had taken Highway 50 from Sacramento, we'd be in Washington by now," Yonah pronounced in disgust.

Djina and Solomon stayed at Nancy Lincoln's cabin where she could blog and he could read *Harry Potter*. Ken, Yonah, and I rode. At mile twenty, Ken backtracked to the cabin. There they loaded up the Footprint and met us at the Bardstown library, where we bid goodbye to Ken.

○═○╷○═○╷○═○╷○═○╷○═○╷○═○╷○═○╷○═○╷○═○╷○═○╷○═○

Solomon began a new annoyance that I stopped before it became ritualized. I wondered why he was so quiet that morning. The answer was that he was thinking about what new behavior would most likely get on my nerves. "He hates it when I stand when he's drinking water. I like when his face turns all blotchy red. But it's kind of dangerous. There's the taking my hands off the handlebars routine, but now he ignores it. The 'I see Jesus on their front lawn' gives him an excuse to bore me with religion. Even *I'm* sick of ranking TV shows. I got it! This will be great!"

We were straining up a medium hill, and I felt a tap-tap on my back. "Solomon, (wheeze) what do you (wheeze) want?"

"Nothing."

"Why'd you (wheeze) tap me?"

"I didn't."

Perhaps I imagined it. But thirty minutes later there it was again. "Stop tapping!"

"I'm not!"

"Stop it!" Our shadow was riding side-by-side with us, so the next time he did it, I caught him. When he denied it, I said, "Don't lie. I saw you."

"Well, it's your fault for sitting too far back on the seat!"

"If you do it again, you will never see your tenth birthday!"

"I'm not talking to you anymore!"

"Good! And stop tapping!"

Six hundred and seventy-five more miles. Six hundred and seventy-five miles including double black diamond grades in the

Appalachians sharing roads with coal trucks that had pictures of cyclists painted on their doors to show the number forced off the road. Six hundred and seventy-five miles of dogs whose owners were still sore about the Civil War. Six hundred and seventy-five miles of a heat that could make the Greenland ice shelf melt in a day.

On Day Fifty-Five, after 3,100 miles on the back of a tandem, the nine-year-old boy was finished, kaput, done. His brother wasn't doing any better. Besides wanting to reroute the rest of the trip onto the interstate, he suggested cycling nights as well. They were sick of days that consisted of waking up at 6:00 AM, wolfing down a crappy breakfast, riding sixty miles in a sauna, eating a crappy dinner, and going to sleep. They were physically, emotionally, and spiritually pooped. Had the bikes spontaneously combusted, they would have cheered.

I found a bike shop where I hoped a mechanic could provide enough life support for The Beast to last until D.C. The owner of Danville Bike fixed the demon drum brake and gave The Beast a complete physical. "Look at this," he called to his assistant and pointed at the middle chain ring. "You don't see these anymore." Apparently the chain ring was a Biopace. Invented in the mid-1980s, the Biopace, with its elliptical shape, was supposed to lessen the dead space when the front crank was horizontal to the ground. Alas, while it worked for slow rpms, it didn't at higher rpms. By 1988, the Biopace was more extinct than the prairie chicken. I had never noticed it because you'd have to be more sensitive than the Princess with her pea to feel the infinitesimal change a Biopace would have on the weight of The Beast. Given The Beast's other oddities, it would have been more surprising if it *didn't* have a Biopace.

While Yonah and I were at the bike shop, Djina and Solomon went to the library. After The Beast's makeover, we picked them up, though it wasn't easy.

"Just five more minutes," Djina pleaded. Djina's mind operates near the speed of light; therefore, time is slower for her. Five minutes for her is thirty by an atomic clock.

"No, we've still got mileage."

"But . . . but," she stammered for the right words, "*blogo ergo sum!*"

"'I blog therefore I am'?"

"Two more minutes, I promise."

Twenty minutes later we were on the road and passed Kentuckian after Kentuckian engaged in the popular pastime of riding sit-on lawnmowers. Surrounding the houses were vast expanses of lawn. A sweat-powered push mower couldn't cut it here. It'd be easier to paint the Taj Mahal with a toothbrush.

As Anonymous once said, he who lives in a glass house shouldn't throw stones, and a grown man wearing a fluorescent-green jersey bicycling in triple-digit weather should not be laughing at anyone, but the sight of middle-aged women astride their lawn mowing steeds, one hand on the wheel, the other clutching a cigarette . . .

We arrived in Berea, Kentucky, at 7:00 PM, but it took an hour to check into a motel because Djina had to sample the wares of each and every one. Guys and gals are built with different blueprints. Guys take the first place that has beds, TV, and breakfast featuring a pink doughnut box. It is the second x-chromosome that contains the "Goldilocks" gene. When walking into a restaurant, a gal surveys the room, calculates which table has the best feng shui, and finagles her way to it. If she's with a guy, he'll do an eye roll, but he better do it out of her sight. Whether he eye rolls or not, she will make him agree that the new table is better. I suppose there were times when I was a kid that my mother didn't make us change tables at a restaurant. I just can't remember any.

So it was with motels. Djina declined motels with pools, breakfast buffets, and comfortable beds. In my impatience, I blundered by offering what I thought was an accurate insight: "You're just like my mother!" Motel after motel we marched right in and then back out. And then came the Berea Hampton Inn. It had an indoor pool with Jacuzzi, a clean room, breakfast buffet with waffle iron, and a computer hooked up to the internet for guest use. "Don't you agree this is the best one?"

The truth was, Djina had vetted the hotels for a single criterion: the best blogging spot. If the Hampton was out of beds, she would have proclaimed, "We'll throw our sleeping bags on the ground!" No shower or toilets? "We'll hose each other down and pee in the bushes!"

She climbed into bed at 2:30 AM.

KILLING TIME
BETWEEN IRONIES

14

BEREA IS "GATEWAY to the Appalachia Mountains." We took a rest day to steel ourselves for this surliest of American mountain ranges. Every blog warned us that the roads through the Appalachians were pot-holed, driveway-wide, steeply graded, and populated by NASCAR-wannabe coal-truck drivers. One blog ominously reported, "If the Rockies are kindergarten, the Appalachians are a post-doctorate fellowship."

Yonah wanted to continue an earlier conversation about Satan. "I don't get it," he said. "If Jesus needed to die for Christian theology to work, you know, his death cleans Christians' sins, then why do they think Judas is bad?"

The day before, I mentioned that at the center of Dante's Hell sat Lucifer munching away on Judas's bones ad infinitum.

"I mean, if Judas didn't give up Jesus, there's no Christianity."

Yonah had a point, and I said, "Without Judas, Jesus continues his life gathering disciples, making miracles here and there, and dies a wise old man. He might even be remembered as a prophet, but none of the Son of God, dying for our sins business. So rather than punishing Judas, are you saying that they should make him a saint?"

"Exactly." If Judas had Yonah Biers-Ariel as his lawyer, he would have gotten off with a five-year sentence in Purgatory.

Thinking this might be his last good buffet breakfast for awhile, Yonah loaded up. Japanese tourists took pictures of his sumo wrestler portions. "Why he not fat like other Americans?"

they inquired and made a list of all he ate. "That fifth or sixth waffle?" Okay, I made the tourist bit up, but could that boy eat!

The Appalachians were interspersed with tobacco plots between hardwood forests. Clouds moving through the mountains gave the ride a mystical feel. The lushness and beauty made Djina's eyes well up. She reminded me of Doodle from James Hurst's "The Scarlet Ibis." Doodle was a housebound young boy who was so overcome at being in nature for the first time, that all he could do was murmur, "It's so pretty, so pretty."

It was Sunday and the coal trucks were observing the Sabbath. To top off a lovely ride, the grades weren't too steep and the downhills were fun. Solomon felt the need to give me a complete account of every cartoon he watched in Berea. At first I didn't mind, for I was happy that he was pedaling with power as he spoke. But after a while, I resented that the retellings were drowning out the songbirds.

"Solomon," I said gently, "You don't need to tell me everything from the show. Just tell me the important parts."

"But it's all important or they wouldn't have put it in. Right?"

Sigh.

"So then SpongeBob said to Crabby, who was wearing a funny apron with green stains on it. Actually, the stains were lots of colors, but mostly green . . . "

About a mile outside of Booneville, rain clouds descended. Djina and the boys stopped at the library, and I went for groceries. Finding no beer, I asked the cashier if it was in a different store or if they didn't sell liquor on Sundays.

"Hon, this here's a dry county."

"So people go to the next county, buy beer, come back, get drunk, and throw the empties on the roadsides?"

"That's right, hon. Did you find everything else you needed?"

Like Sebree's First Baptist, Booneville's Presbyterian Church was bicycle friendly. Behind the church, they built a covered shelter for cyclists. Attached to the shelter was a shower. There was a well-tended lawn for tents. When the heavens burst open two minutes after our arrival, we were happy and dry. Darkness settled in and a cyclist arrived to share the shelter. Stephen, a mechanical engineering student from UC Berkeley, confirmed

Djina's theory of single male cross-country riders under thirty being cool, as he was smart, funny, and—according to Djina—cute. Despite riding 120 miles, he rose to Solomon's mano a mano obstacle course challenge around the tents and over a split rail fence. Though Stephen was faster, Solomon's low center of gravity and familiarity with the course (he'd run it at least ten times) forced Stephen to his VO$_2$ max to beat the nine-year-old.

All in all, we were impressed with this mature twenty-year-old. Especially when I recalled how I was at that age. Though I personally didn't light my farts on fire, my friends did. The only way Stephen let us down was that he didn't know the Cal drinking song. Yonah and Solomon happily filled this academic hole.

The farther into the Appalachians, the more lawn ornaments. Only a tropical reserve had more pink flamingos. Ceramic gnomes guarded Virgin Marys. A goose proudly flew a flag from its butt. Flags abounded. Sometimes Stars and Stripes, sometimes Stars and Bars, sometimes a mixed marriage—both flags flying side by side. It was an election year, and apparently Dexter Miller was popular, judging by the large number of signs proclaiming "Re-elect Dexter Miller, County Jailer."

"While other jailers allow you just a single phone call, I let you keep your cell phone. A cell in a cell. Ha-ha. And ladies, you can always send a cake to your dear ones. Just make it chocolate and remember to cut me a slice. And no saws please. Ha-ha."

Be it ramshackle trailer or well-groomed mansion, there were yard ornaments. However, it was only the trailers that hosted automobile monuments such as 1972 Chevy trucks and pre-Sputnik Ford vans. I imagine that one day all these vehicles will return to the earth. As they say, "Ashes to ashes, dust to dust, metal to ore." But how far behind can the rest of civilization be? How will the Earth look in five thousand years? In geologic time, it's not even a hiccup, but for a species that thinks a seventy-five-year-old building needs a plaque, five thousand years is forever. Will there still be cities? Countries? Will we be speaking one language, a combination of Chinese, English, and Twitter? Will there be peace and goodwill among the Earth's inhabitants, or will the world be suffering from the effects of disastrous climate change? Will we have conquered death through medical technology or by building back-up brains? Will we smash through the speed of light barrier and transport ourselves throughout the universe?

Whatever life is like in five thousand years, I hope—nay—pray there will be something akin to bicycles.

The people of Kentucky were friendly, though their accents were thick. Sometimes a guy would speak for ten seconds before it clicked, "Oh, English." The owner of one store kept a cycling registry that began with the 1976 Bikecentennial. Judging by this registry and the one we signed at the Sebree First Baptist Church, it seems that an average of fifteen hundred to three thousand cyclists cross the United States each summer on the TransAmerica route. With higher gas prices, I had expected the number to be on the rise, but the summer of 2007 looked to be slightly less than a thousand.

We stopped in Chavies for lunch and shared a shade structure with an eighty-three-year-old local. We steered the conversation to global warming. Even here at the mother lode of coal, this octogenarian realized that climate change was not a ploy of elite Yankees and latte-sipping West Coasters to destroy Kentucky's traditional way of life. He saw coal's problems and spoke of the need for the local coal economy to diversify. He signed the petition.

We camped at the Hindman City Park. Solomon was not happy about the "No Camping" signs, for under the tutelage of his parents, he was now a juvenile delinquent. Fortunately, pizza assuaged his guilt. It might be instructive to anyone contemplating a cross-country bicycle trek to examine the clothing situation at Hindman. First, shirts. We didn't take our jerseys off. We peeled them away from the sweat/sunscreen coating that acted like mild epoxy. After removal, we looked for a safe place to put them, for anything within a five-foot radius of the shirts would shrivel up and die quicker than the Wicked Witch of the West after Dorothy doused her with water. Okay, *that's* an exaggeration. The jerseys would not cause death. But someone silly enough to touch one would certainly never be able to reproduce. We put them on a table to dry overnight. Ha-ha. *That's* a joke. At 85 percent humidity, no matter what state of dryness or wetness the jerseys were in, by next morning they were clammy.

Socks. Socks were routinely put in the mesh part of the panniers to be traded for socks from the prior day. The prior day socks were just as dirty and smelly, but they had the advantage of having the sweat dry in them during the day. Since they were clammy by the morning, there was no advantage having a second pair. Both pairs smelled as though they had been washed in Stink-O laundry soap.

Cycling shorts. Suffice to say that Washington, D.C.'s HazMat squad would meet us at the Potomac and take it from there.

The good news about Hindman was that the flies didn't bother us. We stank too much, even for them.

○━○·○━○·○━○·○━○·○━○·○━○·○━○·○━○·○━○·○━○·○━○

A steady light rain fell as we continued through the Appalachians. No one complained, for we needed showers, and it was a respite from the heat. I had a quandary at the rain's onset: put the pasta in the dry pannier or not? I figured the rain would soon stop, so why bother pulling over. Twenty minutes later it was too late to save the pasta, so why bother pulling over. Quandary solved.

We entered the town Bypro for Second Breakfast. Dripping wet, we entered the air-conditioned restaurant whose ceiling fans kept the air conditioning circulating faster. Coffee and hot chocolate inoculated us against pneumonia. Solomon needed some brotherly interaction while we waited for biscuits and eggs.

Solomon: (sprightly) "Let's play the laughing game!"

Yonah: (sourly) "No."

Solomon: (emphatically) "C'mon!"

Yonah: (with anger) "No!"

Solomon: (hurt) "Why not?"

Yonah: (with exasperation) "Because you laugh at everything. It's not fun."

Solomon: (incredulous) "I don't."

Yonah: (really exasperated) "You do."

Solomon: (really incredulous) "I don't laugh at everything."

Yonah: (deep breath signifying ultimate exasperation) "Solomon, you laugh at everything."

Solomon: (innocently) "No I don't. I'm more mature now."
Djina and Matt laugh hysterically. Matt's coffee sloshes over
the rim. Yonah chuckles.
Solomon: (triumphantly) "I win!"

○━○:○━○:○━○:○━○:○━○:○━○:○━○:○━○:○━○:○━○:○━○

If you're a guy, you might be wondering why there is no mention
of sex in this book. If you're a gal, you know that after sweating like a horse for ten hours on a bicycle and then entering
a twenty-one-square-foot tent carpeted with not-washed-since-
June sleeping bags holds about the same sexual turn-on as
walking barefoot on live coals. Okay, but what about hotel rooms?
A Class 5 hurricane could smash through the windows, and the
boys would still be fighting over the remote. They wouldn't notice
anything. But we (read: Djina) didn't want to take chances. So
when we pulled into an Elkhorn City hotel and discovered each
room had only one double bed, I thought: "Two rooms! Djina and
me! Hot dog!"

"You sleep with Yonah, I'll sleep with Solly," Djina said.

"I figured they'd sleep together."

"In this dive? Are you serious? No way. Anything could happen. Someone could steal Solomon." Pause. "Don't you agree?"

She did have a point. Not about stealing Solomon, for after
regaling the kidnapper with tales from the Cartoon Network,
Solomon would be dumped in front of the hotel room with an
envelope stuffed with money and a note pleading to take him
back. No, she was right about the hotel's quality. No offense, but
when a hotel office is manned by a pair of men, and the first
who is in his fifties addresses the second as "Pa," the chances
that the hotel's motto being "cleanliness is next to godliness" is
slim. The rooms consisted of threadbare blankets, lingering sec-
ondhand smoke, and stained sheets that had successfully stared
down bleach since Prohibition.

Breakfast at the hotel's restaurant was biscuits, gravy, and
eggs, all of which were vehicles for generous portions of grease. A
truck pulled into a parking space next to the restaurant window.

The driver unsuccessfully tried to close his dented door five times before the latch caught. The truck's license plate frame read: God Answers Prayer.

"Maybe he should pray for a new door," I ventured.

"Maybe he should buy one," Yonah offered.

"Maybe he has more important things to pray for," Djina weighed in.

"Maybe it's not his truck," said Solomon the Wise and settled it.

The morning ride was laden with long, steep climbs that were difficult due to sore tummies. One climb was so long and steep, The Beast needed to pull over for a rest. Yonah, of course, needed no rest. He was atop the summit with enough time to both start and finish *Harry Potter*. He didn't though because that dumbbell was in my pannier.

The blogs were right about the coal trucks. They accelerated up the mountains to gain momentum so they could go faster on the downhills. There were no roadkills because anything hit by these monsters was instantly vaporized in the manner of E=mc2. Because these guys were paid by the load, not the hour, their incentive to wait for an appropriate place to pass a family of wispy bike riders in their fluorescent-green jerseys was nil. We didn't play games. The moment we heard them, we dismounted and moved off the road. Still, they were competent drivers and never went out of their way to cause us grief. The same could not be said for the driver of a large auto with a vanity license plate that read "BEULAH," who ran Djina off the road. Rather than run The Beast into a ditch as well, Beulah pulled up eight inches from us and yelled, "It ain't legal to ride here! Git off the road!"

After Beulah sped away, Solomon said, "Let's catch her! I want to ask her, 'Does it make you happy to hit and majorly injure someone?'"

"Solomon, you never catch these jerks. Remember the guy who blew his air horn at us? I prayed he'd get a flat."

"I'm going to pray harder. C'mon! Let's go faster." There was an atypical surge of power from the back, and soon we came to a town. Solomon practically jumped off the bike hollering, "There she is!" The Beast accelerated faster than a Ferrari, and we got close enough to yell "Beulah!" but she kept her eyes straight ahead, her hands at 10 and 2, and drove out of our lives forever. Beulah, if by some infinitesimal chance you are reading this, my son has a question for you.

Between Beulah, the climbs, and the coal trucks, the day was tough, but it ended on the happy note of another cycling ministry at the Rosedale Methodist Church. The rain held off until we were lodged safely under a large, covered patio. Though the minister was out of town, his wife made sure our stay was comfortable. Because of the rain, she insisted we sleep in the sanctuary. The sanctuary was intimate and beautiful, three pews wide and seven deep atop a luxurious, red carpet. Large silver goblets and ritual items made of precious metals and beautiful glass adorned the altar.

I found an extremely large Bible opened to the Book of Amos, the Hebrew prophet who castigated the Hebrews not for their lack of piety, but for their mistreatment of those in society who could not fend for themselves. Righteousness was what *Yahweh's* messenger demanded. Twenty-five hundred years later, his message still needs to be preached. Jews, forget that you're the "Chosen People." Christians, don't dwell on Jesus dying for your sins. Muslims, reciting "There is no God but Allah, and Muhammad is his messenger" isn't important. There are only two religious teachings we need: One, take care of the unfortunate. Two, treat others and the Earth with the same respect that you want to be treated. The rest is simply bells and whistles.

●━○┈○━○┈○━○┈○━○┈○━○┈○━○┈○━○┈○━○┈○━●

The minister's wife warned us that the climb out of Rosedale was one of the toughest in the country. "That's what the cyclists tell me," she said. She gestured at The Beast. "That's quite a load you've got. Good luck."

I thanked her for her hospitality and woke The Beast with a strong shove. I muttered, "No way can Sprite and I get this monster over a bump in the road, never mind a mountain." But we got on and pedaled once, which led to a second pedal and then to another, and I knew after thousands of pedals, we'd be over the mountain. I wonder how many things in life are like this.

A person confronts a tough task and cannot imagine doing it, saying, "No way. Impossible." And then he never even tries. But if you go for the seemingly impossible, just one pedal at a time, you can do it. Or not. But at least you tried. That's what counts because no one wants his tombstone to read, "He never tried."

Addendum to that earlier paragraph: Success also matters. If Solomon and I had to walk all the steep grades, we would have quit in the Sierras.

Solomon asked about Rolls-Royces; he wanted to see one.

"Probably the Appalachians aren't the best place to find one," I suggested.

"There! That's one, right?" he exclaimed pointing to a new generation VW Beetle.

"A Rolls is bigger."

The conversation shifted to status symbols and how people define themselves by their things. I told him the story of Tanqueray Gin as taught by my Econ 1 professor. When Tanqueray was first introduced into the US market, no one bought it. The company doubled the price and advertised Tanqueray as the "world's most expensive gin." Stores couldn't keep up with demand. "That, Solomon, is a status symbol."

"How about that one? It's big."

"It's a Buick."

Switching gears, Solomon wanted to know what Djina and I had against Walmart. "We got *Harry Potter* there. And you like their food."

"Not only that," I said, "but Walmart is doing something positive about global warming. They use energy-efficient lighting and are refiguring their transportation to save fuel."

"So why don't you like them?"

"Their prices put local stores out of business. That's part of the reason why so many small towns have dead Main Streets."

"But low prices are good."

I wanted to tell him about union busting and lack of environmental and labor laws in overseas factories, but that might have been too much for a nine-year-old. Anyway, we reached the top of the gnarly mountain, so I had two final words for him: "Hold on!"

The banked curves with recently paved asphalt made rolling down the mountain feel as though we were skiing in fresh powder. Had we cycled across America just to reach this single five-mile downhill, the trip would have been worth it. The land was lush forest and farm. The weather was cool and misty. The air was delicious. Even the deservedly maligned kudzu, the invasive scourge of the South, provided eye candy as it engulfed abandoned building after building. And not a single coal truck.

We stopped for Second Breakfast and spoke with a stereotypical Harley biker whose standard equipment included a denim jacket cut at the sleeves to allow unobstructed views of the assorted tattoos adorning his thick arms, a full score of teeth, and a belly to see him through lean times. His face lit up upon learning we were Californians. Had we heard of the Jesse James Motorcycle Shop in California? Apparently they are the Rolls-Royce of Harley customizing, and he wanted to make a hajj there. He showed us a shortcut. Yonah was ecstatic, but we were a day ahead of schedule, and the biking was so good that Djina and I nixed it.

When the biker left, a lone grandfatherly figure, sitting on our other side, cleared his throat. He'd been waiting to chat. We learned that he had fought in Vietnam with other farm boys and urban poor.

"You think that's who fights in all wars?" Yonah ventured.

"You bet. Lookit the Civil War. Most a us dint own no slaves. Was the rich men start that one. But we took most a the casualties. Ever hear a Robert E. Lee?"

"I've heard of him," Solomon piped up.

"Best general we or the Yankees had 'cause he was smarter 'n 'im, but also 'cause he cared 'bout his men. He was a *real* gentleman. They don't make 'im like that no more. Them crooks in Washington care only 'bout linin' their pockets. Cheney 'n Bush never went to 'Nam. Never seen war. They don't care 'bout people. Just 'bout their oil."

Though I agreed with him, I silently wagered a hundred bucks that *if* this guy voted, it was for Bush, twice.

THE BAR MITZVAH AND THE BEAST

Like cross-country cyclists, long distance hikers have well-known routes they travel. The Appalachian Trail is the granddaddy of epic American trails. In Damascus, the TransAmerica Bike Route crosses the Appalachian Trail. Bicyclists and hikers congregate at "The Place," a hiker/biker hostel built and run by the local Methodist Church. It's a two-story building with five rooms of bunk beds, a reading room stocked with books and games, a lawn where one can sun or relax under a large shade tree, and a box filled with stuff hikers and bikers no longer needed. We scored a few granola bars and a jar of peanut butter. Too bad we couldn't use the real prize. Six—count 'em six—full MSR fuel bottles. The majority of life is killing time between ironies.

There was a swimming hole three miles away in Tennessee, so we bagged another state. Yonah, the cat, tried to get away with dipping his big toe, but Solomon, the dog, splashed him so much, he eventually jumped in. Solomon wanted to jump from the cliffs with the locals, but a few years before, he had nearly killed himself when he slipped jumping from a twenty-five-foot cliff. (Yes, on my watch, why do you ask?) So Solomon had to be content with jumping from a one-meter rock.

Solomon finished *Harry Potter and the Deathly Hallows*, banged the cover shut, and announced, "Voldemort is like Hitler. Hitler wanted the Aryans to rule the non-Aryans, just like Voldemort wanted the 'purebloods' to rule the 'mudbloods.' Hitler didn't look Aryan and Voldemort wasn't a pureblood. They killed everyone who stood in their way."

"They lacked love as kids," Djina said. "They probably weren't breastfed."

"The biggest fanatics are insecure people who prove their devotion by going overboard," I added. "Just don't tell me the ending, or I'll have to kill you."

"Daddy's just joking about killing you," said Yonah. "But if you ruin the ending, I really will kill you."

AMERICAN HERO: HOMER SIMPSON OR THOMAS JEFFERSON?

15

DAY SIXTY-TWO WAS HOT and smoggy as we rolled into Virginia. We were expecting a phone call from KGO radio in San Francisco, which wanted to do a follow-up interview. I prepped Yonah. "They're going to ask you about the trip. For example, 'What did you learn?'"

Long pause. "Nothing."

Could it be that Yonah had cycled 3,500 miles across mountains and deserts, met hundreds of people, saw rural America up close, and learned nothing? Though he possesses an intelligence way to the right on the bell-shaped curve, by the summer of his thirteenth year, Yonah was not a reflective person. For him, the trip was simply an extreme physical challenge. He had met the challenge with panache. Perhaps that was enough.

The interviewer asked Yonah, "What has been a highlight of the trip?"

"The milkshake-to-vegetable ratio has been high. Also I like being in charge of the map. It's kind of a puzzle to figure out."

"Great. Next question: How has the trip changed you?"

Without hesitation, Yonah said, "I learned how my mind can control my body. I don't like biking. But I told my body to do it anyway."

"You don't like biking?"

"Not really."

"So you don't have fun riding, but would you say that biking across the country was worth it?"

"I guess so."

If the radio interview happened as we entered our next town, Christiansburg, Yonah probably would have given a different answer. I announced that we were camping and not staying in a hotel, because the inevitable TV conflicts sickened me. The boys vociferously disagreed.

"It's too hot to camp!"

"Our breakfast food stinks!"

"Whine all you want. We are camping." We passed five or six motels and arrived at Christiansburg's lone campground, close enough to the interstate to hear the cars' talk radio. We circled the gravel parking lot looking for the way to the lawn where we could pitch tents. We circled twice. There was no lawn. The gravel parking lot was the campground.

I cursed, Djina laughed, Solomon got the remote, Yonah his buffet breakfast.

○━○┃○━○┃○━○┃○━○┃○━○┃○━○┃○━○┃○━○┃○━○┃○━○┃○━○

The morning started with a fight over Cartoon Network versus *Court TV*. I unsuccessfully tried mediating with a patient voice and then quickly became stern high school teacher. That also failed, so I kicked the boys out of the room. Everyone's nerves were jangled. We needed vacations from each other.

Moods lifted with easy uphills and long downhills. There were rolling hills and enormous lawns interspersed with immaculate houses and a variety of tasteful lawn ornaments. A Norman Rockwell scene appeared. A mother and daughter, both tan and slender, sat on the front porch, enjoying the cool morning air. The girl was about ten, with her hair pulled back into a ribbon-adorned ponytail. She was fiddling with what appeared to be some needlework or knitting. The mother, with her perfectly coiffed hair, wore orange tennis shorts that matched an orange tube top. She was reading a magazine. The idyllic scene reminded Djina of when the boys were small and the three of them would sit in the hammock under our fig tree and read.

The girl stood up. Her knitting turned out to be a toy machine gun. She opened fire at the plastic Bambi grazing on the lawn. Rat-tat-tat-tat-tat. Norman Rockwell morphed into Diane Arbus.

We lunched at the Icee Shack in Troutville. The 102-degree ambient temperature combined with the 85 percent humidity catalyzed the icees and produced numerous brain freezes. The proprietor felt sorry for us, and unsuccessfully called around town to find us a swimming pool.

Djina's chain went funny and insisted on moving from the big chain ring to the small one. We tried fixing it. She'd go a mile or so, and we'd try again. On the fourth repetition of this cycle, an older man stopped his truck. "Y'all need any help?"

"If you're a bike mechanic."

"I'm a mechanic." And so we met Raymond, Caterpillar earthmover repairman. With his triage, the bike got a little better.

We thanked Raymond, and he offered, "Y'all want to let them boys jump in my pool? I'm just five houses up the road." Ten minutes later we were sipping iced tea in the custom pool he had fashioned out of an old coal car that he had sunk into concrete. He showed us his shop where he was putting the finishing touches on a bathroom he was making for his cabin. His wife was averse to using an outhouse, so Raymond took an old freight container and built a "portable bathroom," complete with wallpaper.

Raymond is a national treasure. This is no hyperbole. This modern alchemist takes discarded items and turns them into useful products. America might have shortages of renewable energy, quality education, and affordable health care, but we have plenty of junk. We need to creatively reuse these materials. We need America's Raymonds to teach us how to turn trash to treasure. How many universities have majors in renewable trash? Zero. If I ever become a multimillionaire, I'm going to endow a chair at Cal to do this.

I don't know if there is a heaven as Raymond believes, but if there is, he'll be there. He offered to drive us the thirty-four miles to Lexington's bike shop, but we declined. Though this would be a serious "reroute," and though Yonah had tired of biking a thousand miles earlier, he was determined to ride every mile from San Francisco to D.C. Djina and Solomon had missed Day One in San

Francisco, and Solomon and I had hitched fifteen miles in the Utah desert, so Yonah was the only one who could honestly say he had cycled the entire country under his own power.

From Raymond's, it was an easy ride to Camp Bethel. I don't know what Christian denomination ran it, but even though they had a religious retreat going on, they still allowed us to camp. It was the fifth accommodation compliments of a religious order. Though Yonah's thoughts on theology were credible, I couldn't imagine atheism becoming a significant societal force until it organizes into something akin to a church or synagogue and partakes in the religious duty of taking care of others. If this ever happens, atheism might have more followers than many religious sects, perhaps even challenging *SpongeBob* for number of devotees. We pitched our tents, were serenaded by crickets, and spent the evening sans TV. A slice of heaven.

Djina called ahead to the Lexington bike shop. It was Saturday, and the owner was going fishing, but he'd be open until noon. Lexington was thirty-two hilly miles away. Djina had only her small chain ring. If we arrived late, we'd have to wait until Monday morning before "Gone Fishin'" was removed from the window.

Djina set her alarm for 5:00 AM, but there was a conspiracy against her on Olympus and the alarm failed to ring. At 5:45 she jumped out of her sleeping bag, skipped yoga, enticed the boys from their bags with hot chocolate and oatmeal, and we were on the road by 6:45. We traveled through the lush rolling hills that Djina loved, but this morning she had none of it. No morning songs. No greetings to birds. She had a broken bicycle. Time after time, the chain slipped and she lurched forward. A couple of times, the chain fell off the chain ring, and she'd fly forward, her bike atop her. She hobbled along for twenty miles, and then the chain snapped; she crashed, banged up her hand, and was done.

The gods tempered their sadistic pleasure at bringing Djina to her nadir by throwing a lifeline. The chain didn't snap in the wilderness, but in front of a gas station. A truck going to Lexington might stop for gas and give her a lift. For ten minutes no one fit the bill, so she went to the cashier and asked if he knew anyone who wanted to make twenty bucks. Five minutes later, Johnny, a sixty-something guy with a tumor-sized tobacco wad, pulled up. Johnny seemed amiable, but I wrote down the license plate number because that's common sense when your wife drives off with a potential ax murderer.

When we met Djina in Lexington, her bike had a new chain. To celebrate, we found a cute little café on Lexington's bustling Main Street. Before going in, we struck up a conversation with a young couple. The gal was as hot as Angelina Jolie. I didn't notice the guy, but Djina later claimed—I'm sure hyperbolically—that he made George Clooney look like a dweeb. We told the couple we were going to Charlottesville via Vesuvius. Apparently, the road out of Vesuvius was hard. The normally understated ACA map proclaimed: "After the town of Vesuvius, there is a very steep, four-mile climb onto the Blue Ridge Parkway." The blogs were a bit more descriptive—from "Vesuvius is the toughest climb on the TransAmerica. We had to walk four times," to "When you see it, you'll be cleaning number two from your pants," to "Vesuvius. Bwa-ha-ha-ha-ha-ha." But we'd heard it before. How hard could it be?

"Don't even try it," the guy said, forcing me to unglue my eyes from Angelina and notice him, a totally buff spin instructor. "You'll walk." Now this was alarming. We'd come 3,500 miles without walking once. There were only three hundred miles to go. I wasn't going to let The Beast be defeated by a steep road.

"Don't worry," he continued, "There's another way to get to the Blue Ridge. Take Highway 60 out of Lexington. It's ten extra miles, but you won't regret it."

We thanked him and went inside to eat. The twenty café patrons lined up at our table to sign our petition. When this scene happens at a Hutchinson, Kansas, café, the battle against global warming will be won.

The Blue Ridge Parkway is a 464-mile Depression-era work project designed to give motorists an aesthetic experience of stunning vistas. The views made for great biking. An extra bonus is the 45-mile-per-hour speed limit. We passed by the road that intersected the Parkway from Vesuvius and peeked down. It was really steep.

"Next time," I told Yonah. He didn't bother to reply.

Clooney told us of campgrounds along the Parkway, but we were on the wrong side of sunset and found nothing. Finally, we pulled into a rest area with bathrooms, water, picnic tables, and a grassy area to set up tents.

"Is this a campground?" Solomon asked.

"Do you see any 'No Camping' signs?"

"But is it legal?"

"Yeah." The tents were up and the sleeping bags unfurled when the ranger came. He didn't ticket us; rather, he rerouted us one hundred yards away to a lawn behind the ranger station. It was still illegal, but he had mercy.

⊙━⊙⊙━⊙⊙━⊙⊙━⊙⊙━⊙⊙━⊙⊙━⊙⊙━⊙⊙━⊙⊙━⊙⊙━⊙⊙━⊙

Though it was a short day, most of it along the exquisite Blue Ridge Parkway, I lost it with Solomon. The back tapping was only the last straw. The first was the Spanish ditty. The first time he sang it, it was cute. Numbers two through ten, while not enjoyable, were tolerable. Ten through twenty, were fleas trampolining on my skin. After twenty, it was hot oil poured into my ears.

Straw two: Sweating up a 6 percent grade and glancing back at Solomon singing and doing motions that involved circling his hands above his head and swaying his body like a hula dancer. Like a hair-triggered rat trap, I snapped at the first back tap.

"Don't yell at him," Djina implored.

"Let's trade places and see how you do."

"He's doing his best."

I snorted and added a new prayer to my morning devotion: "Please, God, let me not kill my youngest son today."

Unlike his father, Yonah felt no compunction to withhold a slug when Solomon crossed the "stop bugging me" line. Solomon would bother him until Yonah gave him a whack on the back. The more he got whacked, the more Solomon asked for more. Kiddie S&M.

Afton has a museum dedicated to cyclists traveling the TransAmerica route. Since 1976, June Curry (aka The Cookie Lady) has operated a hostel for cyclists while collecting memorabilia and stories. I was interested to see who was the youngest person to cycle him/herself across the country. At thirteen, Yonah would certainly be one of the youngest, but there have been younger. It's hard to imagine a younger kid having the mental and physical toughness necessary. Unfortunately, Ms. Curry was ill and the museum closed.

In Afton, Kevin Murphy and Jennifer Oman picked us up and brought us to their home fifteen miles south of Charlottesville. We had been put in contact with Jennifer by Janet Fullwood, the *Sacramento Bee* travel writer covering the trip. Jennifer, Janet's old college roommate, invited us to stay with them when we reached Charlottesville. The majority of their house was dug into the earth to provide enough insulation to keep the house warm in the winter with minimal energy—say, the energy produced by a can of beans and a few matches. (My imagery, not theirs.) Kevin had done quite a bit of the work himself. To make me feel like an even less competent male, Kevin had to go build a lake. (He modestly referred to it as a pond.) Overcoming my shrunken maleness, I swam in the lake, played fetch with the dog, and drank a malted beverage. Diving off the dock at Kevin's lake was more than just a relaxing afternoon; it was a perfect moment: had the good Lord deemed it time to whisk me away right then, I would not have felt in the least bit ripped off by life.

The notion of being ready for death is an interesting one. There are times when I feel that I've lived a full life. I sired a pair of very decent humans and perhaps made a small positive mark on the world. I've had wonderful experiences and shouldn't be greedy. If my life suddenly ended, I'd be content. These moments of mortal lucidity are real, and I'm sure we all have them. But they are not our default settings regarding death. The default is: No!!! Not yet! I still have not figured out life, and I haven't had a best seller! God, I beg you! More time!

If given the opportunity to live forever, would I take it? I'd like to say no. Practically every thinker who has reflected upon this question has answered nyet to eternity, arguing that immortality isn't what it's cracked up to be. Probably they're right, yet isn't the promise of immortality the fuel that drives religion? Death is acceptable as long as there is life afterward, for few of us relish vanishing, the erasure of the being, the end of the soul. On the other hand, while immortality isn't around the corner, in the next few years the reality of an extremely long life may be available due to advances in medical science. Yonah might not only be one of the youngest to pedal across America, he may be one of the first to bike across the country at age 150. (Will 137 years be enough for him to get over his cycling distaste?)

Not only did Jennifer and Kevin invite us to stay at their Shangri-La, they had also agreed to be the receiving address for people circulating petitions on our behalf. During our two months on the road, we had gathered about five-hundred signatures. Over 95 percent of all the people we spoke to signed the petition. Signers included left-leaning vegans who watched the *Colbert Report* and continued along the political spectrum to right-wing hunters who got their news from Rush. Signer after signer told us that when we got to Congress, we needed to tell them to stop the gridlock on global climate change and do something about it. Yet, no matter how well our petition had been received on the trip, we were shocked and awed by the box Jennifer presented to us. It was overflowing with petitions. We guessed there were about five thousand signatures gathered by a few friends and a handful of people who read about us in the newspapers. True, there were not the million signatures we initially hoped for. And true, we weren't going to lead a parade of a thousand bicycles to deliver the petition to our elected leaders. But in the manner that a pollster uses random samples from which to extrapolate, so did we. The vast majority of Americans want Washington to tackle global climate change.

○━○┆○━○┆○━○┆○━○┆○━○┆○━○┆○━○┆○━○┆○━○┆○━○

Kevin and Jennifer gave us a lift to Charlottesville. If you have been following our progress on a map, you might be wondering about the twenty-five miles of the TransAmerica route we skipped when Kevin and Jennifer picked us up in Afton, took us off-route to their home in Faber, and delivered us to Charlottesville. What about the pride of pedaling every last mile? Doesn't this sully the trip? Have you no shame, Mr. Biers-Ariel? To you cynics, I offer the following five rationalizations. Pick your favorite or mix and match.

According to Kevin, who in addition to being the ultimate handyman was also a cross-country cyclist, the road from their house to Charlottesville was too dangerous. Fast traffic, no shoulders, no love lost between drivers and cyclists.

Over the summer, we had already more than made up the lost twenty-five miles through wrong turns and backtracking.

If we had followed Yonah's interstate highway idea, we would already have arrived in Washington two weeks earlier. By interstate, coast-to-coast is three thousand miles. Instead of cheating twenty-five miles, we were ahead eight hundred.

We wanted to see Monticello. If we rode, it would have been impossible to rally the boys for a tour of Jefferson's mansion.

It was the only way to take Kevin and Jennifer out to breakfast.

Onto Monticello. Italy had Leonardo da Vinci. The British had Isaac Newton. We had Thomas Jefferson. He penned the Declaration of Independence, founded the University of Virginia, doubled the size of the country with the Louisiana Purchase, and sent out Lewis and Clark. Monticello was his home, where his genius manifested itself. In the front hallway one is greeted by the clock he invented. In addition to giving the time, it marks the days of the week with a cannonball. His favorite pastime was reading. Not trashy novels or flippant memoirs. He read for knowledge and to shape the intellect because he saw the connection between nurturing a first-rate mind and creating a free and democratic society. His library was the most extensive in the young republic. He built the Library of Congress to make books available to congressional members. If one were to ask Jefferson to define a true American patriot, I imagine he'd say a reader more than a flag-waver.

Jefferson was religious. But his faith wasn't the faith of the Bible as immutable truth. He was a deist who believed a creative force created the universe and then stepped away. Through reason and an understanding of natural laws, one could discover God. His God was not a personal deity one could petition with prayer.

"What do you think of Jefferson's religion?" I asked Yonah.

"I agree with him about reason, but why say God created everything?"

"You think the laws of the universe and life itself are all random chance?"

"It seems more reasonable than God."

"I'm more with Jefferson."

"Why?"

"I don't believe that the perfection and beauty of the universe could come about by random chance."

"That's what Creationists say is the problem with evolution, but natural selection is about random chance."

"Touché. Then let me say the universe with or without God seems equally plausible, so I'd rather go with God because it gives me comfort."

"I think people prefer comfort over truth."

"That's true."

If Jefferson was the man that early Americans held as a role model and wanted to emulate, his modern successor would be . . . Homer Simpson, the American anti-hero of the post-modern era. Don't laugh. Not only has Homer entered the canon of important Americans by having his own postage stamp, but try this memory experiment. Name the five Simpsons. Easy. Homer, Marge, Lisa, Bart, and Maggie. Now name the five rights in the First Amendment of the Bill of Rights. Doh!

While the boys took in *The Simpsons Movie*, Djina and I blogged at the Charlottesville library. The slow computers made us antsy. It was like driving behind a car going fifty-five on an interstate. You're frustrated and pissed until you realize that compared to walking or bicycling, fifty-five miles an hour is really fast.

D.C. OR BUST

16

FOR NEARLY 3,700 MILES, the ACA maps had revealed excellent routes, bike shops, destinations, and had rarely steered us wrong. But it was time to go our separate ways, for the TransAmerica route continued east to the Atlantic Ocean while we were going north to Washington. There was the option of continuing the TransAmerica to Yorktown and then heading up the ACA Atlantic Coast route to Washington. Total mileage: 260 miles. However, we had appointments with various congressional staffs and a Washington Nationals game to attend. Charlottesville direct to D.C. was 150 miles. Even if we had the time, Yonah would not have allowed a 110-mile reroute to be ignored.

As it turned out, the 150-mile stretch between Washington and Charlottesville was a bicycling dark continent. The Charlottesville Bicycle Club published a complicated route that began along the commuters' main artery out of town. There were no shoulders but there was a large hill; hence, our posse of three bicycles, straining at the hill-climbing pace of 3 to 5 miles per hour, slowed down the caffeine-powered commuters who were, as they always are, late. We hugged the white line and pulled over at every opportunity. For the most part, the commuters were patient. But not all. At one pullout, seven cars passed. The last driver blasted us with his horn and waved his middle finger. Two American flag decals adorned his rear window; a Bush-Cheney '04 sticker adorned his bumper.

I speculated. What if I wasn't a tofu-eating, microbrew-drinking wimp, but a macho heavy-equipment operator with Rush on speed dial? Wouldn't I conclude that Bush was a dickhead because his supporters were? Didn't this guy realize that with his bumper sticker he was no longer an average Joe late to work, but an ambassador to an embattled president? If he really wanted to support Bush, he'd have made a lot more points by offering us coffee and scones. The incident reminded me of a time years before when I went through a two-week ultra-religious phase and wore a Jewish skull cap, a *yarmulke*. During this time, I was hyper-conscious of how the world viewed me. I was no longer just a guy, but an advertisement for Judaism. I tried to avoid acting like a jerk because I didn't want people saying, "See. I told you. Jews are dickheads."

Yonah's idea was to put a Bush-Cheney sticker on our car and have me drive like a jerk. There's a future for him as a campaign adviser.

Though the directions were relatively accurate, the "turn left on Ashton and go six miles on gravel road" was not fun. We arrived in Remington midafternoon and found no campground, hotel, or park to sleep in. There was nowhere to pitch tents. Everything was fenced-in or swampy.

"Are there any hotels or campgrounds anywhere?" we asked the woman behind the gas station counter.

"You can get on Highway 29 and in five miles there are a couple of hotels, but I wouldn't stay in either of them. Go five more miles and there's a Comfort Inn."

A customer offered, "The second hotel's not as bad as the first."

US Highway 29 was not on the route, but you have to sleep, and once Yonah heard his mantra—highway—the matter was settled. Highway 29 turned out to be not just any highway but the South's primary road to Washington, D.C. It had a wide shoulder, and the tailwind created by the nonstop line of humongous trucks added 3 to 4 miles per hour to our speed. The blasts of wind from these same trucks, however, shook me as if I had chugged a quadruple espresso. The Biscuit, of course, was ecstatic. It didn't matter if the side mirror of a twenty-ton Peterbuilt came within six inches of his 120-pound body. We were saving miles.

The plan was to go ten miles to the Comfort Inn, but Djina, whose nerves were also quite jangled, needed to exit the highway and was willing to stay in the better of the nonrecommended hotels. The shirtless desk clerk was elbow-deep into a truck engine when we pulled up. He threw on a t shirt and showed us a room. The first impression indicated it needed a coat of paint, but we'd been in worse. After wheeling in the bikes, closer inspection revealed our first impression was overly optimistic. In addition to paint, the bathroom needed a new toilet and sink. The current fixtures had enough cracks and rust that a museum might be interested. Then there was the heart-sized pool of dried blood outside the front door adjacent to the welcome mat.

While I paid for the room, the owner harangued the clerk for giving away the room at sixty dollars instead of the regular seventy dollars.

"Sir, would you mind paying an extra ten dollars more because this is our deluxe room?"

"You're kidding. There's blood outside the door. Also, the towels are filthy. Could you send us some clean ones, ones without hepatitis?" (Unfortunately, I only *thought* the hepatitis remark.)I backtracked a mile down the interstate to pick up sandwiches at a Subway located in a gas station mini-mart. Imagine my surprise when the clerk announced, "The Subway's closed."

"Closed? It's seven o'clock, and I see the food."

"The guy who's supposed to work called in sick. I work for Shell. Sorry."

I hunted through the mini-mart shelves and gathered two boxes of mac and cheese, a can of soup, and a tin of tuna. Back in the room, the stove Ken left us ran out of fuel before the water boiled. I said, "God is telling us the trip is over, go home." Yonah agreed.

⚬▬⚬▬⚬▬⚬▬⚬▬⚬▬⚬▬⚬▬⚬▬⚬▬⚬▬⚬▬⚬

Day Sixty-Nine. For two miles we traveled north on US Highway 29 until we spotted the road a local assured us would take us to D.C. Not only were we traveling without the ACA maps, but we no longer had the directions from the Charlottesville bike club because there was no way we were backtracking along the interstate to Remington. Unfortunately, two hundred yards prior to the turnoff stood a freeway sign: "Washington, D.C., 50 miles." Yonah was apoplectic that we didn't continue on the freeway. But the country road was carless. Djina and I were elated until the road turned south. Again, we begged directions and cycled north until reaching a stop sign where five roads intersected.

A Subaru stopped. Upon hearing we had come from California, the driver exited her car to shake our hands.

"I'm happy to meet you too," I said, "but do you know how to get to Washington?"

"Take that one," she pointed to the road on the far left. "Wait, I've got a map." She opened her glove compartment and maps cascaded out. "You'll need this one too and probably this one. Maybe this." She handed us four maps. "Can I sign your petition?"

Five miles later, again lost. Yonah harangued, "We could be halfway there if you listened to me."

While we were scouring the maps for a route, Janet Fullwood from the *Sacramento Bee* called. "Hi, Djina! Is now a good time to talk for the follow-up story?"

"Hey, Janet, can you MapQuest something for us?" MapQuest didn't help, so we hailed a small pickup truck. The guy pulled out a gazetteer. The hundreds of tiny roads on the page resembled a schematic of the brain's one hundred billion neurons. The guy penned in a road that wasn't on the page.

"It's from a new subdivision. It'll take you through Manassas." And soon we were at a coffee shop in a large mall near the famous battlefield. Even though the boys were Civil War buffs, I knew better than to ask if they wanted to see it. The only thing they wanted to see was the Washington, D.C., Marriot Courtyard. Yonah, who'd been keeping a careful tally of the day's mileage, said, "If we were on the interstate, like I wanted, we'd be ten miles from Washington."

Djina insisted that the coffee shop should not be considered Second Breakfast, only a drink stop. "Fine," I said and ordered a mucho grande coffee frappuccino guzzler weighing in at five thousand calories.

"Whip cream, sir?"

"Just hand over the can, please."

While we slurped drinks, a kindly woman named Barbara began a conversation by telling us that she and her husband rode a tandem. She asked if we needed directional help, but at Manassas we were back on the original Charlottesville-D.C. directions.

"May I look them over?"

"Sure."

She scanned the page, shook her head a couple of times, and asked, "Did a cyclist write this?" I thought about the six gravel miles.

"There's a much better way to get to the W&OD [Washington and Old Dominion] bike trail, which will take you right into Washington." She wrote out the new directions, and I asked, "How far to the W&OD?"

"No more than ten miles."

After religiously following her instructions for twenty miles, the famed bike path was still nowhere near, and the road we were on was not the one less traveled, and there were no shoulders.

"We'd be watching *Court TV* by now, if we went my way," the former navigator huffed.

"Or *SpongeBob*," added his ally.

At a stop sign we flagged down another vehicle. The driver pulled out a map that contained both our current coordinates and the seven-mile-away W&OD. After she drove off, we cursed Barbara. She was a Republican who, although she signed our petition, was a subterfuge. A dirty trick. She once worked for Tricky Dick Nixon. Now she was on Dick Cheney's payroll hired to prevent us from entering the capital to deliver the petitions. She was the devil's mate, Lucifer's whore.

Five minutes after cursing her birth and praying a bolt of lightning would deliver a heavenly justice, she called. "I just wanted to check to see how you all were doing because I checked the mileage and realized that the W&OD is actually much farther than I told you. I hope you haven't gotten discouraged. Tell me where you are, and I'd be happy to swing by with Gatorades." Okay, so "Lucifer's whore" was perhaps a bit exaggerated.

The Washington and Old Dominion railroad ceased running in 1968 and was later converted into a forty-five-mile multiuse trail. We intersected with it and cycled the last twenty-five miles into D.C. car-free. Our nation will convert more unused railroad tracks into trails like this when people stop screaming, "No new taxes" and start screaming, "Tax carbon and put the revenues into 'beyond autos' transportation projects!" When this occurs, the United States will become a leader in combating climate change.

If we demand it today, it will happen tomorrow.

At 4:00 PM, we ate the *official* Second Breakfast at a Middle Eastern restaurant a block off the W&OD. We surged to D.C., the path crowded with commuters. Night was approaching, so we strapped on lights and rode away from the sunset. We turned off the W&OD, swung around a corner, and there on the left was the Potomac River. Against the darkening sky stood a familiar looking edifice, the Lincoln Memorial. The Washington Monument poked up its pointy head in the back.

We stopped, let our bikes fall to the ground, and stared. We made it. Through the power of our bodies, we had traversed four time zones, a desert, nine states, and four mountain ranges: the entire United States. One ordinary family, one extraordinary feat. With no less pride than Super Bowl champions coming home to a ticker-tape parade, we rode across the Potomac whooping the whole way. We slalomed through tourists who checked their wallets when they beheld four bicyclists plowing through the crowds screaming like howler monkeys. At the Reflecting Pond that fronts the Lincoln Memorial, we anointed the front wheels and symbolically ended the trip 3,804 miles from where we dipped our rear wheels in the Pacific Ocean.

"Well, Yonah, Herzl was right: If you will it, it is no dream. You willed it and made it. How do you feel?"

"My legs are tired, my back is tired, and I'm just tired of riding this bike. I'm tired and cranky. All I want to do is get to the hotel and sleep." Yonah stared at himself in the Reflecting Pond.

"What do you see?" I asked after seeing him suddenly smile like a cat finding the door ajar to the canary cage.

"A boy with a helmet of indeterminate color wearing biking shorts and a dirty shirt. He is thirteen years old and in better physical shape than he ever has been. He is not a man, but he is content with having accomplished what most men cannot. I see a tired, cranky boy who is victorious."

"Okay. Let's go," I said.

"Are you kidding?" Djina said. "This is the most amazing thing we have ever done. It's probably the most amazing bike trip any family has ever done. And now that we're finally here, you want to rush us. Let's savor it for a minute."

"It's dark and I don't feel comfortable riding here. I don't even know exactly where the hotel is. We should go."

Though not all of us were happy about leaving, we got on our bikes one last time and rode to the Marriott, where my buddy Jonathan and his son met us. Jon and I quaffed a magnificently delicious beer. Solly had a Sprite. Djina drank a Perrier and cranberry juice mix. And Yonah celebrated with a bottle of Orange Gatorade.

<hr />

I checked myself out in a full-length mirror before leaving the hotel for our meeting at Congressman Edward Markey's office, I was one sorry-looking dude. When you meet with an important government official, you need a suit. I wore a faded green UV-protection shirt with a wrinkled collar. After a good chortle at the shirt, the congressional staff would see the oil-stained cycling shorts and wonder if I had stopped to fix the basement boiler on the way to the office. To make matters worse, my physique resembled that of a scarecrow but more anorexic. All summer, Djina hounded me to eat more because I was losing weight. I didn't believe her; besides, how many milkshakes can a guy drink? But she was right. I had shed twelve pounds. Since I am relatively skinny to start with, I could have been mistaken as an actor playing the role of an Auschwitz survivor. Would the Capitol building security try to direct me to the Holocaust Museum?

The boys didn't look any better. Djina, at least, had a skirt and a blouse. Thankfully, we had showered, so the Capitol building wouldn't be evacuated from a tear-gas scare when we entered.

Yonah and I each held a pannier of petitions as we passed into the hallowed halls of Congress, the metal clips of bike shoes clicked along the marble as we searched for Markey's office. We might have looked lousy, but we walked tall. We had ridden across the country and had something to say.

Markey was then chair of the House Select Committee on Energy Independence and Global Warming. He was the House gatekeeper on climate change bills, but he was out of town. His staff director, David Moulton, came out to greet us. Meeting with congressional staff is not necessarily the political equivalent of kissing your sister since the staff members do much of the congressional work.

We shook hands and sat down. I had a dream that Yonah would clear his throat and begin, "Thank you for meeting with us, Mr. Moulton. We'd like to present you with these petitions and talk to you about how Congress should act to decrease America's carbon footprint."

Well, we can always dream. The truth was that shy Yonah tried to disappear into the plush couch. I started the meeting by presenting one pannier of petitions. Though Mr. Moulton graciously accepted them, the thought crossed my mind that he would put them in the paper recycling bin as soon as we left, because what else could he do with them?

Before I got too depressed thinking about how all our hard work was going to be imminently pulped, he said, "I'd like to hear about your trip."

Yonah might have been shy, but Solomon wasn't. He told Mr. Moulton about turtles and going over Monarch Pass. He described how we rode over a hundred miles in one day twice. Solly told him how hot it was and that Mr. Moulton should get people to build solar power plants in Nevada.

"That's a good idea," Mr. Moulton agreed.

Yonah jumped in and spoke about wind farms in Utah. To illustrate how little Americans conserve energy, he spoke about how cold a lot of the air-conditioned stores were and that it was practically impossible to find recycling bins in much of America. I mentioned how great the W&OD was and how our country needed to tax carbon and build more paths like it.

We told Mr. Moulton about the various people who signed the petitions and how people really wanted to do something about climate change. He seemed quite engaged as he nodded, smiled, and asked questions. After we gave him our spiel, it was his turn.

Throughout the trip, I had pictured the Biers-Ariels as the cutting edge on climate change, but David Moulton knew as much or more about global warming as Al Gore. True he had not bicycled across the country, but we sensed a strong passion in him. He told us how Markey's committee was trying to pass a new energy package, but that there were two obstacles. One, any reorientation of the current energy focus (read: oil) would be filibustered in the Senate. The second obstacle was a veto threat from President Bush, who for the first six years of his presidency questioned the science of global climate change.

According to Moulton, Congressman Markey felt he could make only incremental changes versus the sea change that he knew was necessary. He was taking a two-pronged approach: what was possible under Bush—sort of a global warming triage—and what was necessary to turn back climate change. This second part would need to wait for a president and a Congress ready to undertake the task.

"But the people are demanding the sea change now," I said. "You guys need to go for it. If senators filibuster it, we can vote them out."

"That's a good idea, but right now that probably isn't going to happen." Mr. Moulton smiled at the boys. "Maybe one day you'll run for office and by then you'll be able to vote for what is right instead of what can pass."

We thanked Mr. Moulton, but he stopped us. "No, thank you. You've sent a powerful message to our country. I'm going to tell the congressman about our meeting. He'll be very interested."

We left the office and walked over to Senator Barbara Boxer's office, where we met with her chief of staff, Bettina Poirier. Like Markey, Boxer understands the need to do something significant. And like Markey, her chief of staff was well-informed about climate change. After we had showered her with petitions, anecdotes, and energy insights, she suggested that while she and her colleagues work at the national political level, we the people need to go grassroots to organize, educate, and change ourselves, our schools, and our communities.

Though I suggested that Boxer had to go bigger in her legislation and not be afraid to confront the deniers and filibusters, I thought Ms. Poirier had a point. Going to Washington to speak to Congress was important. What we would do upon our return to California would be equally important.

The takeaway from the meetings was that though there are those in Congress who want to act decisively, they won't unless we make them. We must organize and push them to do what is right. For both the economy and the natural world, the United States needs to once again go big, as earlier generations who fought the Nazis, built the highways, and went to the moon did. It won't be easy and will take a tremendous effort from each of us. The odds for success are not high, and the pain to change to a carbon-neutral nation may be significant, yet if an ordinary family can overcome tremendous odds and physical pain to cross the country on bicycle, why can't America do on a macro-level what we did on a micro-level?

○■○:○■○:○■○:○■○:○■○:○■○:○■○:○■○:○■○:○■○:○■○

Djina, Yonah, and I rode to a bike shop to pack up the bikes for the plane ride home. We arrived at City Bikes at 3:00 PM with plenty of time to make the 7:00 Washington Nationals' game. We didn't worry about leaving Solomon alone in the hotel room. He was equipped with a bag of Doritos, a can of Sprite, and the TV remote.

I was against bringing The Beast home. Don't get me wrong. I appreciated The Beast. I even had a soft spot in my heart for it. After all, Solomon and I had ridden on its back across the country, and despite its cantankerous drum brake and irritating chain jams, it had performed reasonably well. But I longed to be back on my regular bike. Hopefully, one of the shop employees would offer it a good home. One guy offered $100. I had paid $920 for it and put in about $500 of improvements. I couldn't do $100, so I decided to box it up, take it home, and either use it when I needed to taxi Solomon across town or sell it on Craigslist. The two other bikes were boxed in about fifteen minutes. On its own, The Beast decided to end the relationship by applying subterfuge to the boxing process. The Beast was so long that it needed a custom box fashioned from two empty bike boxes duct-taped together. That took thirty minutes. Using a technique not dissimilar from stuffing a sleeping bag into its sack, I crammed that hunk of steel and grease in. More duct tape was applied to close the top, for it kept trying to jump out.

One of the bike guys said, "There's a maximum length that airlines allow. You might want to measure."

"You're kidding."

"It's sixty-two linear inches."

The Beast was sixty-eight. I tried to shorten it, but The Beast refused to budge. Option Two was to ship UPS. No one picked up the phone at the UPS store, and according to their website, shipping would run three hundred dollars. That seemed excessive; I figured if we got to the UPS store, we could get a cheaper rate. We called a taxi van to whisk us to UPS and then to our hotel, but after thirty more minutes, no van. Yonah worried he might miss the first pitch of the Nationals' game. I did a cost-benefit analysis of schlepping The Beast to UPS, paying two hundred to three hundred to ship it, and the hassle of listing and selling it on Craigslist versus the amount of money I'd make. Costs exceeded benefits, so I strode into the shop, found the guy who had offered a hundred dollars and said, "Two hundred and she's yours. I paid almost fifteen hundred dollars for it. She rides great. Take it."

"Okay." We exchanged money but not handshakes, for my hand was bloodied after being stabbed by the chain ring when I had removed The Beast's pedals. It wanted to leave me with one last memento to remember it by.

I was a little sad to say goodbye, for there was history with that bike. And—don't laugh—sometimes I came to think of it as an animate being more than simply a bicycle. But there was no time for sentimentality. We had two boxed bikes to get to the hotel room and make a 7:00 PM game. It was 5:53 when we hailed a cab. One box was wedged into the trunk. It looked like a small snake attempting to swallow a large bullfrog. We wedged the other box into the back seat. Yonah and I wedged ourselves around the box and discovered two new yoga postures. As fate will always have it, as Djina shut her door, the spacious taxi-van we called an hour earlier pulled up to the bike shop looking for us.

"You'd probably call that the hand of the Devil," smirked Yonah.

"Ha-ha-ha," I said, not laughing.

Arriving at the hotel, we pried ourselves out of the taxi with minimal pancreatic damage. We rushed to the stadium, and the boys saw the opening pitch while I stood in line for a six dollar and fifty-cent beer. After the trauma of The Beast, they could have asked sixty-five dollars. I would have paid.

○━○∙○━○∙○━○∙○━○∙○━○∙○━○∙○━○∙○━○∙○━○∙○━○

Djina and Yonah separated from Solomon and me as we museum-hopped the morning of our flight back home. Solly and I went to the Smithsonian's Museum of the American Indian. Once inside, Solomon plugged into a large HDTV, where cartoon renditions of various Creation myths babysat my son and other children, and I found an exhibit on Native American philosophy. Though it is surely a mistake to lump the thousands of Native American tribes into a single philosophy, the museum presented common-alities distilled into seven values: truth, respect, honesty, love, courage, humility, and wisdom. (I wondered, where were money, greed, and power—the trilogy of values that drive most of our lives?) The irony is that the Native Americans, thought of as sav-ages by European Americans, held values no different than any Western religious tradition. If atheists got together and formed a pantheon of values to live by, the list wouldn't look any dif-ferent. As if we needed another proof that no one tradition or religion holds a monopoly on ethics.

Strolling through the exhibit, it was as if I had swallowed a magic slow-down pill. Had I been able to maintain that transcendent feeling when I met up with Solomon, he would have asked, "What happened to you?" and I would have replied, "As Black Elk teaches, 'the seasons form a great circle in their changing, and always come back again to where they were. The life of a man is a circle from childhood to childhood, and so it is in everything where power moves.'" Unfortunately, by the time I picked him up, my eye was no longer focused on the beautiful and profound exhibits, but on my Timex. "Last cartoon. We're late."

We left and though I felt a warmth that the Indian culture was thriving, I also felt melancholy thinking about what Yonah had said about how his rite of passage hadn't changed him either emotionally or spiritually. Probably I expected too much from a thirteen-year-old. I wanted the experience to be profound and life changing. I wanted him to be in such a state of ecstasy that light would emanate from his face, like Moses descending Mount Sinai.

Yonah would not be what I envisioned for him. And then I realized it was my bad. I desired to turn his rite of passage into what *I* wanted instead of letting it be what it was. Though Yonah was unable to articulate how his rite of passage changed him, he already embodied most of those seven Native American attributes. My melancholy lifted. Had there been more European Americans like Yonah and fewer like George Custer, the Native Americans wouldn't have gotten such a rotten deal and the world would possibly be a better place.

The plan was to return to the hotel, grab a taxi, drive to the airport, and fly home. What could be easier? However, the gods needed a final laugh and inserted one last obstacle to surmount. After we had pushed the bike boxes to the Frontier Airlines ticket counter, the clerk informed us we needed to pay eight hundred dollars for our tickets.

"There is a mistake," I said. "I bought these tickets months ago through Travelocity. We even bought carbon offsets," I smugly added.

"Yes," she countered. "I see that they made the reservation, but unfortunately, Travelocity never paid us."

"What are you talking about?" I asked in a trying-to-remain-calm-but-something-is-amiss voice. "I've got the tickets right here." I showed her our four tickets.

"Yes," she admitted, utilizing her the-more-upset-the-customer-gets-the-calmer-I-become voice. "Travelocity issued a ticket, but since they never paid us, you will have to buy your ticket from me before I can let you board."

It took but a second to understand the import of her words, and then not only did my newly minted Native American philosophy wither like a young corn seedling under a 120-degree sun, but everything I ever learned from religious school, years of prayer and meditation, and the wisdom gleaned from the trip immediately and completely flew forth from me into the air-conditioned ether of the airport terminal. The plane was on the tarmac; there was precious little time. My being, which had taken two months to slow to a 10-mile-per-hour pace, was now confronted by the every-second-counts of modern life. I continued conversing with the clerk and thought I was simply trying to get her to understand and empathize with our predicament. An objective observer witnessing the scene would have seen a skinny, middle-aged man shrieking, "I am normally not a screaming lunatic, but we are getting on this plane!"

Before security was alerted, Djina stepped in and commanded me to sit down. Even without training in the seven Native American attributes, she deftly handled the situation and obtained our boarding passes. As the chagrined man of the family boarded the plane, he realized how his wife had been right all along: It would have been insanity to ride across America without her. We never would have made it past Placerville.

Soon we were flying across the country in a fast-forward of the trip in reverse. Djina and the boys read contentedly. The aura of completing the quest glowed from them. *Shtarker* is a Yiddish term for one who doesn't give up, no matter the difficulty of the task. We were *shtarkers*. I had known it would be difficult to bike across America, but the experience itself was a quantum leap harder than what I had imagined. The mountains were significantly steeper and longer than what we had prepared for, the weather was hotter and muggier than any climate I'd ever experienced, and the eight to ten hours a day in the saddle took an emotional toughness that I wouldn't have guessed the boys possessed. Had I known the ride's reality, I don't know if we would have attempted it. But isn't that true with many great accomplishments? When it is not fatal, ignorance is indeed bliss.

I thought about Yonah. Not only did he accomplish this physical feat, but he did it with aplomb, especially given the fact that he dislikes bike riding. That he got up every day to do something exceedingly difficult that he didn't enjoy reflected a great strength of character, but I was saddened that he didn't do something for his rite of passage that gave him joy. Perhaps it was more like a bar mitzvah than I imagined.

"Yonah?" He looked up from his *Mad Magazine*. "Are you glad you did it?"

"I wasn't glad doing it, but yeah, I'm glad I did it."

"Why?"

"If I can do this, I figure I can do anything."

"Do you think it changed you?"

"You always ask me that." His face lit up. "What about you? Did you change?"

The interviewer was now the interviewee. Not for the first time on the trip were the roles of father and son reversed. "I think I did. I didn't turn into an atheist, but I'm less sure of God and the soul and everything. The only thing I can truthfully say is that I don't know anything. I guess that makes me an agnostic."

"So can we stop doing prayers on Friday nights?"

"Sorry. We might not be a family of believing Jews, but we're Jews. You might be an atheist, but you're a Jewish one."

He returned to his magazine. Thirty thousand feet below were the Sierras, and I thought about all the stars on the trip that had lined up for us. No one got sick. Our bodies, especially my knees, held up. None of the bikes suffered irreparable breakdowns. No one was killed or maimed by a car, truck, or other family member. There were no floods or tornadoes. We found the last *Harry Potter*. Had one of these conditions not been met, we would not have made it.

I leaned over to Yonah and said, only half-jokingly, "Clearly, God wanted us to succeed."

He looked up and replied, "Even if He exists, which I doubt, do you really think God cares?"

"My head says no, but my heart says I hope so." I smiled and the budding philosopher burrowed his head back into his magazine.

EPILOGUE

THE WORLD'S LEADING climate scientists believe that an atmospheric concentration of 350 parts per million (ppm) of carbon dioxide is the upper limit before catastrophic climatic change such as the melting of the Greenland ice shelf becomes inevitable. In 2007, the carbon dioxide concentration registered 382 parts per million. Rather than arresting carbon dioxide emissions, we are producing greater quantities every year. By 2011 the concentration had jumped to 392ppm. Clearly, our petition did not slow carbon dioxide emissions. Hand-in-hand with rising carbon dioxide emissions, the earth continues to heat up. The year 2010 tied 2005 as the warmest year since reliable figures began to be recorded in the late 1800s. The third warmest year was 2009.

Both Congressman Edward Markey and Senator Barbara Boxer claimed to be waiting for a new president who would support progressive energy legislation. In Barack Obama, there was hope this new president had arrived. However, Mr. Obama took the oath of office during the Great Recession. From 2008 to 2011, unemployment bounced between 9 and 10 percent, the stock market resembled the rollercoaster hills of the Ozarks, and though polls still indicated that the majority of voters wanted action on global climate change, serious action to bring about a noncarbon energy future was largely ignored both on Main Street and in Washington, D.C.

The irony is that combating global climate change may be the shot in the arm the economy needs. Hundreds of thousands of unemployed could be put to work with weatherization and other energy conservation jobs. Building Big Projects such as solar arrays in Nevada and wind farms in the Midwest will require both skilled and unskilled workers, as will building a smart energy grid. Rebuilding city transportation systems to encourage alternates to automobiles is desperately needed. There is so much infrastructure work that could be done to provide work and decrease our carbon footprint. We just need to give our government the green light. These projects need to begin now. If we wait until the economy gets better, they may never happen.

In addition to climate change moving to the political back-burner since our ride, China has recently emerged as the world's largest emitter of carbon dioxide. The time when the United States was the most important country to regulate is over. It is critical that the nations of the world work together to reach a consensus that can be enforced. Unfortunately, this cooperative spirit still seems far off.

●▬○▬●▬○▬●▬○▬●▬○▬●▬○▬●▬○▬●▬○▬●▬○▬●

Since 2007, the Biers-Ariel boys have grown up. Though it was difficult for Yonah to articulate how the trip changed him, indeed it had. He returned to California with a new maturity and self-confidence. There was not a single time during high school when I had to remind him to attend to his work or his chores. My role as parent changed. Rather than actively guiding or teaching him, I stepped back and made myself available when he needed me, which wasn't often. Mostly we played chess. He pushed himself to excel at what interested him: school and debate. Whatever he didn't want to do, he didn't do. For example, since the night we rode into Washington, D.C., he has taken exactly one recreational bike ride. Recently, he ceased being an atheist and became an apatheist, someone who just doesn't care if there is a God or not. In August, 2011, he happily went off to college.

Like his brother, Solomon decided against a bar mitzvah. While he did not have the same gripes against religion as Yonah had, he wasn't interested, and we didn't push it. Still, when he turned thirteen, he needed to undertake a rite of passage. He decided to do a long backpacking trip from the southern end of the Sierra Nevada in Kings Canyon to Yosemite. Djina and I accompanied him while Yonah chose to stay home. It was more fun for Yonah to work in a law office and scan documents than to climb 13,000-foot peaks. At three weeks long, the backpacking trip was significantly shorter than the bike trip, but the extraordinarily high levels of precipitation that year made it much more harrowing. Instead of gathering signatures on a climate petition, Solomon raised money to send ten children from war-torn countries to a summer camp called Vacation From War. The trip ended less than a month ago, so it is too early to say how he has changed from it. I will say that I believe that the rite-of-passage trips our children took were powerful, positive influences, and I highly recommend something like them for every young teen.

As for Djina and me, we both work in our same jobs and watch our retirement portfolios shrink. I still commute to work on my 1991 Giant Cadex, which has over 50,000 miles on it. Djina still rides her bike and started a new hobby of beekeeping. As far as combating climate change, we put solar panels on the roof, and every year I attempt to teach my students that climate change is real and we must fight it. Sometimes I am successful, often I am not. I came to the realization that you can't force people or governments to change until they are ready. My great hope is that this book will nudge a few people to be ready.

STATISTICS

Miles: 3,804
Miles per day (average): 63
Vertical miles: 30
Days over 100 miles: 2
Days over 100 degrees Fahrenheit: 41
Days of rain: 1 (plus an hour of hail)
Average speed: 10.6 miles per hour
Maximum speed (The Beast): 45 miles per hour
Minimum speed (The Beast): 2.1 miles per hour
Gallons of Gatorade (total): 99
Calories consumed (per capita): 345,000
Pounds of French fries (Solomon): 15
Total revolutions of bicycle cranks (per capita): 1,331,400
Number of ibuprofens (Matt): 14
Turtles saved: 3
Deer saved: 1
Days without stove fuel: 17
Flats: 13
New tires: 7
New chains: 2
New spokes: 5
Rebuilt wheel: 1
New pedals: 2 pairs
New shoe cleats: 1 set
New bike gloves: 3 pair
Broken chain ring bolt: 1
Front derailleur overhaul: 1

PETITION
FOR COOLING OUR PLANET

WHEREAS

The single greatest challenge human beings face is imminent climate change caused by the increasing atmospheric carbon dioxide brought on in large part through the burning of fossil fuels.

WHEREAS

The United States of America has 5 percent of the world's population but is the single largest contributor of carbon dioxide at 25 percent.

WE, THE UNDERSIGNED, REQUEST AND URGE

President Bush, the United States Congress, state governments, local communities, and individual Americans to significantly reduce our country's carbon dioxide emissions by:

- Dedicating the necessary resources to become the world leader in nonfossil fuel energy production and technology.
- Adopting conservation as the first energy solution.
- Raising automobile mileage standards to a minimum of 40 mpg.
- Building transportation systems that double current mass transit trips.
- Encouraging biking and walking as means of transportation.
- Eating more of a plant-based diet.

Dedicating the necessary resources to become the world leader in nonfossil fuel energy production and technology. On May 25, 1961, President John F. Kennedy spoke before a joint session of Congress and audaciously set a goal to send a man to the moon by the end of the decade. Audacious because at the time, John Glenn had yet to orbit Earth. Yet, if the United States wished to retain its world leadership in the face of the Soviet Union's successful space program, the Apollo Program was necessary. On July 20, 1969, Neil Armstrong

MATT BIERS-ARIEL is author of *The Triumph of Eve and Other Subversive Bible Tales*. He teaches high school English and lives in Davis, California, with his wife and two sons.

PETITION
FOR COOLING OUR PLANET

took the first step on the moon. This impossible goal was reached in a mere eight years because the United States dedicated itself to reaching it. At its peak, the Apollo Program employed four hundred thousand Americans and required the support of over twenty thousand industrial firms and universities.

Dealing with global climate change requires audacious leadership. Though the United States is the economic and military leader in the world, it has not dedicated its might to this issue. If the United States were to launch a program as aggressive as the Apollo Program, it would not only earn its right to call itself the world leader in dealing with climate change, but such a program would provide millions of new jobs and reinvigorate the United States' moribund economy. *Adopting conservation as the first energy solution.* Conservation is still the low-fruit to decreasing carbon emissions. Americans are energy hogs. Compare the United States to Japan. The average America uses 8.35 tons of oil equivalent (TOE) to support a per capita income of $44,000. Japan uses 4.13 TOE to support a per capita income of $39,000. We use twice the amount of energy for about a 10 percent income advantage. Denmark's per capita income is higher than the United States' at $47,000 and they do it on 3.64 TOE. Denmark accomplishes this when their national thermometer hovers below freezing all winter. Clearly, the United States has a lot of energy fat to shed. Without inventing any new technology, the United States could tomorrow or the day after tomorrow, shrink its carbon footprint by 50 percent.

Building transportation systems that double current mass transit trips. Over half of all US commuters commute to work in single-occupancy vehicles except in areas where good mass transit systems are available. Enough said.

Encouraging biking and walking as means of transportation. Americans have the world's biggest posteriors. Let's get off our butts.

Let's do it now.